D0375001

Building a Winning Sales Management Team

The Force Behind the Sales Force

Andris A. Zoltners
Prabhakant Sinha
Sally E. Lorimer

ZS Associates, Inc.

This publication is designed to provide accurate and authoritative information in regard to the subject matter covered. It is sold with the understanding that the publisher and authors are not engaged in rendering legal, accounting, or other professional service. If legal advice or other expert assistance is required, the services of a competent professional should be sought.

Published by ZS Associates, Inc.
1800 Sherman Avenue, Suite 700
Evanston, Illinois 60201

www.zsassociates.com

Text design, typesetting, and project management: Books By Design, Inc.

Library of Congress Control Number: 2012939603

ISBN: 978-0-9853436-0-6

Contents

Preface

Great salespeople are a key asset for a successful sales organization, but great *managers* of those salespeople are worth even more. That's why we call a winning sales management team "the force behind the sales force." If a company has a poor salesperson, it will lose market share in one territory. But if it has a weak first-line sales manager, it risks losing market share in all the territories that the manager is responsible for. In time, the salespeople in those territories will drift without guidance, disengage from their jobs, or lose motivation and allow their skills to plateau. Frequently, good salespeople who work for weak managers ultimately leave the company.

We believe that too many sales organizations underinvest in their sales management teams. We have observed companies focusing their sales force improvement efforts either toward the bottom of the sales organization to make salespeople more effective or toward the top of the organization to make sales executives savvier. Too little time and attention, and too few resources, are directed toward the first-line sales managers in the middle who are a critical link in the corporate chain and a key point of leverage for driving sales force performance.

The sales force is a key focal point in the challenge to drive profitable revenue growth in an ever-changing business environment. We see first-line sales managers (FLMs) as pivotal players in driving sales force success. FLMs act as a critical link between salespeople, customers, and the company through three roles: people manager, customer manager, and business manager. In a people manager role, FLMs have influence over who sells for the company and whether the best salespeople stay, how (and how quickly) salespeople improve, how motivated salespeople are, and how well the sales force embraces change. In a customer manager role, FLMs can execute key sales process steps, take the lead in selling to large customers, and help strengthen customer relationships by bringing skills, experience, and credibility to the sales process. In a business manager role, FLMs connect headquarters and the field. They ensure that sales force activity stays aligned with corporate goals by adapting company strategies and allocating resources appropriately for local markets and by reinforcing company culture in the field. They communicate what's happening in the field back to headquarters so that company strategies and plans stay aligned with customer needs. A winning sales management team that executes these three roles well is a powerful force behind the sales force—and a key success factor in driving sales performance.

We wrote *Building a Winning Sales Management Team: The Force Behind the Sales Force* to help you harness the power that a winning sales management team can bring to the sales force. The book fills a void in the information available for helping sales organizations succeed. There are books that help salespeople improve their selling techniques, books that help first-line sales managers become more effective coaches, and books that help sales leaders address a range of sales management issues, including several that we have written on topics such as sales force design, sales force incentive compensation, and sales force effectiveness. But until now, there were no comprehensive books that combined practical insights with academic rigor to help sales leaders and their direct reports (for example, regional sales directors who oversee FLMs) do a better job of defining, creating, and enabling the FLM team.

Through our consulting work, time and again we see the high impact that FLM effectiveness has on sales force success. We have observed and participated in projects across industries and companies all over the globe that focus on improving FLM effectiveness. These projects include the following:

- **Redefining the FLM role to align with a new sales strategy.** Implementing the role change required redesigning FLM competency models, hiring profiles, development programs, support data and tools, and reward structures to reinforce the new role.

- **Adjusting FLM span of control and reporting relationships.** The new sales organization structure improved coordination of sales activity for customers while allowing FLMs time and bandwidth to coach and manage salespeople to bring expertise to customers.

- **Identifying the characteristics and competencies of a company's most successful FLMs.** Once identified, programs and processes were implemented to propagate the success characteristics and competencies throughout the sales management team.

- **Designing and facilitating customized development workshops for FLMs.** The workshops focused on skill improvement and reinforced best practices in critical sales effectiveness areas.

- **Enhancing FLM motivation by redesigning incentive plans.** In addition to an improved plan design that aligned more closely with the FLM role, new goal-setting processes created district sales goals that were challenging, attainable, and fair.

We expect projects like these will boost revenue by 10 percent or more in the long term.

Writing this book has been a continual journey of learning. We started with a single-chapter overview on the topic of the sales manager for our last book, *Building a Winning Sales Force* (AMACOM, 2009). We enhanced the material from that chapter with what we've learned from our consulting experiences and began testing our ideas for improving sales manager effectiveness with sales executives in courses that we teach at Northwestern University's Kellogg School of Management and at the Indian School of Business. In September 2010, we held a two-day Summit for Sales Executives at Kellogg called Building a Winning Sales Management Team.

As momentum for writing the book grew, we formed a Sales Management Advisory Board consisting of 19 successful sales leaders from leading companies in a variety of industries. Board members shared with us countless ideas and best practices for building a powerful first-line sales management team to drive sales force success. In addition to sharing their thoughts and stories with us individually, board members met six times over a 19-month period to collaborate and brainstorm solutions to difficult sales management issues. The experience, creativity, judgment, and practical examples that board members provided became a core element of the book. With the board's help, we took our existing ideas and theories and made them practical and actionable for sales leaders, and we developed several new frameworks relevant to the challenges that sales leaders face in today's environment.

How the Book Is Organized

Building a Winning Sales Management Team: The Force Behind the Sales Force is not a silver bullet. Instead, it lays out a logical and thoughtful approach for building and sustaining sales force success. The book describes eight FLM success drivers. These success drivers involve key sales leader decisions and sales management programs, systems, processes, and tools that together define, create, and enable the sales management team. After an introduction in Chapter 1, the heart of the book is structured into eight chapters that each focus on one key FLM success driver. The chapters are organized into three major sections:

- **Section I, "Defining the FLM's Job."** By anchoring the FLM job around your sales force strategy, this section suggests approaches for bringing excellence to three key FLM success drivers: defining the role (Chapter 2), sizing and structuring the team (Chapter 3), and creating the success profile (Chapter 4).
- **Section II, "Creating a Strong FLM Team."** This section shows you how to build a team of talented sales managers using two key FLM success drivers: selecting talent (Chapter 5) and enhancing competencies (Chapter 6).

- **Section III, "Enabling the Right FLM Activity."** This section shares strategies for enabling quality FLM activity through three key FLM success drivers: supporting critical activities (Chapter 7), managing performance (Chapter 8), and motivating and rewarding success (Chapter 9).

Chapter 10 of the book discusses two primary topics: the responsibility FLMs have for enabling successful sales force transformation and improvement in a changing sales environment, and how sales leaders can enable FLMs in their role as facilitators of change.

The book concludes with a self-assessment tool that you can use to determine your priorities and start improving the FLM success drivers for your sales organization today.

Readers who desire a complete look at how to build and sustain a winning sales management team can read all the chapters sequentially. Readers who are looking to solve a particular issue or concern can start by reading Chapter 1 and then jump directly to the chapters most relevant to their needs. Readers who need help with determining where to start can read Chapter 1 first and then complete the assessment tool provided at the end of the book to identify the highest-impact priorities that deserve urgent attention.

Acknowledgments

This book is the result of a collaborative effort between numerous individuals, including the members of our Sales Management Advisory Board, the sales leaders we have worked with through our executive education programs and consulting projects, and the talented staff at ZS Associates.

Thank you to our Sales Management Advisory Board. This board, which was created for the purpose of writing this book, consisted of 19 successful sales leaders from a broad range of industries. Corporate board members included Chris Ahearn (TPG Capital), John Barb (International Paper), Sandy Cantwell (Cardinal Health), Liza Clechenko (BP), Amy Davalle (Smith & Nephew), Cathy Fischer (consumer packaged goods and durable goods industry), Chris Hartman (Boston Scientific), Jeff Heard (newspaper industry), Denise O'Brien (ARAMARK), Lance Osborne (AFLAC), Quinton Oswald (SARcode BioScience), Jay Sampson (Machinima Inc.), Greg Schofield (Novartis), Fred Wagner (Johnson & Johnson), Helmut Wilke (Microsoft Corporation), and Conrad Zils (General Electric). Three board members from ZS Associates—Marshall Solem, Linda Vogel, and Tony Yeung—were instrumental not only in contributing insights; these individuals also helped us design agendas, develop content for discussion, and facilitate brainstorming sessions at the six board meetings.

We are grateful to Northwestern University's Kellogg Executive Education Department for providing a fertile environment for ideas to flourish. Thousands of executives have participated in our programs at Kellogg and at the Indian School of Business. Our classroom interactions with these individuals have been invaluable for turning our theories and frameworks into practical sales force management tools.

As consultants, we have worked personally with executives, sales managers, and salespeople at more than 400 companies all over the world. The clients of ZS Associates have helped us discover, develop, test, and refine many of the concepts described in the book. Because of confidentiality, many of the people and companies must remain anonymous, but we owe a great deal of gratitude to all those who have used their experience, creativity, judgment, and guidance to help us develop and enhance our ideas.

We would also like to thank the people of ZS Associates, the consulting firm that we founded in 1983. ZS Associates today has more than 2,000 employees across 20 offices in North America, Europe, and Asia. ZS employs some of the finest consultants and businesspeople in the world, and they have contributed to the book immensely. Chad Albrecht, one of the world's leading experts on sales incentive compensation, made significant contributions on the topics of FLM motivation, rewards, and incentives. Other ZS consultants who contributed ideas and examples for specific chapters and who evaluated our frameworks based on their creativity and practical knowledge of what works in the real world include Angela Bakker Lee, Julie Billingsley, Ty Curry, Lauren Lamm, Pete Masloski, Alysa Parks, Stephen Redden, Scott Sims, and Kelly Tousi. The ZS members of our Advisory Board—Marshall Solem, Linda Vogel, and Tony Yeung—made valuable contributions throughout the book. Ashish Vazirani read the entire manuscript and made suggestions for enhancing the book's clarity and value across a range of industries, based on his experience working with high-tech companies and on his knowledge of sales channel strategy and management.

We were very fortunate to have several research and editorial assistants working with us on this project. Preeti Panwar used her artistic talents to create the book's 90 illustrations. Sugandha Khandelwal led the ZS Knowledge Management team in uncovering examples and supporting research. Shelley Gabel reviewed the manuscript many times for accuracy and consistency and was instrumental in coordinating the meetings and ongoing communications with the Sales Management Advisory Board.

Thank you to Meredith Rosen, who led the book's production and marketing efforts. Meredith reviewed the entire manuscript for clarity and content, suggesting revisions based on her sales management knowledge. She created detailed book production and marketing plans and kept us on track to meet every deadline, using her outstanding project management skills and attention to detail. We also greatly appreciate the efforts of the ZS Marketing team and Neil Warner, who designed the book jacket cover. We also thank ZS partners Bob Buday (who wrote an outstanding book proposal) as well as Nancy Benjamin and the team at Books By Design.

Without the efforts of these fine collaborators, this book would not be in your hands today.

CHAPTER 1

How a Vigorous Sales Management Team Helps You Win in the Marketplace

The Impact of the Sales Manager

As a sales leader charged with driving sales performance, which of the alternatives shown in Figure 1-1 do you prefer?

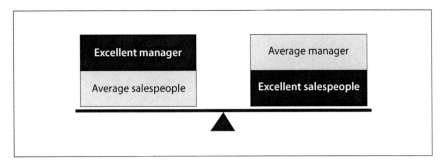

Figure 1-1   Which Sales District Do You Prefer?

Many sales leaders argue that having excellent salespeople is more important than having excellent managers. They say:

- "Managers aren't the ones who are selling, they are the ones managing, and not all salespeople follow their managers. A manager can tell a salesperson to do something, but at the end of the day, it's the salesperson's talent and effort that drive results."

- "Customers don't care who the sales manager is—they just want an excellent salesperson who can deliver what they need."

- "Replacing one average manager is much easier than replacing an entire team of average salespeople."

- "It's the salespeople—not the managers—who make sales and ensure we achieve goal. That's why at our company, many salespeople make more money than their managers."

Other sales leaders believe that having excellent managers is what's most important. They say:

- "Excellent salespeople win sales and can help you make this year's sales goal, but eventually they retire, get promoted, or get wooed away by a competitor. Excellent managers develop excellent salespeople and are there to keep developing excellent salespeople."
- "An excellent manager constantly recruits the best talent, coaches salespeople to continuously improve, motivates them to succeed, and keeps talented salespeople on the team and engaged in their jobs."
- "An excellent manager can make a team of average salespeople excellent by managing to the strengths and improving the weaknesses of different team members."
- "Without a strong manager, even a team of excellent salespeople will start to disengage and go astray—an entire district can quickly get out of control."
- "Salespeople take their job because of the company but leave or stay because of their sales manager."

Since 1987, we have been teaching an executive-level course entitled Accelerating Sales Force Performance at Northwestern University's Kellogg School of Management as well as in other global venues. During the course, we often ask the sales leaders in attendance which of the two alternatives shown in Figure 1-1 they prefer. After asking thousands of sales leaders this question, we have found that the vote is nearly evenly divided.

In the short term, a team of excellent salespeople with an average manager easily outsells a team of average salespeople with an excellent manager. But over time, excellent salespeople who work for an average manager are likely either to disengage from their jobs (channeling their talents and energies toward personal endeavors) or to set their own priorities for what selling activities to focus on (possibly diverging from what may be most important for customers or the company). Many excellent salespeople get promoted or retire, or they quit because their average manager is holding them back. And when excellent salespeople leave, an average manager is likely to replace them with average salespeople. Average managers rarely surround themselves with excellent salespeople, as they may be unable to recognize talent or may be intimidated by excellence. It is often said that "first class hires first class; second class hires third class."

In the long run, average managers bring all of the salespeople that they manage down to their level. On the other hand, excellent managers bring excellence to all their territories. Great managers may inherit average salespeople, but in the long run they counsel, coach, motivate, or replace salespeople until their entire team is excellent.

Clearly, the best sales forces have both great salespeople and great managers—and the best way to get both is to start with excellent managers. A strong sales management team is the force behind a great sales force.

Two Case Studies: How Sales Managers Impact Performance

When one company conducted an assessment of its first-line sales managers (FLMs), it saw clear evidence that sales manager coaching improves district performance. The company had a large sales force with a few hundred sales districts. Districts in which salespeople were consistently coached by their managers outperformed other districts on goal achievement by a significant margin (see Figure 1-2).

When another company conducted an assessment of its sales managers, it discovered that the quality of the sales manager has a big impact on performance when a salesperson leaves a territory and has to be replaced. The company identified two groups of managers—one group of top performers and another group of average performers—using a combination of competency model assessment data, historical performance rankings, and input from salespeople's upward evaluations of their managers. Then the company compared the performance of new salespeople who were hired to fill vacant territories by managers in each of the two groups. Twenty months after coming on board, more than 90 percent of the salespeople who had been hired by top-performing managers had maintained

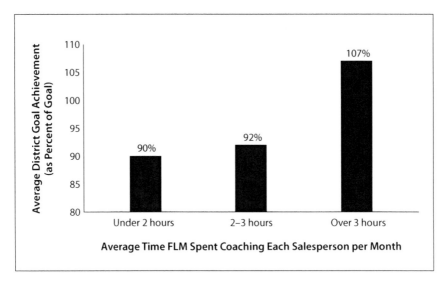

Figure 1-2   The Impact of Sales Manager Coaching on District Goal Achievement at One Company

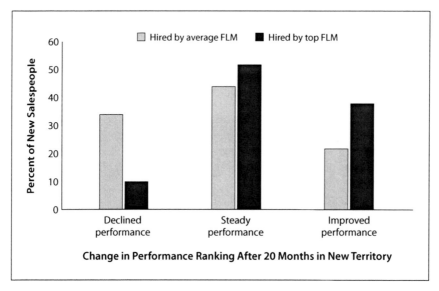

Figure 1-3 The Impact of the Sales Manager on the Success of New Salespeople at One Company

or improved the performance ranking of their territory. In the same time frame, more than a third of the salespeople who had been hired by average-performing managers experienced a decline in their territory's performance ranking (see Figure 1-3). The company attributed this difference to two characteristics of top-performing managers: (1) top-performing managers were better at identifying and attracting talented salespeople, and (2) they were better at helping new salespeople get off to a strong start through effective coaching and support.

Inconsistency in the Sales Management Team

When a salesperson is excellent, performance is excellent in a single territory. When a first-line sales manager is excellent, that manager will coach, counsel, motivate, or replace salespeople until performance is excellent across the entire district or region. Consistent strong performance by a company's sales management team is critical for sales force excellence.

When companies assess their sales management teams, they often discover serious deficiencies in the competencies of some FLMs. Assessments can be based on input from several sources, including evaluations using sales manager competency models, sales leaders' observations, salespeople's view on the effectiveness of their managers, and rankings on metrics such as district quota attainment.

Examples of assessments conducted by two companies illustrate how performance is too often inconsistent across FLMs, leading to lost sales opportunity.

Example 1: Revealing Sales Manager Inconsistency at a Hospital Supply Company

A hospital supply company conducted an assessment in which salespeople completed upward evaluations of their FLMs on several managerial competencies (see Figure 1-4). The evaluations were anonymous, and the results were not identified by individual manager but rather were used to produce an overall assessment of the quality of the sales management team. Sales leaders discovered and were concerned that the average rating that salespeople gave their managers was nowhere near "excellent" for any of the seven competencies that they felt were critical to sales manager success. In fact, managers were rated below "average" on four competencies. Leaders were also concerned that the distribution of scores on most competencies followed a disturbing bimodal pattern; Figure 1-4 shows the pattern for the leadership competency. While many salespeople gave their manager an "excellent" rating on leadership, almost equally as many gave their manager a "poor" rating and relatively few gave their manager an "average" rating. This bimodal trend occurred for the other managerial competencies as well. The

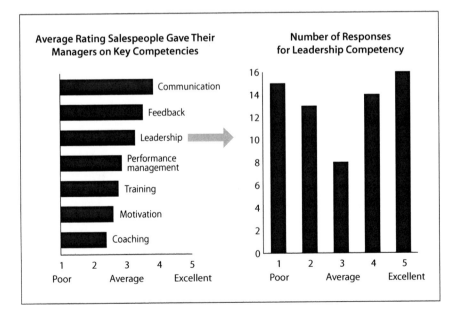

Figure 1-4   How Salespeople Rated Their Managers on Seven Key Competencies at a Hospital Supply Company

survey results confirmed sales leaders' hypothesis that the sales force was carrying a number of weak managers.

Regrettably, too many sales organizations don't assess the capabilities of their FLMs, and many fail to provide the necessary development programs needed to address FLM deficiencies. Too often, companies retain poor managers for too long.

Example 2: Identifying Opportunities for Sales Manager Improvement at a Software Company

A software company's assessment of its sales management team demonstrates the diagnostic power of assessment to uncover the underlying causes of sales force effectiveness and reveal improvement opportunities. The assessment showed that the company's management team was fairly strong, yet it also helped the company discover an important way to boost effectiveness and improve sales results.

The company used a sales competency model assessment to learn about the effectiveness of its FLMs. The model defined two categories of competencies that sales managers need to succeed at the company: *knowledge* (such as understanding of products, customers, and markets) and *skills* (such as selling, planning, and communicating). The model also recognized that FLMs need to be not only *proficient* in these areas but also good at *coaching* their salespeople to develop competency with knowledge and skills. An assessment team collected feedback on each manager's behaviors related to the job competencies by gathering input from each manager's direct supervisor, his or her direct reports, and self-evaluation. Based on the input, each FLM was rated at a "basic," "skilled," or "advanced" level of competency for proficiency and coaching of knowledge and skills. As in the previous example, the results were not identified by individual manager but rather were summarized across managers to produce an overall assessment of the FLM team (see Figure 1-5).

The company's sales leaders were pleased to see that for all four competency categories, more than 80 percent of managers were rated "skilled" or "advanced." The greatest opportunity for improvement was in the coaching abilities of sales managers. The ratings for FLMs' *proficiency* of knowledge and skills were higher than the ratings for FLMs' ability to *coach* others on knowledge and skills (that is, the categories have a larger percentage of managers rated "advanced" and a smaller percentage rated "basic" as compared to the coaching categories).

These results helped sales managers understand that they had been succeeding too often by *doing* the work with their salespeople, rather than *teaching* their people how to do it themselves. Renewed emphasis on the importance of coaching for successful sales management helped this company improve results. One year later, the company observed higher salesperson proficiency on the core

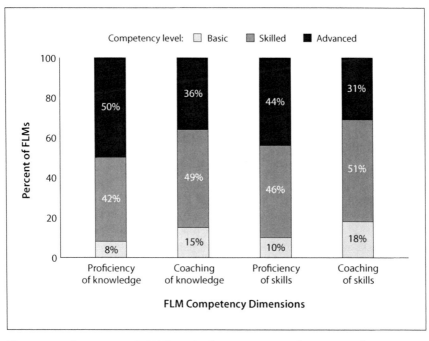

Figure 1-5   Assessment of FLM Team Performance in Four Competency Categories at a Software Company

competencies and had realized an increase in the number of deals in the pipeline as well as higher deal close rates.

The Critical Role of the Sales Manager

The job of the first-line sales manager is arguably the most important job in the entire sales force. Sales leaders tell us:

- "If your first-line management is broken, the entire sales force will be ineffective." (Helmut Wilke, Vice President Sales, U.S. Western Region, Enterprise and Partner Group at Microsoft Corporation)
- "In any sales force, you can get along without the vice president of sales, regional sales directors, and the training manager, but you cannot get along without the district [first-line] sales manager." (Andy Anderson, former Vice President of Sales and President of U.S. Pharmaceuticals, Searle U.S.)

Top sales leaders determine the direction for the organization, but it is the FLMs who ensure that the strategy is executed.

Taking on a Role Different from a Salesperson

Most FLMs are former salespeople. They know what it takes to succeed as a salesperson and therefore are capable of earning the respect of those who report to them. However, a promoted salesperson quickly discovers that the job of sales manager is very different from the job of salesperson.

Consider what happened to John, a super-salesperson who, after several years of stellar sales performance, was promoted to sales manager. As a salesperson, John had an exceptional work ethic and a strong customer focus. He was highly achievement-oriented, competitive, and confident, and he would do anything to get his customers what they needed. When John was promoted to manager, he expected all of his salespeople to be just as hard-driving and achievement-oriented as he was. When he became frustrated with the work styles and performance of some of the people in his district, he told them, "Either make quota or you're fired." On big deals, John would take charge of the relationship himself, using his "super-sales skills" to close the deal. When customers made difficult or even unreasonable requests of the company, John would call someone at headquarters and demand that the company deliver whatever the customer wanted.

Unfortunately, many of the traits that had contributed to John's success as a salesperson worked against him as a manager. John didn't know how to give salespeople constructive feedback. He undermined salespeople's motivation and confidence and, at the same time, weakened their relationships with customers by getting too involved in the sales process. His demanding attitude irritated people at headquarters with whom he had to work. John made his quota during his first two quarters as manager, but by the third quarter, two of his salespeople had left the company, and the district's annual quota was in jeopardy.

Sales leaders share their thoughts on the challenges that salespeople face when making a transition from salesperson to manager:

- "Many super-salespeople who get promoted to manager become 'helicopter managers' who hover over their salespeople and insist on being involved in every deal. This can create some short-term successes, but in the long run, the best managers are those who coach, train, and teach their entire team to be successful," observes Chris Ahearn, a Senior Advisor at TPG Capital and a former Senior Vice President of Sales and Marketing for temporary housing provider Oakwood Worldwide.

- "When salespeople are promoted to manager, one of their biggest challenges is learning to start *leading* people and to stop *doing* the sales activity themselves," says Denise O'Brien, Vice President of Business Development for Global Sales and Client Development at professional services company ARAMARK.

- "The job of manager is not just a bigger job — it's a totally different job than salesperson," says Helmut Wilke, who has led sales teams at Sun Microsystems, Extreme Networks, and Microsoft. "Many salespeople who become managers miss the freedom and excitement that they enjoyed as salespeople. When a deal closes, the salesperson is a hero; when a deal is lost, the manager often gets the blame."

For the right individual, a sales management job can be very rewarding. However, some salespeople are successful in sales because they are independent, action-oriented, and impatient — traits that can work against their success as a manager. Because many salespeople who are contemplating a move to management don't have a clear idea of what the job entails, it's important for sales leaders to communicate their expectations clearly and screen candidates thoughtfully, assessing each candidate's skills and interests relative to the job requirements.

Good salespeople differ from good sales managers in many important ways (see Figure 1-6). Salespeople are successful when they meet customer needs while at the same time achieving the company's financial goals for their territories. Sales managers also succeed by meeting customer needs and achieving objectives linked to company goals. But the manager is not the hunter, the playmaker, or the center of action. Managers contribute to customer and company success when their team of salespeople is successful. Managers are coaches, not players; they

Good Salespeople	Good Sales Managers
Listen to and are an advocate for customers	Listen to and are an advocate for salespeople
Do it themselves	Teach and coach others how to do it
Strive for personal success	Strive for team success
Control	Motivate
Make each transaction successful	Make the district or region successful
Strive for strong short-term results	Strive for strong short- and medium-term results
Focus on customer needs	Focus on customer needs

Figure 1-6   A Comparison of Good Salespeople and Good Sales Managers

achieve their objectives through others. When a salesperson gets promoted to manager, it's no longer about "me" — it's about "the team."

Research by Dawn R. Deeter-Schmelz (Ohio University), Daniel Goebel (Illinois State University), and Karen Norman Kennedy (University of Alabama at Birmingham) sheds light on why many good salespeople fail as managers. The researchers examined the characteristics of effective sales managers from the perspective of both salespeople and sales managers. Through interviews, they asked 58 salespeople and managers from a range of industries what they felt were the attributes of a successful sales manager and why. Although the salespeople and managers agreed on some attributes, subtle differences between the salespeople's and sales managers' responses revealed a common reason why sales managers fail. Salespeople want their manager to be a supportive resource, someone who *enables the sales process* by helping them do their job better. Managers see themselves as *participants in the sales process*, and they feel that their own credibility and reputation are important for success. Too many sales managers have a difficult time sacrificing their own ego needs to give salespeople the help and support they need to do their jobs effectively. In most situations, managers who view their role as sales process "enablers" rather than sales process "participants" are more likely to be successful.

Connecting Headquarters and the Field

"Sales managers are the critical link between salespeople, customers, and other departments within our company," says Liza Clechenko, a former Vice President of Sales, East/Gulf Coast at BP. "Everything comes together at the sales manager level." As Figure 1-7 shows, sales managers act as a hub that connects the field (salespeople and customers) to headquarters (the company).

In their connection with the field, FLMs interact directly with salespeople, as they have primary responsibility for selecting, building, leading, managing, and rewarding the team responsible for maintaining customer relationships. Sales managers also have at least an indirect (and sometimes a direct) role in working with customers.

In their connection with headquarters, FLMs act as intermediaries to facilitate a bidirectional flow of information. FLMs are the voice of the company to the salespeople they manage. Salespeople, in turn, convey that voice to their customers. At the same time, when salespeople need something from the company for themselves or for their customers, sales managers play a central role in helping them navigate the organization in order to secure the needed resources. So, sales managers are also the voice of salespeople and customers to the company.

Implementing Key Sales Force Decisions and Programs

FLMs play a key role in the sales force as implementers of many sales force decisions and programs. A sales manager's set of responsibilities often includes these:

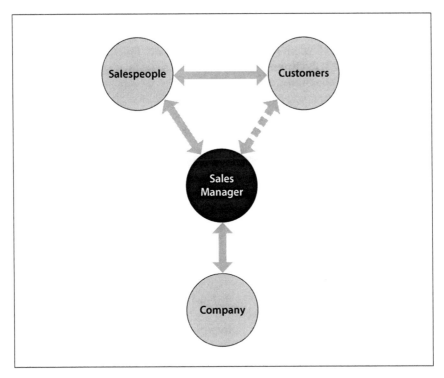

Figure 1-7   The Role of the Sales Manager

- Ensuring that salespeople understand their responsibilities and territory assignments
- Helping salespeople execute the appropriate selling process
- Recruiting, training, and coaching salespeople
- Helping salespeople make the most effective use of customer research, data and tools, and targeting information
- Promoting a culture of success and providing leadership
- Implementing incentive and motivation programs
- Keeping the team aligned with company goals and strategies through performance management, goal setting, and communication

The role of the sales manager as an implementer of sales force decisions and programs is especially critical during times of transition. Conrad Zils, Global Director, Commercial Center of Excellence for GE Healthcare, who worked with many different GE businesses in a former role as Global Director of Sales Programs and Sales Force Effectiveness, talks about the critical role that first-line sales managers played when several of GE's businesses implemented significant sales force changes in 2009 and 2010. In response to the financial crisis and challenging economic conditions, several sales forces in GE Capital's business were forced to downsize and refocus priorities on profitability. Shortly after that, GE Healthcare's business underwent a major organizational transformation to align the sales force around key customers and customer segments, rather than products and individual business units.

According to Conrad, "First-line sales managers played a critical role in helping salespeople deal with uncertainty. Salespeople feared the unknown, and our front-line managers were the first place salespeople turned when they had questions. We kept sales managers informed and aligned with the new direction and vision, so they could provide answers and keep sales force retention and engagement at high levels."

Driving Sales Force Productivity

FLMs are a critical driver of sales force productivity (see Figure 1-8). They impact salesperson quality and activity directly through their role as people managers and indirectly as implementers of key sales force decisions and programs. As a result, sales manager performance affects company financial results in a tangible way.

At the beginning of our executive sales management course, we ask the sales leaders in attendance: "What sales force productivity issues are you currently faced with?" Our initial purpose for asking the question was to learn about sales leaders' needs so we could tailor course content appropriately. In 1995, we began building a database of responses to our question; by 2010, we had captured and categorized more than 2,400 responses from sales leaders from a broad variety of

Figure 1-8   How First-Line Sales Managers Affect Productivity and Results

industries, countries, and selling environments (see Figure 1-9). Many responses directly identify the sales management team as a major source of concern; other responses point to issues that FLMs have direct influence over.

All sales force productivity issues listed in Figure 1-9 can be addressed, at least partially, by improving the sales management team. Sales managers directly

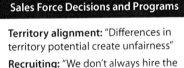

First-Line Sales Managers (FLMs)

Inappropriate structure
- "Not enough managers to support the sales force"
- "Too many types of sales specialists reporting to managers"

Too little training and support
- "Not enough management training to support sales force growth"
- "Sales managers get promoted but are not properly trained"

Weak competency
- "Inconsistency in the way that sales managers manage their teams"
- "Managers struggle to stay on top of everything"

Misdirected activity
- "Managers don't spend enough time coaching"
- "Managers 'do' rather than 'manage'"

Sales Force Decisions and Programs

Territory alignment: "Differences in territory potential create unfairness"

Recruiting: "We don't always hire the 'right' salesperson"

Training: "Need to ramp up new salespeople faster"

Targeting: "Not targeting enough high-potential customers"

Data and tools: "Better use of data can help us drive the business"

Performance management: "Salespeople need more feedback"

Goal setting: "Sales goals are not realistic"

Salesperson Quality and Activity

Quality
- "The sales force lacks key skills"
- "Turnover of good salespeople is high"
- "Huge disparity between our best and weakest salesperson"

Activity
- "Salespeople sell only products they are comfortable with"
- "Too little time with key decision makers"
- "Need to improve quality, not quantity, of sales calls"

Figure 1-9 Examples of Challenges That Companies Face in Areas Under the Direct Influence of Sales Managers

impact *salesperson quality* and retention through their roles as recruiters, coaches, and trainers. They influence *sales force activities* through their roles as coaches, leaders, motivators, and managers of performance. They also have responsibility for implementing many *sales force decisions and programs* that impact salespeople and their activities. Because of the many important roles that sales managers play, investments to improve the quality of the sales management team will certainly enhance company financial results.

The Ever-Changing Role of the Sales Manager

The job of FLM is perhaps more difficult today than ever before, as continuous change in the business environment impacts the sales organization. Some changes originate in forces external to the company: an environment of advancing technology, intensified competition, and a changing world economy; customers who are more knowledgeable and make buying decisions based on business value; a workforce of tech-savvy sales talent with new attitudes about work and life priorities. Other changes come from inside the company, as companies launch new products and strategies and focus on constant improvement and cost-cutting initiatives, often in response to external changes. All of these changes create new challenges for FLMs.

Chris Hartman, Vice President, Central Zone, Cardiology, Rhythm and Vascular Group at medical device company Boston Scientific Corporation, talks about several new challenges that sales managers faced in 2010:

- **More knowledgeable customers:** "The Internet provides customers easy access to information about products and pricing. A quick web search may enable a prospective customer to learn instantly about a price you've offered a customer on the other side of the globe."

- **Increasing numbers of Gen Y employees in the workplace:** "Today's manager is challenged to deal with a new generation of salespeople who have different priorities and goals, place greater value on work-life balance, and shun traditional business communication methods like newsletters, voicemail, and even email, preferring to stay connected through social media such as Twitter and Facebook."

- **Increased workload:** "As companies cut costs, they reduce management staff and ask managers to increase their span of control. With more people to manage, managers are working longer hours. At the same time, expectations for responsiveness have increased, as mobile communication technology keeps people connected anywhere and anytime."

- **Increased emphasis on compliance and regulatory concerns:** "In a world where technology enables transparency of information, sales managers need to be constantly aware of rules and regulations and keep a keen eye on compliance. An innocent email can easily cause considerable damage to a company."

These new complexities further increase the already difficult challenge of building a winning sales management team.

Establishing and Sustaining a Vigorous Sales Management Team in a Changing Sales Environment

The quality of the sales management team affects sales force productivity and success, yet too often companies underinvest in developing their FLMs. When sales managers come into their jobs (usually after having been successful salespeople), they are expected to know how to manage, sometimes with minimal guidance and support. Too few companies focus enough energy and resources on developing and maintaining a top-notch sales management team. As Amy Davalle, Vice President of Sales — West at medical device company Smith & Nephew, observes, "When budgets get tight, management development programs are often one of the first things that companies cut to save short-term costs, and they end up paying for this in the long term."

The Importance of Aligning Sales Management Team Decisions with Sales Force Strategy and Design

FLMs play a critical role in ensuring that sales force strategy is executed effectively. For this reason, sales leaders need to anchor their approach for building a winning sales management team with a winning sales force strategy and design. This strategy includes decisions such as these:

- Which customer segments should the sales force sell to, and what is the right value proposition for each segment?
- What is the best sales process for meeting customer needs in each targeted market segment?
- What is the right size and structure for the sales organization?

It is essential to align sales management team decisions with the right sales strategy and design. According to Quinton Oswald, CEO of SARcode BioScience and a former Vice President and Business Unit leader for Tissue Growth and Repair at Genentech, "Because sales managers are a critical link between sales strategy and execution, you can't define the sales manager's role in isolation. When we changed our sales strategy and design at Genentech to better meet the needs of local markets, we had to realign the role of sales managers as well. We increased our expectations for the role. In addition to coaching, counseling, and managing the performance of their people, sales managers had to become local general managers who could develop business plans and allocate resources effectively. By defining strategy and tying the FLM role to the strategy, the sales management team became a valuable vehicle for executing strategy to achieve company goals."

Three Core Elements of Building a Winning FLM Team

This book lays out an approach consisting of three core elements for establishing and sustaining a vigorous sales management team:

1. *Defining* the FLM job that best facilitates execution of the sales force strategy
2. *Creating* a strong team of FLMs with the talents and competencies that can drive success
3. *Enabling* the right FLM activity for leading the sales team to drive results

Anchored by sales force strategy and design, the approach enables you to win in the marketplace with a sales management team that helps your sales organization achieve its goals in the face of a continuously changing sales environment (see Figure 1-10).

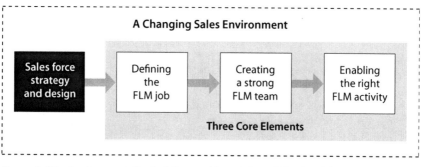

Figure 1-10   An Approach for Building and Sustaining a Winning Sales Management Team in a Changing Sales Environment

The FLM Success Drivers

This book describes eight key FLM success drivers, organized into three sections that correspond to the three core elements. The success drivers include the decisions that sales leaders make and the programs, systems, processes, and tools that they use to define, create, and enable the FLM team to drive sales force performance. Each chapter provides approaches, examples, and practical advice for executing one of the FLM success drivers. A concluding chapter addresses strategies for managing change across the success drivers (see Figure 1-11).

The FLM success drivers are introduced here. More detail is provided in the next eight chapters.

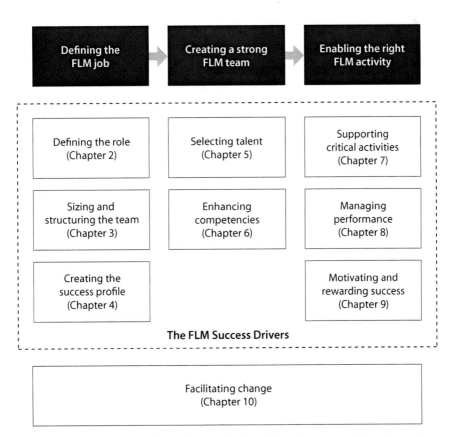

Figure 1-11 An Approach for Building a Winning Sales Management Team Through Eight Key FLM Success Drivers

Section I: Defining the FLM Job

Three FLM success drivers help you create a blueprint for a winning sales management team. The three chapters organized around these success drivers address the following topics:

Defining the Sales Manager's Role (Chapter 2)

- Three roles for FLMs in driving district success
- The right focus on managing salespeople, customers, and the business
- Steps to defining and implementing the FLM role
- Ensuring that FLMs focus on both long-term and short-term success

Sizing and Structuring the Sales Management Team (Chapter 3)

- The right span of control
- The best sales force reporting structure
- Managing a structure to achieve business objectives
- Managing with different types of sales specialists

Creating the Sales Manager Success Profile (Chapter 4)

- Characteristics (personal qualities) and competencies (skills and knowledge) that drive FLM success
- Discovering FLM success characteristics and competencies
- Using the success profile to create and enable the FLM team

Section II: Creating a Strong FLM Team

Two FLM success drivers help you recruit and develop a talented team of first-line sales managers. The chapters in this section address the following topics:

Selecting the Best Sales Management Talent (Chapter 5)

- Role of characteristics and competencies in FLM selection
- Looking for internal versus external FLM talent
- Strategies for finding, selecting, and attracting talent
- Selecting those with the right management characteristics, not simply those who are the best salespeople
- Strategies for retaining management talent and keeping the best salespeople

Enhancing Sales Management Competencies (Chapter 6)

- Training and development content for new FLMs to learn the job
- Content for current FLMs to develop skills and adapt to change
- Prioritizing FLM development needs
- Blending learning methods for highest impact at appropriate cost

Section III: Enabling the Right FLM Activity

Three FLM success drivers help you enable and encourage the sales management team to perform the right activities for driving sales force success. The three chapters in this section address the following topics:

Supporting Critical Sales Management Activities (Chapter 7)

- Processes and systems, support people, and data and tools for enhancing FLM efficiency and effectiveness
- Support that benefits salespeople, customers, and the company without adding unnecessary overhead
- Dashboards and metrics to help FLMs improve performance
- Helping FLMs prioritize to minimize time spent on less-productive tasks

Managing Sales Management Performance (Chapter 8)

- FLM success factors that are critical to manage
- Best metrics for managing FLM performance
- Processes for managing FLM performance that drive results
- Early signs that an FLM is in trouble and steps to take to effect change

Motivating and Rewarding Sales Management Success (Chapter 9)

- The motivators of successful FLMs
- Defining a motivating FLM job and creating a culture of success
- Using recognition to increase FLM motivation and engagement
- Financial rewards that enhance short-term and long-term FLM motivation

Aligning the FLM Success Drivers

It is impossible to create a winning sales management team without strong alignment of the decisions that define, create, and enable the team. Team quality is sacrificed when, for example,

- The FLM role requires managers to spend five days a week with salespeople and customers; yet the company does not provide managers with the tools and support they need to complete all their administrative responsibilities efficiently.
- The FLM selection process does not screen candidates for a competency such as coaching ability; yet new FLMs receive no training on how to coach.
- The FLM performance management process focuses on developing the team for long-term success; yet sales managers earn most of their pay through incentives tied to quarterly sales results.
- The FLM role suggests that sales managers spend two days a month in the field with each salesperson; yet budget constraints have led to an average span of control of 15 salespeople per manager.

As you manage the FLM success drivers that define, create, and enable your sales management team, check that your decisions are consistently aligned with one another and support your sales force strategy.

Recognizing the Need to Change

FLMs play a critical role in providing input for and implementing sales force change. The book's last chapter addresses the following topics:

The Sales Manager: An Essential Facilitator of Change (Chapter 10)

- The critical role of the FLM as a facilitator of sales force change
- Changes impacting sales forces today
- How companies are responding with sales force transformations or evolutionary sales force improvements
- How sales leaders can enable FLMs in their role as facilitators of change

The book concludes with a self-assessment tool that you can use to determine priorities for improving the FLM success drivers for your sales organization. By adapting to the changing environment, and continually improving the FLM success drivers, your sales force can gain competitive advantage by capitalizing on a frequently overlooked productivity opportunity—the sales management team—*the force behind the sales force.*

Glossary

Every selling organization has its own unique vocabulary. Terms such as "salesperson," "sales management team," and "customer," for example, can mean different things in different contexts. At the same time, what one company calls, for example, a "salesperson" another may refer to as a "sales professional" or a "sales representative." To enhance clarity for readers, we provide here a glossary of several terms that we use frequently throughout this book. You may wish to mentally substitute the terms your company uses—for example, substitute "district sales manager" (DSM) for "first-line sales manager" (FLM)—to make the ideas more accessible for your situation.

Company   Generally refers to the selling company. Equivalent terms in some contexts include "seller" or "selling company."

Company leaders / Executive leadership team   The highest levels of leadership within a company, generally those to whom the top sales executives report—for example, a divisional general manager, a COO, or a CEO.

Customer   A current or potential buyer of a company's products and services (equivalent to a client, buyer, decision maker, or purchaser in some contexts). We use the term "customer" when referring to both the customer organization (the buying company) and specific individuals within the customer organization who influence buying decisions.

First-line sales manager (FLM)   A manager within a sales force to whom salespeople report directly. Equivalent terms in some contexts include "district manager" or "region manager."

Prospect   An organization or a person who is a potential buyer of a company's products and services but has not yet made a purchase. Generally we use the term "customer" to refer to both current customers and prospects; however, when it is important to distinguish between the two, we use the term "prospect" to differentiate those customers who have not yet purchased from the company.

Sales leaders / Sales leadership team   Includes second-line sales managers (SLMs) and others above them within the sales organization hierarchy. For example, in a large sales force with FLMs who report to regional directors who report to a sales vice president who reports to a divisional general manager, the regional directors and sales vice president together comprise the "sales leadership team." In a smaller sales force with FLMs who report to a national sales director who reports to a divisional general manager, the national sales director is considered the "sales leader."

Sales management team   All the first-line sales managers in a sales force. This term is used commonly in larger sales forces that have many FLMs with similar job responsibilities. The term is less common in smaller sales forces with just a few FLMs or with FLMs with diverse job responsibilities; however, the ideas in this book apply equally to sales management "teams" of any size and composition.

Salesperson   A person in the sales force who has direct responsibility for selling to customers or prospects. Equivalent terms in some contexts include "sales representative," "sales professional," "seller," "sales agent," "account manager," or "account executive."

Defining the First-Line Sales Manager's Job

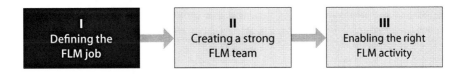

I	II	III
Defining the FLM job	**Creating a strong FLM team**	**Enabling the right FLM activity**

The Focus of Section I

Building a winning sales management team starts with developing a first-line sales manager (FLM) job definition that enables the best execution of your sales force strategy. Three FLM success drivers, discussed in Chapters 2 through 4, help you define the right job for enabling sales force success.

Defining the Sales Manager's Role (Chapter 2)

"First-line sales managers should see a clear link between their role and daily activities and the overarching company goals and strategies," says Chris Hartman, Vice President, Central Zone, Cardiology, Rhythm and Vascular Group at Boston Scientific Corporation. By defining the FLM's role, sales leaders create a blueprint that helps sales managers focus their time effectively to drive both long-term and short-term results. The FLM job includes three distinct roles: people manager, customer manager, and business manager. A series of prescribed steps can help you discover the optimal mix of roles for managing your sales force to drive the best possible results.

Sizing and Structuring the Sales Management Team (Chapter 3)

The right span of control and reporting structure for FLMs ensure appropriate development and management of salespeople and proper coordination and control of sales activity. Several proven approaches can help you determine how many salespeople and what types of sales specialists should report to each FLM. By providing good support mechanisms and revisiting reporting structure decisions when business needs change, sales leaders overcome the inevitable stresses that a sales management structure creates.

Creating the Sales Manager Success Profile (Chapter 4)

A sales manager success profile defines the characteristics (personal qualities) and competencies (skills and knowledge) that drive success in the FLM role. Several approaches can help you discover the most important FLM success characteristics and competencies for your sales environment. Then, by using the profile as a template for aligning FLM selection, development, support, performance management, and motivation programs, you can build a potent sales management team that enables your sales force to win in the marketplace.

What Sales Leaders Say About Defining the FLM Job

Helmut Wilke   Vice President of Sales, Western Region, Enterprise and Partner Group, Microsoft Corporation

"The job of manager is not just a bigger job; it's a totally different job than salesperson." Helmut has served in many sales leadership roles in the high-tech industry. Prior to his position at Microsoft, he was a Senior Vice President at Extreme Networks and Sun Microsystems.

John Barb   Former Vice President of Sales, xpedx, International Paper

"It's critical to be very clear on what the role of the sales manager is and to align the competency model, selection process, development and support programs, metrics, and reward systems with role expectations." John's career at International Paper has spanned many business units and positions, including procurement, finance, marketing, sales, sales management, and executive leadership.

Amy Davalle   Vice President of Sales — West, Smith & Nephew

"You need to be very clear on what you want your FLMs to focus on. They are likely to gravitate naturally to the role of customer manager. But is this where you want them to spend their time?" Amy has held various positions in sales and sales management, most recently at Smith & Nephew and Guidant.

Sandy Cantwell   Vice President of Sales Operations, Cardinal Health

"With the dynamics and speed of change today, it is critical that FLMs engage as change facilitators." Sandy's healthcare industry experience includes roles in field sales, sales leadership, sales operations, and human resources. She has facilitated multiple sales strategy and sales organization restructurings, automated sales forces, and built centers of excellence for sales performance and incentive management.

Cathy Fischer   Executive-level marketer in consumer packaged goods and durable goods

"Sales management span of control can be higher when a company provides its salespeople with strong support for executing a well-defined sales process." Cathy led a sales team of 500 people dedicated to meeting the needs of a major retail customer. The team included merchandising, field sales, and headquarters sales roles and was aligned to match the customer's buying organization.

Marshall Solem   Principal, ZS Associates

"The best reporting structure when multiple sales specialist teams share customer responsibility depends on the size of each team and the need for coordination between teams. A good structure brings customers expertise by allowing FLMs to meet the unique coaching needs of each specialist role, and facilitates a coordinated sales effort when that's something customers value." Marshall leads the Sales Solutions Practice at ZS, focusing on sales force design, territory alignment, incentive compensation, and sales force effectiveness.

Fred Wagner   Vice President, Customer and Logistics Services, Johnson & Johnson

"Our division manager [FLM] competency model declares our profile of what it takes to succeed in the FLM role. It helps us select people for the role who fit with our strategy. . . . It helps us identify strengths and weaknesses in FLMs and allows us to have competency-based discussions with individuals through the performance management process." Prior to his current role, Fred was a Vice President of Sales at Johnson & Johnson's Ethicon Endo-Surgery division.

Liza Clechenko Former Vice President of Sales, East/Gulf Coast, BP

 *"Change orientation is an important competency for all FLMs. . . . We expect FLMs to develop and seek out solutions, enlist and motivate others around change, and drive change programs to successful conclusions."* Liza has held various leadership positions within BP in sales and frontline operations, human resources management, and strategic program development. She has led transformation initiatives across IT, human resources, and sales functions.

CHAPTER 2

Defining the Sales Manager's Role

Enabling Execution of Sales Strategy

"It used to be that good sales managers were only *people managers*, responsible for selecting, building, leading, managing, and rewarding a team of salespeople," says Chris Hartman, Vice President, Central Zone, Cardiology, Rhythm and Vascular Group for medical device company Boston Scientific Corporation. "Most sales managers were former salespeople who could coach others effectively, and as long as they delivered the numbers, not much else mattered. But today, rapid change in the environment in which managers have to lead creates a need for managers to be more than just good coaches. They also have to be good general *business managers.*"

"On our sales team, AVPs [first-line sales managers] spend most of their time as *people managers* who do the day-to-day management and coaching of their salespeople. Additionally, some AVPs are *customer relationship managers*," says Denise O'Brien, a Vice President of Business Development, Global Sales and Client Development, at professional services company ARAMARK. "For example, one AVP leads a team of sellers who focus on our largest 'mega' accounts in a specific segment of the business. The sales process for these customers is complex, and the AVP works with the customer and the salesperson throughout the sales process. The AVP also helps to develop the relationship with the customer, for example by meeting with the customer's CFO to discuss strategy."

"The role of the first-line sales manager varies across the multiple sales divisions in our company," says Sandy Cantwell, Vice President of Sales Operations at Cardinal Health. "In one division, sales managers are both players and coaches. They spend 70 percent of their time selling (for example, managing large deals and negotiating with customers), and 30 percent of their time coaching and managing a team of reps who service customer needs. In another division, sales managers are more like general managers for a city or market. They manage the sales team and also play an integral role in local operations."

First-line sales managers (FLMs) play three roles—people manager, customer manager, and business manager. The emphasis placed on each role depends on business needs. In some sales organizations, FLMs are primarily *people managers*. In others, the *customer manager* or *business manager* role is important as well for enabling execution of sales strategy.

The Focus of This Chapter

This chapter helps you *define* the right FLM role for your sales organization. The chapter is organized around four main topics:

- The importance of defining the FLM role for keeping your sales management team focused on the right business priorities.
- The responsibilities and impact of the three sales manager roles: people manager, customer manager, and business manager.
- A three-step process for defining the right mix of these roles and finding the highest-impact FLM activities for your sales environment.
- The importance of FLMs as essential facilitators of sales force change—an ongoing responsibility that cuts across all three roles.

Subsequent chapters help you *implement* the FLM role successfully by aligning the other FLM success drivers—team size and structure, sales manager characteristics and competencies, manager selection processes, development programs, support systems, performance management processes, and motivation programs and rewards—around the role definition.

When building a winning sales management team, defining the FLM role and its relative emphasis on people, customer, and business management is a critical FLM success driver and a first step in defining the FLM job (see Figure 2-1).

Keeping Sales Managers Focused on Business Priorities

By defining the FLM role, sales leaders help managers stay focused on the activities that are most important for executing company sales force strategy.

The FLM role must fit within the context of the larger sales organization. According to Liza Clechenko, a former Vice President of Sales, East/Gulf Coast at BP, "An effective sales team works like a well-oiled machine with clear role definition and clear accountability between roles from senior level to frontline representative and sales/customer support."

FLMs have multiple demands on their time and can be pulled from all sides. When salespeople need something from the company, they often go to their manager for help in securing the needed resources. At the same time, when the company needs something from the sales force, it relies on FLMs to ensure that the task gets done. FLMs who have selling responsibility face additional time management challenges, as they need to prioritize customer responsibilities along with people and business management responsibilities.

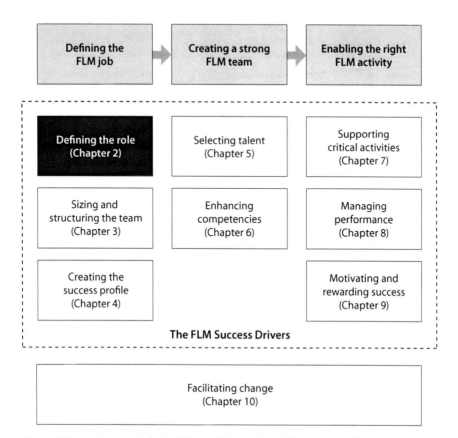

Figure 2-1   An Approach for Building a Winning Sales Management Team

To simultaneously meet the needs of salespeople, customers, and the company, sales managers have to make choices about how to spend their time. Some of the work required to sustain long-term district success is challenging. For example, "developing people and formulating business strategies are difficult and messy tasks that are quite often outside of a manager's comfort zone," says Chris Ahearn, a Senior Advisor at TPG Capital. Other work required of FLMs is easier to do (especially work that relates to the manager's prior job as a seller) or has urgent deadlines (see Figure 2-2). Without a clear definition of what work is most critical to their role, FLMs too often choose to focus on the easy or urgent work, leaving inadequate time for the difficult work that is essential for long-term success.

Sales leaders encourage role clarity for FLMs by continuously communicating and reinforcing the FLM role through the other FLM success drivers. "It's critical

FLM Responsibility	Difficult Work with Long-Term Impact	Easy or Urgent Work
For salespeople	Give a poor performer tough feedback Coach the salesperson to improve	Focus on results without coaching on how to achieve them
For customers	Visit a challenging prospect Help the salesperson develop the relationship	Respond to a service request Nurture the relationship myself
For the business	Tailor sales strategies for local needs	Attend meetings Respond to emails

The constant pull toward easy or urgent work can leave too little time for difficult work with long-term impact.

Figure 2-2 Examples of Work That Sales Managers Might Choose to Spend Time On

to be very clear on what the role of the sales manager is and to align the competency model, selection process, development and support programs, metrics, and reward systems with role expectations," observes John Barb, a former Vice President of Sales for xpedx, a distribution business within International Paper. Without a consistent message about what activities are critical to the FLM role, it's easy for sales managers to get pulled off track, focusing on tasks that are urgent or within their comfort zone, rather than on what is most important for driving long-term sales performance.

The Sales Manager: Managing People, Customers, and the Business

Sales managers are ultimately accountable for achieving sales and profit objectives that help the company attain its financial goals. To accomplish this, FLMs play three main roles that connect salespeople, customers, and the company: a people management role, a customer management role, and a business management role (see Figure 2-3). All three roles influence sales success, and the emphasis placed on each role depends on the selling environment.

As people managers, FLMs oversee a team of (typically) 7 to 12 salespeople. As customer managers, FLMs play a role in the sales process to drive success with

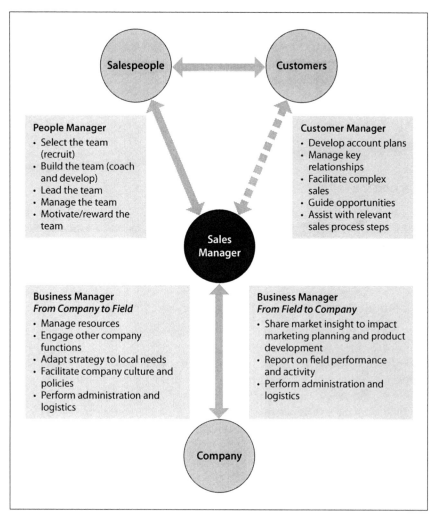

Figure 2-3   Three Main Roles of Sales Managers

customers. As business managers, FLMs have a bidirectional flow of responsibility. First, FLMs must ensure that company strategies, resource allocation, culture, and policies get implemented effectively in the field so that sales force activity stays aligned with company goals. Second, they must ensure that what's happening in the field (with salespeople and customers) gets communicated back to the company so that company strategies and plans stay aligned with customer needs.

A People Manager: Enabling the Sales Team

Sales managers succeed when their people succeed. The best way for FLMs to have high long-term impact on sales team performance is by coaching, educating, and motivating their people to succeed on their own. As the old Chinese proverb states, "Give a man a fish; you have fed him for today. Teach a man to fish; and you have fed him for a lifetime."

As people managers, FLMs must select, build, lead, manage, and reward a team of salespeople, ensuring that the team executes the right sales activity, meets customer needs, and achieves company results.

Selecting the Team

The best FLMs create a team of winners, starting with selecting the right people for the team. Hiring and retaining the right team is perhaps the most important responsibility a sales manager has. Chris Hartman of Boston Scientific recalls, "When I was a district manager, my former boss told me: 'When I see a bad salesperson, I don't ask, 'Who is that slacker?' I ask, 'Who *hired* that slacker?'"

Building the Team Through Coaching and Development

Once the salespeople are selected, good FLMs focus on how to coach and develop the team for success. "The best FLMs find ways to 'cross pollinate' ideas through peer-to-peer learning and teaching," says Chris Ahearn of TPG Capital. "This builds deep capability and competency across the team and enables new salespeople who join the team to ramp up much faster."

The best managers understand each salesperson's strengths and weaknesses and tailor coaching and development appropriately for the individual. And when faced with major changes — for example, significant new product launches, a changing economy, or a selling process transformation — good FLMs help their people successfully navigate the changing waters.

Leading the Team

As leaders, sales managers use their knowledge and insight to develop a clear and effective vision and then influence their team to share that vision and to work to achieve common goals. "I need to lead from the front and set a good example," says an FLM in the retail business of an insurance company. "My team looks to me for direction and guidance, and I'm no longer 'one of the guys.'"

Managing the Team

Good FLMs are decisive and consistent in managing their salespeople. They know how to define and organize the work that needs to be done. "One of the toughest transitions for new, inexperienced FLMs is shifting from working for themselves to leading and driving results through others. Good managers are not micromanagers. They delegate appropriately to team members," says Sandy Cantwell of Cardinal Health.

Good FLMs empower the team while setting high performance standards and monitoring performance against those standards. Through their role in the performance management process, FLMs help sustain and continuously enhance sales force performance.

Rewarding the Team

Good FLMs reward team members for their commitment, hard work, and results. Although companies usually centralize financial reward programs (bonuses, commissions, salary increases), sales managers typically have some input as to which rewards are appropriate for their people. More importantly, they have responsibility for giving out nonfinancial rewards, such as appreciation and recognition. Good FLMs understand what motivates different members of the team, and they match the right rewards with the right people.

What Makes a Good People Manager?

Over a period of several years, one of the authors asked his MBA students to describe the characteristics of the good managers and poor managers for whom they had recently worked (see Figure 2-4). These students were relatively new to their careers and came from a variety of industries and job functions, including sales. Good managers excelled in all five categories of activities required for enabling an effective sales team: they were good at selecting, building, leading, managing, and motivating and rewarding their team of people.

Most sales management jobs have a significant people management component, as a strong team of salespeople is critical for an FLM's success. In one pharmaceutical sales force, the people manager role is the fundamental focus of the job. Salespeople in this sales force need deep product and customer expertise so they can inform physicians about the benefits and side effects of the company's line of prescription medications using communication that is consistent, accurate, and within regulatory guidelines. FLMs have an important role in coaching and managing salespeople to ensure appropriate quality of sales force activity. The FLM job description is dominated by people management activities, such as providing leadership and direction; coaching, counseling, and mentoring salespeople; attracting, retaining, and developing salespeople; rewarding positive results; aggressively managing performance deficiencies; ensuring sales messages are delivered accurately; and fostering teamwork. Ultimately, the sales manager's job is to achieve district sales results.

Good Managers	Poor Managers
Select the best team	**Are not careful when selecting the team**
Identifiy and attract the best talent	Hire weak people
Build the team's competence and help people grow	**Allow team to atrophy over time**
Train, coach, and counsel	Do not set achievable objectives
Measure progress and provide feedback	Demand improvement without coaching team members on how to improve
Fight for promotions for team members	
Manage their people	**Work for themselves**
Define clear objectives, strategy, and roles	Micromanage and try to do everything
Delegate and empower	Are inconsistent
Listen, discuss, and are open	Are indecisive or unavailable when decisions need to be made
Back up their people	
Lead for their company	**Work for themselves**
Increase productivity continuously	Take credit for the team's success
Live company values	Set a poor example of behavior
Communicate market conditions and employee feelings and sentiments	Make excuses or blame poor performance on external factors
Manage expenses and resources	
Reward and motivate	**Create poor morale**
Create a positive work environment	Are unethical
Are interested	Exhibit favoritism
Are fair	Play political games
Recognize and reward their people	Are thoughtless

Figure 2-4   Characteristics That Distinguish Good People Managers from Poor People Managers

A Customer Manager: Selling and Managing Customer Relationships

In addition to their people management role, FLMs at some companies are expected to sell. Selling responsibilities can include:

- Participating in steps of the sales process where the manager's skills and experience add value—for example, helping with negotiations on large deals.

- Participating in sales situations where the manager's involvement adds credibility. For example, in small start-up companies, sales managers and even the CEO often participate in the sales process.
- Bringing resources from other company functions (customer service, manufacturing, or finance, for example) to the customer during the sales process.
- Maintaining primary responsibility for selling to the company's largest customers or for selling to customers with whom the manager already has a strong relationship.
- Assisting salespeople on difficult sales calls or on sales calls to new or strategic accounts.
- Ensuring consistent implementation of sales strategy within global accounts. Denise O'Brien of ARAMARK explains, "Salespeople on global account teams focus on the needs of specific locations of the multilocation account; managers must understand the impact of what happens in the entire global account and manage the broader sales activity—connecting each of the individual locations and keeping the global strategy in mind."

Many sales managers enjoy retaining some selling responsibility. Selling is something that they are typically quite good at and that new managers especially are very comfortable with. In addition, selling helps managers stay connected to the marketplace and customers.

In some environments, manager involvement with customers is an integral part of the sales process. For example, a large sales team at a supplier of home improvement products to the retail building industry is responsible for meeting the needs of the supplier's largest customer, a national home improvement chain. The supplier's sales team structure mirrors the retailer's buying organization: salespeople are aligned with the retailer's buying districts, which include 8 to 10 retail stores each, and region managers (FLMs) are aligned with the retailer's buying regions, which include four or five districts each. While salespeople build and manage relationships with their counterpart retail district buying managers and with personnel in individual retail stores, the supplier's region managers are expected to spend approximately half of their time in the role of customer manager, building and maintaining relationships with regional-level buyers. The matching of individuals with sales responsibility at the supplier to individuals with buying responsibility at the retailer occurs at all levels—up to the top leadership—of both organizations.

The danger of giving FLMs selling responsibility is that they may spend too much time on selling tasks that a salesperson should do (tasks that are well within their comfort zone) and not enough time managing their team (an activity that can be stressful and may challenge their skills, especially when dealing with poor performers). The best FLMs limit their customer management time to tasks and customers that are appropriate for managers (such as those listed above). They coach and manage their team to perform customer management tasks that are appropriate for salespeople, and they encourage team members to pursue professional development opportunities that can help them improve competency at those tasks.

A Business Manager: The Critical Link Between the Company and Its Salespeople and Their Customers

Good FLMs need to be more than just good managers of people and customers. They must also excel in their role as business managers in order to successfully connect the field to the company. "As business managers, sales managers help to keep the sales force focused on the bigger picture," says Helmut Wilke, a sales leader who has worked for companies such as Sun Microsystems, Extreme Networks, and Microsoft. "The best sales managers think like 'company guys' not like 'sales guys.' A good salesperson closes a deal, makes a commission, and moves on to the next deal. A good manager, on the other hand, sees the bigger picture and can judge the best way to use resources, taking into account the cost to pursue a deal and the likelihood of success." In their role as business managers, FLMs act as a critical link between salespeople and customers and the company.

From the Field to the Company: Communicating Field Opportunities and Concerns

On one side of the business management role, an FLM's responsibility flows from the field to the company. By sharing with the company the knowledge gained through interactions in the field, FLMs enable development of more effective company marketing and sales strategies and plans. An FLM needs to do the following:

- **Share market insight to impact company marketing strategy and planning.** "Sales managers play a key role in managing the pipeline, developing quotas, and tracking performance," says Jay Sampson, former General Manager, U.S. Emerging Media Sales at Microsoft. According to sales leader Helmut Wilke, "Sales managers are a critical source of current market information. Through their day-to-day interactions with salespeople and customers, managers learn what the competition is doing and can report back to the company so that appropriate marketing and product strategies can be developed." In the words of Quinton Oswald, CEO of biopharmaceutical company SARcode BioScience and a former sales and marketing leader at Genentech: "FLMs are the best customer feedback source we have, especially when things are changing."

- **Report on field performance, activity, and morale.** Salespeople are empowered. Yet the company wants to know that they are happy, are doing the right things, and are on track to achieve goal. FLMs keep the company informed about the morale and activity of their people and their performance on key results metrics, such as sales growth, goal attainment, and performance in key accounts. For example, in the IBM sales organization, "cadence" reports measure progress against key goals. These reports are used as tools to manage weekly calls between FLMs and their supervisors (and between other levels within the sales organization as well).

From the Company to the Field: Implementing Strategy, Resource Usage, Culture, and Policy

On the other side of the business management role, an FLM's responsibility flows from the company to the field. FLMs are responsible for ensuring that company strategy, resources, and culture get implemented and managed effectively. Managers need to do the following:

- **Manage sales force resources.** As business managers, FLMs are often responsible for managing resources that the company provides to the sales force. This can include physical assets such as cars, computers, telephones, demonstrator equipment, and office space. It can also include informational assets, such as databases and insight into company strategy. Many sales managers are expected to manage a budget for their operating expenses as well, including items such as relocation, collateral, travel, training and meeting expenses, and office supplies.
- **Secure resources from other company functions.** At a business information company, input from more than 800 members of the sales organization revealed that a consistent attribute of top-performing salespeople and managers was a good understanding of the internal organization to resolve issues with product teams, marketing, and accounting. Good FLMs know how to navigate the internal organization to support their salespeople. In addition, "good managers enable and teach the salespeople on their teams how to navigate the company and get resources, rather than trying to own it all themselves," says Chris Ahearn.
- **Tailor strategy and resources for local markets.** "Adapting corporate sales strategies and resource allocation decisions for local needs is a key part of the sales manager's job at Genentech," says Quinton Oswald.
- **Enable company culture and ensure policy compliance.** FLMs are responsible for ensuring that the company culture gets propagated throughout their district. They must share the vision for a success culture with their

team and reinforce that vision with constant communication, consistent actions, and appropriate rewards for behaviors that align with the culture. As business managers, FLMs are also responsible for ensuring compliance with company policies and external regulations, a responsibility that has increased in importance as communication media such as email, the Internet, social networks, and texting provide powerful methods for sales organizations to share information broadly and rapidly.

Minimizing Administrative and Logistical Requirements: Focusing the Business Manager's Role on High-Value Activity

"Sales managers too often get pulled into functions that others in the company should be doing—logistics, service, and pricing, for example. It's a real challenge to get them out of hand-to-hand combat and pull them up to a 30,000-foot level where they can add value through their leadership," says John Barb of xpedx.

FLMs, especially top performers, may be asked to participate in numerous internal meetings and phone calls, to respond to a plethora of emails, or to be on multiple internal task forces—all of which take managers out of the field and away from their people and customer management responsibilities. Too often, the role of business manager requires FLMs to participate excessively in logistics and administration. If the processes for securing resources from other company functions, ensuring policy compliance, reporting on local performance through cadence calls with company leaders, and submitting and managing local budgets, for example, are not streamlined, the burden on sales managers can accelerate rapidly.

When we asked 37 sales leaders (including attendees at one of our sales executive courses and several members of our Sales Management Advisory Board) how FLMs in their sales forces spend their time, a consistent trend emerged: more than three-quarters of responders said that FLMs spend too much time on low-value business management activities (administration and logistics) and too little time on people management. On average, the leaders felt that sales managers should shift a half day each week from business management to people management activity. The consensus was that, although some business management activities are important for long-term success (sharing market insight and developing local business plans, for example), the business management role also requires many low-value, time-consuming tasks that are easy for managers to do. The urgent nature of these tasks often prevents managers from performing higher-impact but harder people management activities.

By taking a close look at how FLMs spend their time, companies often discover that time-consuming processes can be made more efficient or that some low-value business management tasks can be eliminated, simplified, automated, delegated to cheaper resources, or outsourced.

Defining and Implementing the Right Sales Management Role at Your Company

What is the right mix of people, customer, and business management responsibilities for first-line sales managers at your company? In most sales forces, FLMs play all three roles—people manager, customer manager, and business manager—to some extent. There is considerable variation across different industries and selling environments in the amount of time that FLMs spend in each role. The typical time allocation and some insights on the business conditions under which each role is emphasized provide a benchmark to help you determine what the ideal time allocation is for your sales managers (see Figure 2-5).

Role	Typical Time Allocation	Some Conditions Under Which Time Allocation Should Be Greater Than the Typical Range
People Manager	30%–55%	**Allocate more than 55% to People Manager role when:** • The sales process is simple, streamlined, and consistent • There are many inexperienced salespeople due to rapid sales force growth or high salesperson turnover • It is important to closely control sales activity
Customer Manager	25%–40%	**Allocate more than 40% to Customer Manager role when:** • The sales process is complex, multistep, and customized or involves multiple decision makers • Customers value a relationship with someone with authority • There are too few key accounts for a dedicated key account manager • Managers have unique expertise (for example, in pricing or negotiating)
Business Manager	20%–35%	**Allocate more than 35% to Business Manager role when:** • The sales process requires participation of other company functions • Managers control local budget and resources • Dynamic events, rapid change, or local conditions require significant adaptation of sales strategies

Figure 2-5   Benchmarks for the Time Sales Managers Should Spend in People, Customer, and Business Management Roles

Regardless of the amount of time they spend in the roles of people manager, customer manager, and business manager, FLMs at all companies have one responsibility in common: they are expected to deliver results. The philosophy of how to accomplish this may vary, but at the end of the day, sales managers succeed in their jobs when they accomplish revenue and profit objectives that help the company achieve its financial goals.

The three-step process shown in Figure 2-6 can help you define and implement a high-impact FLM role for your sales force—a role that includes the right mix of people, customer, and business management activity.

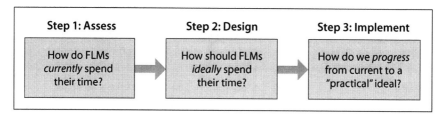

Figure 2-6   Three-Step Process for Defining and Implementing the Right Sales Manager Role

Step 1: Assess How Sales Managers Currently Spend Their Time

"One of the easiest and most eye-opening analyses that sales leaders can do is to take a look at how sales managers (and salespeople) are spending their time, either by surveying the sales force or by asking managers or salespeople to track their activity for a period," says Ty Curry, a principal at sales and marketing consulting firm ZS Associates. "Very often, such analyses reveal easy-to-implement effectiveness improvement opportunities." Here's how to do an assessment for your FLM team:

1. **Develop a list of specific job tasks.** Consider organizing the list around the three sales manager roles (use Figure 2-3 as a starting point for task definition).

2. **Include tasks for each role from the following categories:**
   a. Tasks with direct value to customers and the company—for example, coaching salespeople (people manager), nurturing relationships with key customers (customer manager), and tailoring sales strategies for local needs (business manager).
   b. Tasks that have indirect customer and company value and are necessary to keep the business functioning—for example, completing compliance

administration for HR (people manager), following up with customers to ensure satisfaction (customer manager), and attending important internal company meetings (business manager).

c. Tasks that sales managers devote considerable time to, even though they have low company and customer impact—for example, answering emails, following up on requests from headquarters, and some internal meetings.

d. Tasks that allow managers to grow professionally—for example, attending training and participating in development opportunities that are important for long-term success.

3. **Use an effective but efficient method of capturing the data.** If possible, use data from the customer relationship management (CRM) or other electronic system that tracks how managers spend their time. Supplement that data by asking managers to keep a journal of how they spend their time for several weeks or by administering a survey that asks managers to estimate how much time they spent on each task in recent weeks.

4. **Use the results of the assessment as a baseline** for defining the current FLM role.

The results of an FLM time survey for a sales force that sells custom business software solutions revealed an opportunity for enhancing effectiveness (see Figure 2-7). Sales leaders were concerned that FLMs devoted a full one-third of their time to internally focused less-valuable activities (internal communication and reporting, internal projects, and home office administration). They either eliminated or reassigned some of these activities, allowing FLMs more time for coaching while participating in customer-related activities with their direct reports.

Step 2: Design How Sales Managers Should Ideally Spend Their Time

With a baseline assessment in place of how FLMs currently spend their time, look for opportunities to reallocate time to the activities that have the greatest impact on successful execution of your current and future sales strategies. For example:

1. **Think about how your sales environment is changing.** Consider also how that change is affecting customers and salespeople. Ask questions such as these:

   • What sales management activities are most important for meeting customer needs—both today and in the future?

   • What management activities encourage salespeople to spend their time on activities that align with customer needs and company goals?

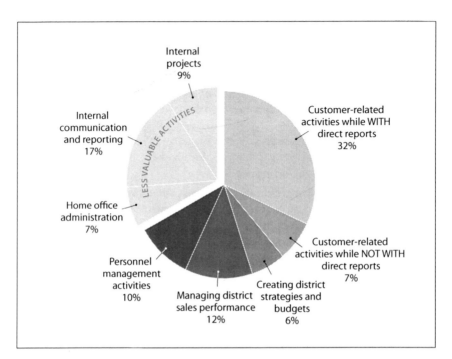

Figure 2-7 Results from an FLM Time Survey in a Sales Force Selling Custom Business Software Solutions

- What management activities help keep sales force motivation high?
- How are customer needs changing relative to sales force skills and experience? What sales management activities help salespeople keep their skills current and aligned with evolving customer and company needs?

2. **Identify time traps.** Time traps are tasks that have low customer and company impact relative to time spent. Look for ways either to take these tasks off the FLM's plate or to help FLMs accomplish them more efficiently, so that energy can be directed toward more valuable management activities. Here are a few examples.

  - In a people manager role: If FLMs can spend less time dealing with performance issues for people who should not be in the job, they will have more time to spend recruiting talent and coaching salespeople who have potential to improve.
  - In a customer manager role: If FLMs can spend less time jumping in to close sales that salespeople should handle themselves, they will have more time to spend nurturing relationships with key customers.

- In a business manager role: If FLMs can spend less time doing administrative work, they will have more time to spend tailoring strategies to local needs and allocating resources for maximum impact.

3. **Learn from your best-performing managers.** Identify managers who have the strongest results after taking into account differences in district or region potential (use techniques such as the performance frontier analysis described in Chapter 4). Identify a group of managers with average results to be used as a basis for comparison. Conduct interviews or focus groups with each group of managers, or observe managers from each group in the field to learn what activities they engage in. By comparing the activities of successful managers with those of average managers, you can discover points of difference that will help you define a role that drives sales success.

4. **Consider a zero-based approach.** A zero-based approach can provide useful insights and a good benchmark for how FLMs should spend their time. This approach ignores the assessment results from step 1 and instead designs the FLM role from scratch. Start by making a list of all the people, customer, and business manager activities that need to get accomplished—the essential work. Evaluate and prioritize the activities, figure out which ones are best accomplished by FLMs (and which ones should be handled by someone else), and then allocate FLM time to appropriate tasks in priority order. The advantage of a zero-based approach over incremental approaches is that FLM time allocation reflects needs and benefits rather than history. Because the approach provides a fresh perspective, it can help sales leaders find creative ways to improve FLM effectiveness and identify tasks that should be taken off the FLM's plate. Zero-based thinking helped one pharmaceutical sales force eliminate many headquarters requests for time from sales managers and salespeople. Although well intentioned, these requests were taking too much time away from customers. Sales leaders implemented an initiative called Drop Everything and Sell. For three months, they limited field participation in headquarters-focused activities and only allowed conference calls between headquarters and field personnel before 7 am or after 5 pm. This gave leaders better clarity around which requests were most valuable so that when the initiative ended, they could start layering back in the things that mattered most.

Step 3: Implement the Progression from Current to Ideal

Several action steps can help you move your FLM team from the current way of spending time to a more ideal focus on critical job tasks.

1. **Identify gaps** between how sales managers currently spend their time (step 1) and how they should ideally spend their time (step 2); develop strategies for closing those gaps, focusing on two goals:

- Helping sales managers move to the ideal allocation of time across the three roles: people manager, business manager, and customer manager.
- Helping managers shift how they spend their time within each role away from low-value tasks and toward high-value tasks.

2. **Communicate expectations to sales managers, and involve them in the implementation process.** Listen to their input about what tasks are most important and valuable to customers. Through their involvement, managers will begin to see the new role definition as their own, not as something passed down from headquarters.

3. **Look for a "practical ideal"** if you discover that the ideal role definition cannot be implemented. Acknowledge that FLMs will have to spend some time on activities that are not mission-critical and help them accomplish these tasks as efficiently as possible, or delegate the tasks to another resource, to help FLMs get as close to the ideal as possible. Allow some flexibility when implementing the practical ideal to account for varied district requirements and FLM skill levels.

4. **Reinforce role expectations** by aligning the FLM success drivers around the new role definition. For example:

   - Align your sales manager selection profile with the ideal role definition, and select managers who have the right characteristics to be successful in the job.
   - Train and coach managers on the competencies they'll need to carry out the role successfully.
   - Provide managers with the support data, tools, and processes that can enable their success.
   - Align performance management, goals, metrics, motivation programs, and rewards for managers with the ideal role expectations.

Periodically review the FLM role description, and adapt it as business needs change. "Our FLM job description is a living document that we continually update to keep relevant, not a static list for the HR file," says one sales leader. "We review the document every quarter and tailor it to current business strategies. The document provides a guideline for managers on what is most important and how to best allocate their time. We also share the document with salespeople so they understand what their manager is trying to accomplish."

The Sales Manager as an Essential Facilitator of Change

The world of sales is changing. The recipe for sales success is more complex than ever, as sales organizations (and therefore sales managers) face many changes (see Figure 2-8).

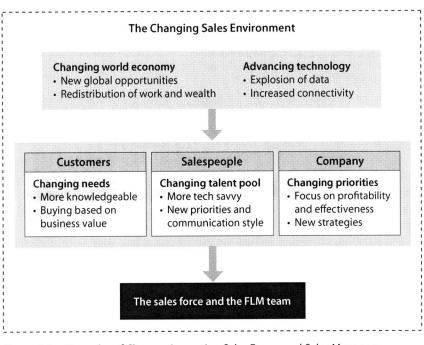

Figure 2-8   Examples of Changes Impacting Sales Forces and Sales Managers

The changing sales environment includes a new world economic climate. Companies have new opportunities in global markets, while facing the challenge of intensified competition and a redistribution of work and wealth across industries, countries, and continents. Change in the environment is also fueled by rapidly advancing technology that enables a more connected world while creating an explosion of available data. All of this change impacts *customers*, as their needs and buying processes evolve and the new technology-enabled world allows them to be better informed about competitive options. Change impacts *salespeople*, as a changing talent pool brings a new tech-savvy generation into the workforce, requiring managers to supervise people who have different preferred communication methods and dissimilar attitudes about work and life balance. And finally, change impacts the *company*, as — in response to all of these external changes — it launches new business strategies, while seeking to discover creative ways to continually improve profitability and effectiveness.

The commitment of the first-line sales management team is critical for responding to these and other changes successfully. "Some of the best advice I got when we implemented a selling process change was to get the managers involved early," says one sales leader. "We brought FLMs in and put them through a change management process. We focused on 'why are we doing this?' to encourage FLMs to make the program their own and take accountability for implementing it with their people."

FLMs are essential facilitators of sales force change. Without the engagement of the sales management team, any sales force improvement or change initiative is destined to fail.

FLMs have responsibility both for helping the company design changes that impact the sales force and customers, and for implementing change within the sales force. This responsibility impacts all three of their job roles: people manager, customer manager, and business manager. As people managers, FLMs can help to shape company changes that enable their people to succeed. Then, using their leadership skills, they can encourage their teams to accept and embrace change, changing their own behaviors so that others are inspired to follow in their footsteps. As customer managers, FLMs can help the company design change that addresses customer needs. They can provide continuity for customers and can ensure a smooth transition so that the company's relationship with important customers remains strong. "You always want to make sure that sales managers have the information they need to explain the rationale for change to a customer," says Jay Sampson, former General Manager, U.S. Emerging Media Sales at Microsoft. And as business managers, FLMs are the primary source of company information to their team—the first place salespeople go for answers. At the same time, FLMs play a key role in facilitating communication from the field to the company, letting management know if new strategies work in the field and sharing feedback on how customers react to change.

At many companies, sales managers go through change management training to help them understand what to do as leaders during times of change. "With the dynamics and speed of change today, it is critical that FLMs engage as change facilitators," says Sandy Cantwell. "We help our FLMs embrace change by providing proactive training. We devote significant time and content in FLM training classes to change management concepts."

An excellent first-line sales management team embraces its responsibility as a change facilitator to drive long-term sales success for a company. The final chapter of this book discusses strategies that sales leaders can follow to support the sales management team in this critical responsibility.

Conclusion

By defining the FLM role, sales leaders align the day-to-day activities of FLMs with the sales force strategy, thus enabling a sales organization that drives high performance. Defining the right FLM role requires three activities:

- Finding the right mix of people, customer, and business management responsibilities for FLMs in your environment.
- Helping FLMs focus their time on high-impact tasks that will drive both short- and long-term success.
- Implementing the role by aligning the other FLM success drivers around the role definition.

The remaining chapters of this book focus on how these success drivers, when aligned around the FLM role, will help you build a winning sales management team.

CHAPTER 3

Sizing and Structuring the Sales Management Team

The Challenge of Sizing and Structuring the Sales Management Team

Rick, the Vice President of Sales at a manufacturing company, has just received budget approval to add 12 salespeople to support the launch of a new product line. His existing sales force has 100 salespeople and 10 first-line sales managers (FLMs), giving each manager 10 direct reports. The hiring of 12 more salespeople will give each FLM an additional 1 or 2 salespeople. Rick wonders if his FLMs have time to manage the additional personnel. The new product line already adds to their workload. FLMs will have to learn the new products and selling process, recruit and train the new salespeople, realign sales territories and quotas, and develop a business plan for selling the new product line in their markets. Then, on an ongoing basis, managers will have additional work helping salespeople identify new opportunities and sell and service the new product line. The added workload means that FLMs will have less time for coaching their people, planning their business, and nurturing customer relationships. Rick wonders what impact this change might have on the sales of current product lines. Should he add an additional FLM to help keep the management workload under control? If he does that, he can add just 10 instead of 12 salespeople. Rick wonders which strategy is best for the bottom line:

- Add 12 additional salespeople and increase FLM span of control to 11 or 12 people.
- Add just 10 additional salespeople and 1 additional manager so that FLM span of control remains unchanged.

Karen, the Vice President of Sales at a medical technology company, is restructuring her sales force to better meet the needs of customers. She is splitting the current sales force's responsibilities into two distinct roles: sales specialist and clinical specialist. Sales specialists will focus on selling and closing deals, while clinical specialists will perform technical product demonstrations and provide customer support and training. By splitting the sales role, customers will benefit from increased sales force knowledge and expertise. Karen can hire experienced sellers of capital equipment to work as sales specialists, and people with medical or nursing backgrounds to serve as clinical specialists.

Karen wonders what the structure change means for the role of her first-line sales managers. Should FLMs manage both clinical and sales specialists so they can facilitate communication and ensure a coordinated sales effort for the customer? Or should sales and clinical specialists each have their own dedicated FLMs who share their skills and backgrounds and can coach and manage them effectively? Karen is concerned that it will be hard to find FLMs who can manage people in both types of roles, yet she wants to ensure that customers get the coordinated effort they desire. Karen wonders which strategy is best for the bottom line:

- Have a single FLM team with sales and clinical specialists reporting to a common manager.
- Have two separate FLM teams: one for sales specialists and one for clinical specialists.

The decisions that Rick and Karen are facing illustrate typical challenges that sales leaders must tackle when they resize or restructure their sales forces. The right size and structure for the sales management team encourages the appropriate development and management of salespeople and the proper coordination and control of sales activity so that the sales force can meet customer needs and achieve company objectives. FLM team size and structure also impact costs. It is important to understand the value that a sales manager brings relative to his or her cost. By influencing both the top and bottom line, decisions about the size and structure of the sales management team have a significant impact on profits.

The Focus of This Chapter

This chapter discusses how to size and structure the sales management team after you've determined the right number of salespeople. It will help you answer two key questions:

- **Size.** How do you figure out what span of control is right for your FLM team?
- **Structure.** How do you determine the best reporting relationships between salespeople and managers, particularly when there are multiple sales roles?

After answering these two questions, you'll be able to define each manager's scope of responsibility and create a sales force organization chart that shows each manager the specific people he or she is responsible for managing. The size and structure of the sales management team is a key FLM success driver and an important part of defining the sales manager's job (see Figure 3-1).

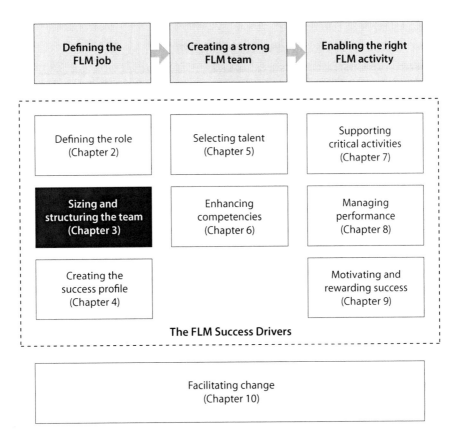

Figure 3-1 An Approach for Building a Winning Sales Management Team

Sizing the FLM Team: Determining the Right Span of Control

The number of salespeople that report to a first-line sales manager—the span of control—varies across sales forces. FLMs typically manage 7 to 12 salespeople, but we have seen sales forces with as few as 3 and as many as 50 salespeople reporting to each FLM. The number of levels of management within a sales organization also varies. In many smaller sales forces, FLMs report directly to the sales organization leader, such as a national sales director or vice president of sales. In larger sales forces, there are usually additional levels of management—such as regional or divisional managers or directors—between the first-line sales manager and the top sales leader. And some specialized sales organizations have structures that include matrix reporting—for example, a product specialist sales

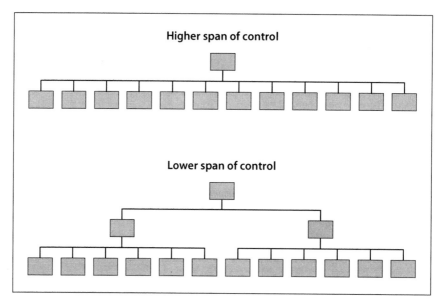

Figure 3-2   Two Span of Control Choices for a Team with 12 Salespeople

team reports to the managers of geographic sales districts but also has a "dotted-line" relationship to a manager in the product organization.

Figure 3-2 illustrates the concept of span of control using a simple, hierarchical reporting structure. For a given number of salespeople, a higher span of control creates a flatter organization with fewer managers, while a lower span of control requires more managers and can require more layers.

The Impact of Span of Control on Productivity

Span of control decisions affect both the costs of maintaining the sales force and the revenues it generates. A flat sales organization with high management span of control creates efficiency. On the other hand, an organization with a lower span of control allows managers to spend more time with each of their people and with key customers. If this time is used well, the sales organization becomes more effective. A sales force will lose productivity if the management span of control is either too small or too large (see Figure 3-3).

Factors Influencing the Optimal Span of Control

The right span of control is tied to how time-consuming the people, customer, and business management tasks are for a given FLM job. Span of control varies

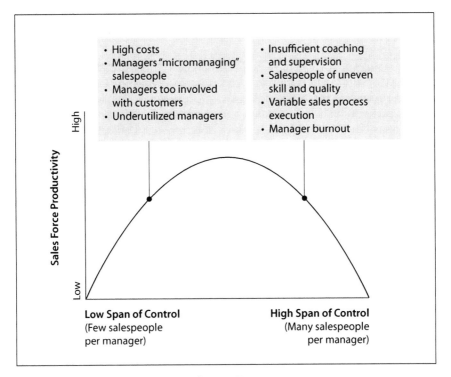

Figure 3-3   What Is the Right Span of Control?

across industries and sales forces and can even vary across managers within the same sales force, depending on differences in geography (for example, urban versus rural), local customer needs, and sales force capabilities.

Several factors affect the time that FLMs need to spend both with the people who report to them and on other managerial tasks; these factors therefore influence the right span of control. Many of the factors are related to job complexity. When managerial tasks are simple and fairly standardized, they require less time, and a sales organization can have fewer managers with a higher span of control. When managerial tasks are complex and diverse, FLMs need more time to carry out their roles effectively as people, customer, and business managers, and a lower span of control is more appropriate. FLM job complexity is closely tied to customer needs; generally, the FLM job is more difficult when the customer buying and decision processes are more complicated.

Sales force capabilities also impact span of control. A higher span of control is possible in sales forces that have salespeople with strong capabilities and experience, because salespeople can work more independently without a manager's frequent coaching and supervision. Excellent FLM and salesperson hiring and training programs enhance sales force capability.

Additionally, the level of sales force support affects span of control. Higher span of control is possible in sales forces that have effective sales force support processes, systems, and resources—for example, defined processes for engaging other company functions in the sales process, strong information systems, and support staff for helping FLMs accomplish lower-value tasks. Strong support allows managers to get tasks done more efficiently or to offload some work to other resources, thus enabling them to operate with a higher span of control.

Some key factors that impact span of control, organized around the three FLM roles, are listed in Figure 3-4.

Sales management span of control can be quite high when a company provides its salespeople with strong support for executing a well-defined sales process. For example, a consumer packaged goods company has a force of approximately 200 part-time merchandisers who perform activities such as stocking shelves, setting up displays, and conducting inventories in stores of a major national retailer. The company provides extensive support to help these part-time employees do their jobs. New merchandisers go through a structured screening, on-boarding, and training process. All merchandisers get instruction about what activities to perform in which stores and how often. Merchandisers are managed largely by activity metrics (for example, how many calls they make and what activities they complete), which are tracked using a sales force automation tool. Because the job is well defined and has significant supporting mechanisms, the merchandising force operates effectively with an unusually high span of control of 50 salespeople per manager.

The ideal sales management span of control typically decreases as the complexity of the customer's buying and decision process increases. For example, in GE's Healthcare division, the sales force sells primarily to local and regional hospitals and has relatively few large national or international customers. A typical span of control could be 8 to 12 salespeople per manager. The Energy division, on the other hand, sells to large utilities, global oil and gas companies, and multinational industrial organizations. Selling to these customers requires global or strategic account teams to coordinate highly complex, custom solutions. Sales managers may supervise an average of six to eight global or strategic account managers (GAMs or SAMs) each.

"Cultural considerations sometimes impact span of control decisions as well," says Conrad Zils, Global Director, Commercial Center of Excellence for GE Healthcare. "In India, where an opportunity to manage people can be critical to retaining top talent, we'll consider having a slightly deeper organization with fewer direct reports per manager."

Low Span of Control
(5–8 salespeople per manager)

High Span of Control
(11–14 salespeople per manager)

Complexity and Time Required for People Management	
Complex sales process that requires extensive salesperson coaching	Simple sales process that requires minimal salesperson coaching
Many inexperienced salespeople	Mostly experienced salespeople
Many poor-performing salespeople	Few poor-performing salespeople
Growing sales force or high sales force turnover	Stable sales force size or low sales force turnover
Team selling or salespeople with dissimilar roles	Individual selling or salespeople with all the same role
Company wants close control of salespeople	Company wants to empower salespeople
Limited HQ support for hiring, training, performance management	Extensive HQ support for hiring, training, performance management
Complexity and Time Required for Customer Management	
Complex sales process, large deals, long sales cycle	Simple sales process, small deals, short sales cycle
Multiple executive-level buying decision makers	Individual lower-level buying decision makers
Customized solutions	Standard solutions
Dynamic environment and sales process	Stable environment and sales process
Products in the early life cycle stages	Products in harvesting mode
Manager has large selling role	Manager has small selling role (is primarily a coach)
Complexity and Time Required for Business Management	
Need for coordination with other company departments	Little or no coordination with other company departments
Many business management tasks (budgeting, planning, reporting, etc.)	Few business management tasks
Limited HQ support for business management tasks	Extensive HQ support for business management tasks

Figure 3-4   Key Factors That Impact Ideal FLM Span of Control

Approaches for Determining the Span of Control

Two types of approaches can help you determine span of control.

- An assessment approach that considers customer and sales force feedback, industry benchmarks, and financial guidelines
- A workload buildup approach that links span of control to the time it takes FLMs to complete tasks required for their role

Assessment Approach

Four tests provide insights about the right span of control from the perspective of different stakeholders: customers, salespeople, competitors, and company financial leaders.

Customer test. Are managers spending enough quality time with important customers and prospects? If key account customers are demanding to see more of your managers, if critical key account prospects are not pursued adequately due to lack of management time, or if the sales process slows down because managers aren't executing their tasks or providing approvals in a timely fashion, consider reducing the span of control to allow managers more time for customer management. On the other hand, if managers are spending too much time with small customers or on selling tasks that should be performed by salespeople or customer service and support personnel, consider increasing the span of control to make better use of your managerial talent.

Sales force test. When there are either too many or too few managers, morale suffers, and turnover of good managers and salespeople can be excessive. Your company's most successful salespeople and managers are a good source of input for span of control decisions. Ask them to reflect on their personal experience. If your span of control is too large or too small, you'll hear about it from the sales force (see Figure 3-5).

Most likely, span of control varies across your sales force. Even though the average span of control is 10, for example, some managers may have 12 salespeople reporting to them, while others have only 8. Talk to good salespeople and managers from districts at both ends of the spectrum. What do they say? What span of control seems to work best? In making your assessment, be sure to control for differences in the potential and geography of different sales districts, as well as for the skill set and experience of the FLM; an exceptional FLM may be able to effectively handle a larger span of control than what is ideal for the rest of the sales organization.

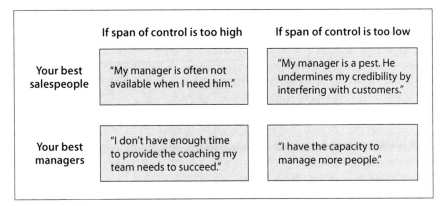

	If span of control is too high	If span of control is too low
Your best salespeople	"My manager is often not available when I need him."	"My manager is a pest. He undermines my credibility by interfering with customers."
Your best managers	"I don't have enough time to provide the coaching my team needs to succeed."	"I have the capacity to manage more people."

Figure 3-5   What the Sales Force May Tell You About Span of Control

Competitor test. Compare your company's investment in sales managers with that of your competitors. Look at industry surveys for benchmarks. If your span of control is significantly different from industry norms, consider whether the deviation is justified. Think about how your sales force measures up to competitors on the dimensions in Figure 3-4. For example, if your sales managers manage more inexperienced people and get less support from headquarters than others in your industry, your span of control should be below the industry average. On the other hand, if your sales process is more streamlined and you have well-developed hiring and training programs compared to others in the industry, your span of control can be higher than the industry average. Benchmarking to comparable sales forces helps you learn from the experience of others, enabling you to make a more informed span of control decision. However, you must recognize that a comparable benchmark is not necessarily the right answer for your organization and should not be used as a substitute for bringing insight and original thinking into your decision process.

Financial test. Although span of control decisions have an impact on both revenues and costs, financial leaders at most companies will focus on the cost side of the equation when making span of control decisions. You'll need to look at sales force costs to determine how many levels and managers the company can afford and still keep costs in line with the sales budget. Break down sales force expenses by category, and compare spending to value added. For example, how much do you spend on salesperson compensation versus sales manager compensation each year? Is this spending in line with the value added by salespeople versus managers? If manager compensation seems out of line with value added, look at manager salary levels. Are they appropriate? Sometimes companies overpay their managers and then have to settle for a higher-than-ideal span of control to stay within their budget. By benchmarking to comparable sales forces, you ensure that FLM compensation is in line with the market. Some companies benchmark FLM pay levels (as well as pay levels for other positions) against others in their industry annually; this is especially important when there are dynamic changes occurring in the industry or in the general economy.

If cost-focused analysis suggests a span of control that you feel is unmanageable, bringing the revenue side of the equation into your analysis can help you negotiate a larger sales budget that enables a more manageable span of control. Two approaches can be useful. First, take advantage of the variation in span of control across your sales force to gain insight about the sales and profit impact of span of control decisions. For example, compare sales and profit results in districts with 12 salespeople to those in districts with 8 (while controlling for differences in potential and geography as well as the skill and experience of the FLM, as mentioned previously). You may be able to demonstrate that a lower span of control, although more costly, generates higher revenues and is therefore more profitable. Second, an analytic approach such as workload buildup (see the next section) can help you evaluate the consequences of span of control decisions for the time available for high-impact sales manager activities such as coaching and developing salespeople—activities that are directly linked to long-term sales success.

A Workload Buildup Approach

Workload buildup analysis (see Figure 3-6 for a simplified example) is an effective and fairly easy method for developing a good estimate of the right span of control for your sales organization. The analysis links span of control to the time it takes managers to complete all the activities required to do their job effectively.

The analysis is structured around the definition of the sales manager's role. Six steps are required:

1. Estimate the average annual hours that a sales manager works. Do not include time away from the job for holidays, vacations, or personal time. In the example in Figure 3-6, sales managers work (on average) 12 of the 13 weeks in each quarter.

2. Estimate the annual hours each manager needs to perform work that is constant (in other words, work that does not vary with the number of salespeople or accounts managed). Often, as shown in the example, work in the *business manager* category is constant. For example, every manager needs to attend certain meetings or complete specific administrative tasks every quarter.

3. Subtract the constant time (from step 2) from the total work time (from step 1) to estimate how much time managers have available to spend with salespeople and customers.

4. Estimate the total annual management work that is tied to the number of salespeople in the sales force. This *people manager* work can include time for tasks such as coaching, performance reviews, and hiring. To develop your estimate, specify the activities that a manager should perform for each salesperson, estimate the average amount of time these activities require per year, and multiply by the number of salespeople. Improve the accuracy of your estimate by organizing your analysis by the experience and performance level of the salespeople (as in the example).

5. Estimate the total annual management work that is tied to the number of customers (and prospects). This *customer manager* work can include activities such as account planning, customer visits, and assisting salespeople with important sales process steps. To develop your estimate, specify the activities that a manager should perform for a customer, estimate the average amount of time these activities require per year, and multiply by the number of customers. Improve the accuracy of your estimate by organizing your analysis by customer segment (as in the example).

6. Add the total time required for people management (from step 4) to the total time required for customer management (from step 5). Divide the result by the time available per manager for people and customer management (from step 3) to determine how many managers you need. Divide the total number of salespeople by the number of managers needed to calculate span of control.

The data required to implement this approach can be based on both field input and external benchmarks.

Additional Benefits of a Workload Buildup Analysis

A workload buildup analysis is not only helpful for determining management span of control; it can also help sales leaders in two specific situations.

When sales leaders want to identify opportunities for improving productivity. At the company used in the example (see Figure 3-6), sales leaders were shocked to learn that sales managers spent a full 15 days a quarter on business management activities, including some meetings and administrative work that had low value to customers and the company. They sought to eliminate some of these activities and to outsource others to lower-paid administrative staff, leaving FLMs with more time for high-value activities. If enough low-value activities can be eliminated or

Step 1: Estimate average annual hours worked per FLM

Weeks/Quarter	12	
Days/Week	5	Available hours/year/FLM **1,920**
Hours/Day	8	

Step 2: Estimate average annual hours of fixed work per FLM

Business Manager	Activity	Days/Quarter	Hours/Year
	Resource Management	6	192
	Meetings/Training	6	192
	Administration/Logistics	3	96
	Business Manager: Hours needed per year (per FLM)		**480**

Step 3: Subtract to get annual hours per FLM available for people and customers

Step 1 – Step 2 = 1,440

Step 4: Estimate total FLM work that varies with the number of people

People Manager	Experience/Performance	Number of People	Days/Quarter	Hours/Year
	New	20	6	3,840
	Experienced			
	High performer	20	3	1,920
	Average performer	40	5	6,400
	Low performer	20	1	640
	Total number of salespeople	100		
	People Manager: Hours needed per year (total)			**12,800**

Step 5: Estimate total FLM work that varies with the number of customers

Customer Manager	Account Type	Number of Accounts	Days/Quarter	Hours/Year
	Key accounts (A)	61	1.00	1,952
	Key accounts (B)	292	0.25	2,336
	Other select accounts	7,300	0.00	–
	Customer Manager: Hours needed per year (total)			**4,288**

Step 6: Calculate the number of FLMs needed and span of control

(Step 4 + Step 5) / Step 3 =	**12 FLMs needed**
Total number of salespeople / FLMs needed =	**8.4 span of control**

Figure 3-6   An Example of Simplified Workload Buildup Analysis

outsourced, FLMs can handle a higher span of control. "As senior leaders, part of our job is to ensure that excessive administrative requirements do not creep into the sales manager's job," says Chris Hartman, Vice President, Central Zone, Cardiology, Rhythm and Vascular Group for Boston Scientific Corporation. "We allow headquarters groups (such as Marketing) to schedule conference calls with the field on Mondays and Fridays only. That way, managers can devote three days a week without distractions to their salespeople and customers in the field."

When sales leaders do not have complete control over span of control decisions. Sometimes, sales leaders need to figure out the best way for FLMs to operate with a span of control that is larger than ideal. Occasionally in an effort to control expenses, company leaders decide how many managers the sales force can afford, and they dictate that decision to sales leaders. At one healthcare company, the sales management team was a major target of the company's effort to control expenses. Over a 15-year period, the span of control increased from 5 to 6 salespeople per manager to 12 to 15 salespeople per manager. Workload buildup analysis helped the company prioritize FLM responsibilities so it could make the best of a suboptimal situation. For example, should it let more poor performers go to free up management time? Should it cut back on the number of days per quarter that FLMs were expected to work with salespeople? Or should it find ways to reduce FLM administrative time? Workload buildup analysis helps assess these trade-offs so that management time can be directed in the best possible way, given span of control constraints.

As companies increase span of control, they can provide sales managers with more support to help them cope with the greater demands on their time. When one company eliminated several sales management positions, it hired a pool of administrative assistants to support the sales force, allowing the remaining managers to offload some of their administrative work. Another company hired a sales analyst for each region—a person with strong analytical skills who could take on certain number-crunching and report-creation responsibilities, thus giving sales managers time for managing more people. Companies can also hire regional coaches or trainers to help sales managers with their people-development responsibilities or can ask HR to play a larger role in sales force recruiting, thus freeing up management time to supervise more people.

Adapting Span of Control to Changes in Sales Force Size

The cost and disruption associated with adding or cutting an FLM position can be quite high. The change not only affects the manager whose job is added or eliminated; it also impacts the many salespeople and customers who will need to be reassigned to a different manager. In some cases, branch offices or other resources also need to be added or eliminated. It is usually best to avoid ongoing disruption of the sales management team structure as you expand or downsize the sales force, even if it means that span of control may not be ideal for a time. Look ahead one to two years when planning your span of control, and avoid knee-jerk reactions that create costly disruption for the sales force.

Increasing Span of Control as the Sales Force Expands

If you are creating a sales force from scratch or if you plan to gradually expand your sales organization, begin with a lower span of control and plan to increase it over time. This enables you to put your long-term management team in place from the start, giving each FLM a defined scope of responsibility (for example, a specific geographic area or set of customers) that will not be disrupted repeatedly during the critical growth period. FLMs get to know the customers and business they are responsible for and can add salespeople appropriately as their business expands. Because FLMs start with a lower span of control, they have more time for recruiting and training new salespeople. As the team gets larger and more experienced, the proportion of newly hired salespeople naturally declines and the span of control increases. Be sure to manage the expectations of the existing management team from the start; managers should know that their span of control will increase with time, so that they can plan accordingly.

Workload buildup analysis is useful for developing the right span of control strategy for a sales force expansion. In the example in Figure 3-6, it takes a manager six days a quarter to hire, coach, and train a new salesperson, but less time to manage an experienced person. Thus, as the mix of new and experienced salespeople changes, the management time requirement changes. With more experienced salespeople and fewer new ones, a manager can handle more salespeople.

Linking Span of Control Decisions to the Future Outlook When Downsizing the Sales Force

If you are downsizing a sales force, the best strategy for managing span of control depends on the likely future outlook for the sales force. If downsizing is expected to continue for the foreseeable future, consider cutting back proportionately more managers than salespeople from the start (therefore increasing span of control temporarily). That way, management costs are reduced right away and the remaining managers can be assured that their jobs are safe and that continued disruption to their responsibilities will be minimized. On the other hand, if the decline in sales force size is likely to be temporary, consider keeping more of the management staff in place and reducing span of control temporarily. For example, a sales force in the building business was forced to downsize in a sluggish economy. Because company leaders expected that sales positions would be reestablished when markets rebounded, they kept the sales management team intact, thus avoiding the expensive temporary closure of branch offices and allowing the sales force to be better positioned for growth when the economy turned around.

Taking Advantage of Manager Turnover to Effect Change

The best geographic deployment of sales managers changes over time, as company product lines evolve, the competitive marketplace changes, and demographics shift. Evaluate the distribution of your sales management team relative to market opportunity annually, and make changes if appropriate.

Manager turnover creates opportunity to redeploy managerial effort without relocating managers or significantly disrupting the sales force. When a manager leaves a geographic location, don't automatically assume that the position should be filled in that same location. Evaluate the potential that can be realized by rehiring in that location, and compare it to the potential that is possible by redeploying the resource to another geographic area. "We view sales force turnover as an opportunity to redeploy resources to the areas of greatest impact," says Chris Hartman of Boston Scientific. "We make decisions about how to deploy managers (and salespeople) deliberately. We reevaluate our plan every year as market needs and company priorities change."

Structuring the FLM Team: Determining the Right Reporting Relationships

The reporting structure of the sales management team defines the organization chart for the sales force. The reporting structure affects how the sales management team will coordinate and control sales activity to meet customer needs and accomplish business objectives. The possible reporting structures depend on the span of control and also on the roles that salespeople play — generalist or specialist — and the needed interaction between those roles.

Generalist or Specialist Roles for Salespeople

Some sales forces employ only generalist salespeople who perform all selling activities and sell all products and services to all types of customers in a territory. Other sales forces include one or more specialist salespeople who specialize in specific selling activities, products, or markets. Consider some examples:

- Activity specialization
  - Telesales people find prospective new customers; they turn good leads over to field salespeople, who follow up on those leads and convert them to customers.

- Some salespeople are account managers who handle the overall sales process and bring in specialists to handle any steps that require specific expertise (such as a specialist who creates technical design or a specialist who handles pricing and financing).

- Product specialization
  - Some salespeople sell products, and others sell services.
  - Some sell product or service line A, while others sell product or service line B.

- Market specialization
  - Salespeople are organized into industry vertical teams, with each team specializing in an industry segment, such as high tech, healthcare, or government.
  - Some salespeople sell to large customers, and others sell to midsize customers.

Many sales forces include a mix of generalists and different types of specialists. Companies with very large sales organizations and broad, complex product lines can have a wide array of generalists and specialists. IBM, for example, has created a highly specialized sales force structure to bring the needed expertise to its customers. More than 40,000 people are organized into many different sales divisions with dozens of different types of sales specialists structured around markets, products, and activities. In addition, the company relies on thousands of business partners—distributors, value-added resellers, service providers—to sell many of its products in many different markets.

The mix of generalist and specialist salespeople affects how well the sales force can meet customer needs and achieve company objectives. The decision depends on many factors, including the complexity of the sales process, salespeople's skills and abilities, and company objectives and strategy. Although this complex decision is largely outside the scope of this book, readers who want additional information can consult *Sales Force Design for Strategic Advantage* (Zoltners, Sinha, and Lorimer, 2004) or "Structuring the Sales Force for Customer and Company Success" (Zoltners, Sinha, and Lorimer, published in the *Oxford Handbook of Strategic Sales and Sales Management*, 2011).

Your options for the reporting structure of the sales management team depend on whether your salespeople are generalists or specialists.

Reporting Structures When Salespeople Are Generalists

If all salespeople have similar job responsibilities, the reporting structure is typically defined geographically. For example, a seller of bottled water has a national sales force of 900 route salespeople who sell the company's full product line and perform all sales and service activities for all types of customers; the structure includes 33 route salespeople in the Orange County/San Diego market (see Figure 3-7). Reporting relationships are defined geographically: salespeople report to branch managers (FLMs), each of whom is accountable for the total business in a specified county or metropolitan area. Reporting relationships for those in management levels above the FLM—market managers and regional sales directors—are also defined geographically.

A geographic reporting structure of generalists provides clear accountability for customers and the sales process, because just one manager is responsible for overseeing all of the business in a geographic area. The lines of communication are unambiguous, and the career path is straightforward. FLMs can live close to the people they manage, minimizing travel time and costs and maximizing the time managers can spend with their salespeople and with customers. Geographic reporting keeps sales management costs down, making it possible for the company to sell profitably at a price that is attractive to customers.

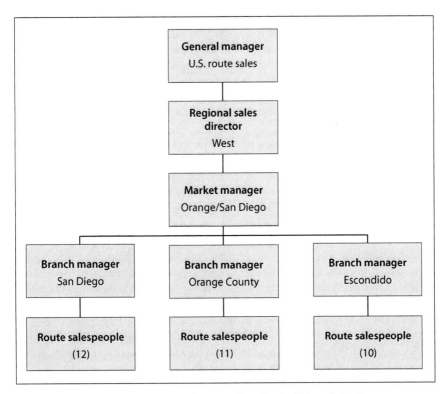

Figure 3-7   Geographic Reporting Structure for a Bottled Water Sales Force

Reporting relationships in a geographic reporting structure are determined based on several factors:

- The ideal span of control, as determined using the methods described earlier in this chapter.

- Travel efficiency. Which FLM is closest (by drive time or air travel, if required) to each salesperson? An FLM in a compact, urban district may be able to handle more people than an FLM in a rural district with high travel requirements.

- A desire to keep trade areas together under the control of a single FLM. For example, because of economic ties within a metropolitan area, it may be best to give, say, all of Orange County to one FLM and all of San Diego to another (see Figure 3-7), even if it means that their span of control will not be exactly equal.

- The experience of the FLM. At Microsoft, career considerations sometimes influence span of control decisions. Jay Sampson, former General Manager, U.S. Emerging Media Sales at Microsoft, says, "When we identify an exemplary salesperson who has high potential for career advancement, we may give him or her a smaller team of salespeople to manage to build his or her experience. When we hire managers from outside the company who already have management experience, we expect them to manage a full load of salespeople right away." But be prepared to make span of control adjustments when an experienced FLM leaves and is replaced with a new FLM.

Although geographic reporting is logical from a business and efficiency standpoint, geography is not the primary factor for determining reporting structure in all generalist sales organizations. Insurance company AFLAC has a unique approach for matching salespeople to first-line managers based on sales team culture. For example, a highly competitive salesperson will be most successful working for an FLM who has established a competitive team culture, while a salesperson who is motivated by helping people will do better on a team with a more nurturing culture. Some FLMs are especially skilled at training and developing new college recruits; others do better managing experienced people. According to Lance Osborne, Vice President, Pacific Territory Director at AFLAC, "Value and culture are more important than geography when matching the right salesperson with the right manager." And because AFLAC has a very large sales organization, geographic separation of salespeople is generally not an issue. The approach works well in AFLAC's unique sales environment; however, geography determines reporting relationships in most generalist sales organizations.

In key account sales forces, the structure of a customer's buying organization can influence sales force reporting relationships. A seller of consumer packaged goods, for example, has a key account sales team that sells to a major national retailer. The sales team is structured around the retailer's buying organization, reinforcing a strong partnership between the selling company and its largest customer. Salespeople are aligned with the retailer's districts (which include 8 to 10 stores each), and region managers are aligned with the retailer's region managers. The span of control and reporting relationships in the sales force mirror the reporting structure of the customer's buying organization.

Reporting Structures When Salespeople Are Specialists

Reporting structure decisions become more complex when a sales force has specialists—different sales roles for different products, markets, or sales activities. Recall that Karen, the Vice President of Sales at a medical technology company, has two types of specialists in her sales force: sales specialists (who sell and close deals) and clinical specialists (who perform product demonstrations and provide customer support and training). Karen is considering two alternative reporting structures (see Figure 3-8).

The best reporting structure in a sales force with specialists depends on the relative importance of the sales manager's role as a *people manager* versus a *business* or *customer manager* (see Chapter 2).

Alternative 1 makes sense if sales managers function largely as people managers. The structure enables regional managers to reinforce the activity expertise and focus of their people. Sales specialists have a different success profile and

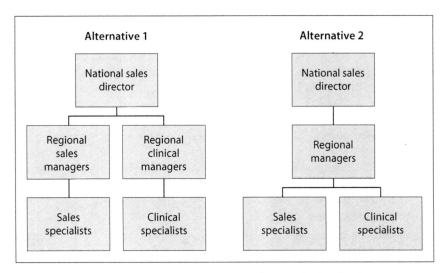

Figure 3-8   Two Alternative Reporting Structures for a Medical Technology Sales Force

require different competencies than clinical specialists. With alterative 1, sales leaders can select regional managers who share the profile and competency of the people they will manage, enabling managers to be more effective coaches. This alternative also allows managers to develop an agenda for regional meetings that focuses around issues relevant to the role. This may be the best option in situations where the sales manager role focuses mostly on people management (rather than business or customer management) and where it will be difficult to find a single manager who can manage and coach both types of specialists effectively.

Alternative 2 makes sense if sales managers function largely as business or customer managers. This structure encourages customer focus because regional managers can manage the entire sales process for customers, including both sales and clinical effort. If customer success requires coordination between sales and clinical specialists, regional managers can facilitate that coordination. Sales specialists and clinical specialists who share customers will likely work more closely together and resolve conflicts more quickly when their manager is accountable for the total customer experience. Alternative 2 also enhances flexibility at a regional level to shift resources or resolve conflicts as needed across the two specialty groups without having to go to the top of the sales organization for approval. This alternative has one additional advantage: it creates geographically compact sales regions that require less travel for managers. If the sales manager role focuses largely on business or customer management (rather than people management) and it is possible to find a single manager who can manage and coach both types of specialists effectively, alternative 2 may be the best option.

Sales organizations that have multiple types of product specialists who share customers face a dilemma similar to the one shown in Figure 3-8. A structure in which product specialists report to their own dedicated FLMs aligns with a sales manager's role as a people manager who reinforces the product expertise and focus of the sales force. But if customers value a unified or bundled offering from the company, then it may be better for product specialists to report to a common FLM who can facilitate the coordination needed to deliver that offering.

As a general rule of thumb, when there are multiple types of sales specialists who share customers,

- Have FLMs manage a single type of sales specialist when they are primarily *people managers* who reinforce the product or activity expertise that is important to customers or when a single FLM cannot master all competencies required to manage multiple types of specialists effectively.

- Have FLMs manage multiple types of sales specialists when they are primarily *business* or *customer managers* who facilitate the coordinated sales effort that is important to customers and when a single FLM can master all competencies required to manage multiple types of specialists effectively.

Overcoming the Stresses of a Reporting Structure with Specialists

Whichever structure you choose for a sales force with specialists, there will be challenges that you'll need to overcome. If specialists who share customers report to different FLMs (as in Figure 3-8, alternative 1), you'll need to implement processes, systems, or programs to encourage coordination across specialists to ensure that customer needs are met. Several mechanisms can successfully enable customer focus and coordination efficiency when specialists have separate FLMs. These include the following:

- **Sales process and information support.** Create defined sales processes that specify the steps where specialists need to collaborate, and provide customer and opportunity management systems that enable the sales force to access a centralized source of customer information and improve the efficiency of information exchange between specialists who are responsible for common customers.
- **Hiring and culture.** Hire cooperative and team-oriented people who can work together to meet customer needs. Strive to build a culture of trust, respect, and teamwork.
- **Mirrored territory alignments.** Give the specialists who share customers identical sales territories, or mirror small groups of territories (for example, match three product A specialist territories to two product B specialist territories). This enables specialists who share customers to work together as a team to provide coordinated customer effort.
- **Incentives.** Offer occasional team-based incentives (such as spiffs or sales contests) that encourage a culture of cooperation among specialists who work with common customers.

If multiple types of specialists report to common FLMs (as in Figure 3-8, alternative 2), you'll need to implement processes, systems, or programs that enable the product or activity expertise that customers value. Several mechanisms can encourage sales force expertise and focus when multiple types of specialists share the same FLMs, including these:

- **Training and development.** Because FLMs need to manage a more diverse group of people, they'll need more training to understand a broader product line, more types of customers, or many dissimilar selling tasks. Salespeople, too, will require excellent training, because their manager may not have the depth of skill and knowledge to coach them effectively in all of their specialized responsibilities. Some sales forces have field trainers who can assist FLMs with coaching and training of specialized competencies. For example, according to Sandy Cantwell, Vice President of Sales Operations at Cardinal Health, "The FLMs in our sales force that distributes medical-surgical products are expected to manage the sales team and play an integral role in local operations. Because the scope of responsibility is relatively broad, we provide local field trainers who support some aspects of coaching and development that the FLMs used to do."

- **Information and support.** Because FLMs have a broader range of responsibility, they cannot know every detail of the tasks that their people are expected to perform. They must rely on excellent information support from the company for enabling salespeople to perform their specialized duties. This can include detailed product information, "how to" guidance for critical selling activities, good target lists, and processes for enabling specialists to share market and customer knowledge with their peers. FLMs may also need extra support in running regional or district sales meetings, because of the diverse needs and perspectives of the different salespeople who report to them.

An additional concern when FLMs supervise multiple types of specialists is that because managers have more choice of how to spend their time, they may choose to work within their comfort zone, rather than on what is most important. For example, a regional manager in the medical technology sales force (see Figure 3-8, alternative 2) who comes from a clinical background may spend more time coaching her clinical specialists, since that is where her strengths lie; at the same time, a manager from a sales background may feel more comfortable working with his sales specialists and focus his efforts there. When FLMs supervise multiple types of specialists, it is especially critical that manager hiring, development, support, evaluation, and reward systems reinforce how managers should spend their time so that all specialists get the management attention they deserve and so that management team effort is directed toward the right activities for driving customer and company success.

Case Study: Finding the Right Reporting Structure at a Healthcare Company

A healthcare company that sold diagnostic testing supplies used three types of sales specialists to reach its markets: physician specialists, hospital specialists, and retail pharmacy specialists. The three specialist teams had historically been managed as separate sales organizations, each with its own dedicated team of regional directors and district managers. Each district manager was responsible for approximately 10 people (see Figure 3-9, structure A). This structure had worked well for years, but changes in the market environment were bringing about a need

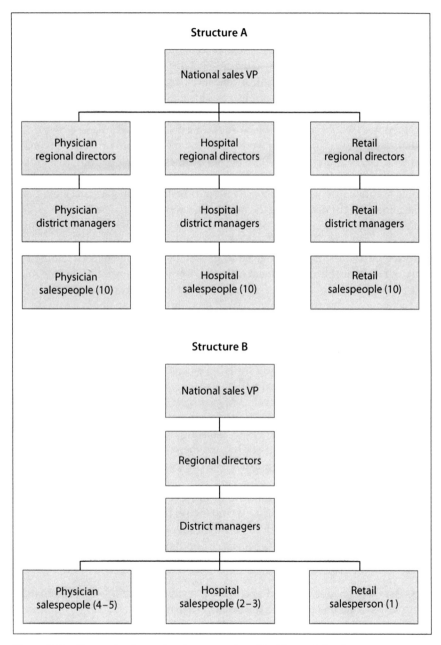

Figure 3-9 Alternative Reporting Structures for a Healthcare Sales Force

for change. As customers demanded better coordination of sales efforts across physicians, hospitals, and retail pharmacies in a local area, the company considered a new sales force structure that could better meet this need.

The new sales organization structure brought the formerly separate, siloed divisions together at a low organizational level. Each district manager was given responsibility for all types of specialists in a local market. This gave each manager four or five physician specialists, two or three hospital specialists, and one retail specialist who would cover all the business in a defined local area (see Figure 3-9, structure B). District managers were asked to take on more of a business management role as coordinators of the overall business in their regions, in addition to their people management role. Span of control was reduced to eight or nine people per manager, giving managers more time for business management and for dealing with the diversity of the people they were responsible for.

With the new structure, the coordination of sales efforts across local physicians, hospitals, and retail outlets did improve, as did business results. Unfortunately, however, district managers struggled to master all the competencies required to carry out their people management role effectively. Managing and coaching multiple types of specialists required a broad range of skills and knowledge. Physician specialists got a disproportionately large amount of management attention, in part because they were the largest group, but also because most managers came from a physician market background and were most comfortable coaching and guiding others in that role. Hospital specialists got a fair amount of management attention, but not enough. Clearly, the retail business suffered the most as a result of the reorganization. Selling to retail pharmacies was very different from selling to physicians or hospitals, and very few managers had any experience in a retail selling role. And because only one of their eight or nine people sold to this market, managers didn't see enough benefit to investing time to understand the market; instead they chose to focus their efforts elsewhere. With the retail specialists getting almost no attention and guidance, the company's retail business ultimately began to suffer.

The company eventually modified the sales force structure again, first putting the retail specialists back under separate, focused district managers, and a few years later, doing the same with the hospital specialists (see Figure 3-10). Three factors helped to ensure that the necessary coordination continued to take place within the new management reporting structure:

- The three groups reported to common regional directors, thus eliminating the silos that had existed in the original structure.

- Territories across teams had common borders (for example, one retail territory mirrored the geography of five physician territories) to make it easier for salespeople to work together as a team.

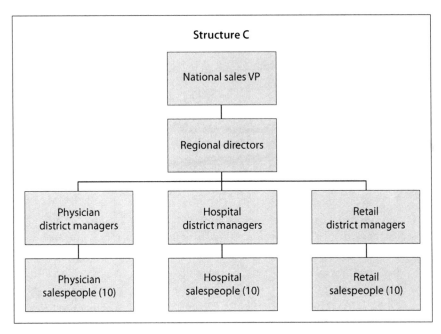

Figure 3-10   A Third Reporting Structure for a Healthcare Sales Force

- A small element was added to the incentive compensation plan to reward salespeople on the success of the entire team.

Two lessons are evident in the healthcare company's story. First, reporting structures need to be dynamic, evolving as the market does and as the company's product portfolio changes. Structures must also adapt as company leaders learn from experience. By trying different management structures and archiving the learning by documenting successes and challenges, leaders create institutional knowledge that enables better future decision making. There isn't one perfect structure that can last forever, and flexibility is necessary for maintaining a good sales management structure over time.

A second lesson that the healthcare company's story demonstrates is that structure change is sometimes necessary to bring about culture change. The coordination that the healthcare company desired would likely never have developed had sales leaders not forced it with the structure change. Leaders had implemented various programs to encourage coordination under the silo structure of the past, with very little success. The structure change was a bold move necessary to create a true team culture within the sales organization. Once that culture took root, the management structure that initially encouraged the focus on overall business management was no longer needed, and a structure encouraging better people management could be put back in place.

Conclusion

An excellent sales management team is a critical driver of sales force success, yet it is also an expensive resource that needs to be deployed in a smart way for achieving strong bottom-line results. Finding the right size and structure for your sales management team, and making that team size and structure work, requires four actions:

- Using analytic approaches such as workload buildup analysis to determine a management span of control that optimizes sales force efficiency and effectiveness.
- Providing the right support mechanisms (for example, centers of excellence that provide administrative or HR support and sales force data and tools) to help sales managers do their jobs better and to enable the span of control and reporting structure to work.
- Adapting span of control and reporting structures appropriately as customer and company needs change.
- Aligning sales force processes, systems, and programs (for example, sales support tools, sales force hiring and training processes, and incentive and goal-setting programs) with the sales force structure and using these systems, processes, and programs to overcome any stresses that the sales force structure creates.

By sizing and structuring the sales management team appropriately, sales leaders ensure the appropriate development and management of salespeople and the proper coordination and control of sales activity, enabling the sales force to meet customer needs and achieve company profit objectives.

CHAPTER 4

Creating the Sales Manager Success Profile

Two Sample Success Profiles

A sales manager success profile defines what *characteristics* (personal qualities) and *competencies* (skills and knowledge) are needed for individuals to be successful in the first-line sales manager (FLM) role. Two examples illustrate.

The sales organization at Ethicon Endo-Surgery defines three categories of characteristics and competencies that its division managers (FLMs) need to carry out their role (see Figure 4-1).

Leading the Team	Driving the Business	Building Relationships and Adding Value
• Team leadership • Holding others accountable • Developing the team	• Drive for results • Decision making and judgment	• Focus on the customer • Strategic initiative • Influencing others

Figure 4-1   The FLM Success Competency Model at Ethicon Endo-Surgery

"Our division manager competency model declares our profile of what it takes to succeed in the FLM role," says Fred Wagner, a former Vice President of Sales for J&J's Ethicon Endo-Surgery division. "It helps us select people for the role who fit with our strategy, and it enables us to identify who should be a manager and who adds more value as an individual contributor. It helps us identify strengths and weaknesses in FLMs and allows us to have competency-based discussions with individuals through the performance management process."

At GE, which employs over 5,800 first-line sales managers across a global portfolio of diverse businesses, a Sales Leader Capability Guide identifies and defines the capabilities necessary for success as a GE sales manager. The guide, which is organized around seven categories of capabilities (see Figure 4-2), helps GE sales leaders understand and communicate FLM success factors. It also helps leaders identify the best FLM candidates, locate FLM development opportunities and support resources, identify and manage FLM strengths and weaknesses, and recognize and reward the capabilities that drive FLM success.

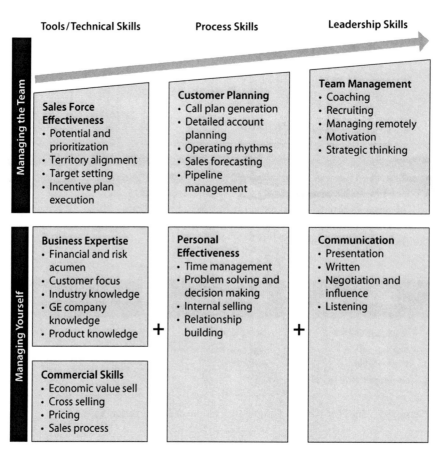

Figure 4-2   An Overview of GE's Sales Leader Capability Guide

The Focus of This Chapter

This chapter shows you how to create a sales manager success profile that includes the FLM characteristics and competencies that will drive success in your sales environment. The chapter is organized around two main topics:

- The elements of a good sales manager success profile.
- Effective approaches for identifying the right FLM characteristics and competencies for your sales environment.

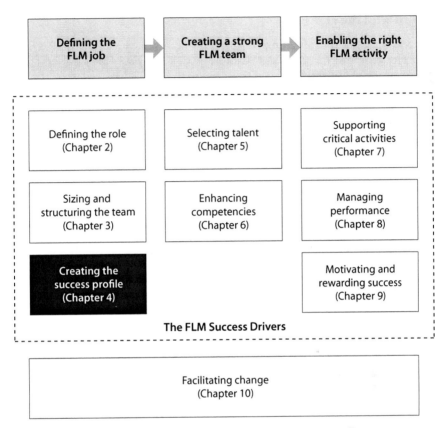

Figure 4-3 An Approach for Building a Winning Sales Management Team

The right profile is a critical FLM success driver. Creating a profile that specifies the characteristics and competencies required for FLM success is a key step in defining the FLM job (see Figure 4-3).

The Elements of a Good Sales Manager Success Profile

A good FLM success profile defines what is required of managers to enable effective execution of the sales force strategy. It aligns with the FLM role, distinguishes competencies from characteristics, and is both focused and forward-looking.

Aligns with the FLM Role

Success characteristics and competencies differ across the three FLM roles: people manager, customer manager, and business manager. A good FLM success profile aligns with the desired role. At Ethicon, *developing the team* helps an FLM succeed as a people manager, *strategic initiative* enables success as a business manager, and *influencing others* is important for achievement as a customer manager. At GE, *team management* is important for success as a people manager; *business expertise, internal selling*, and *relationship building* are important for carrying out the role of business manager; and *commercial skills* and *customer planning* enable achievement as a customer manager. Some characteristics (such as *decision making and judgment* in the Ethicon profile) and some competencies (such as *time management* in the GE profile) may be important for multiple FLM roles.

Distinguishes Characteristics from Competencies

Bruce Nordstrom, former Chairman of the department store known for its impeccable service, once described the importance of distinguishing between characteristics and competencies when hiring salespeople: "We can hire nice people and teach them to sell, but we can't hire salespeople and teach them to be nice." When asked who trains Nordstrom's salespeople, Bruce replied, "their parents." Similarly for sales management positions, job *competencies* can be learned and developed, but an individual will only be successful if the right personal *characteristics* for the job are inherent in the candidate's personality, character, and aptitude. To get the right characteristics (for example, empathy or integrity), you have to hire the right people. Then you can develop and nurture the right competencies in them (for example, coaching skills or market/company knowledge) by providing developmental programs that train, mentor, coach, support, manage, and motivate around those competencies.

P&G once distinguished between competencies and characteristics in its management success profile. The profile defined skills and knowledge required for functional excellence in a managerial role (competencies) as well as what leaders called the "what counts" factors: the intrinsic traits—such as leadership, initiative, follow-through, and critical thinking—that company leaders believed could predict job success. Rather than focusing on the experience and background of candidates, P&G leaders looked for the "what counts" factors when hiring and selecting for sales management and other positions. Then they provided developmental programs to help recruits build the competencies required for job success.

The FLM success profiles used by GE and Ethicon include a mix of characteristics and competencies. At GE, capabilities such as *listening, problem solving*, and *decision making* are largely characteristics of individuals; these are difficult to train and take long periods of time to develop. Capabilities such as *commercial skills, team management,* and *industry, company,* and *product knowledge,* on the other hand, are competencies that can be cultivated in individuals through the right programs. At Ethicon, *drive for results* and *strategic initiative* are characteristics that the company screens for in the FLM selection process, while *developing the team* is a competency that could be developed after individuals are selected for the FLM role.

Typical Characteristics for an FLM Success Profile

Figure 4-4 provides a representative list of characteristics that can enable FLM success in each of the three roles. The list was compiled by looking at the FLM success

| | Importance for Success as a . . . | | |
Characteristic	People Manager	Customer Manager	Business Manager
Interpersonal Abilities • Empathetic • Good listener • Leader • Organizationally savvy • Good at influencing others • Approachable • Decisive • Responsive	★★★	★★★	★
Drive for Results • Goal-oriented • Self-motivated • Competitive • Organized • Ambitious	★	★★	★★★
Conceptual Abilities • Problem solver • Strategic thinker • Analytical • Good judgment • Ability to learn and innovate	★	★★	★★★
Customer Focus	★★	★★★	★★
Integrity • Ethical • Trustworthy	★★★	★★★	★★★

Figure 4-4 Sample Characteristics in FLM Success Profiles and Their Importance for Different Sales Management Roles

profiles used by many different sales forces. These qualities are, for the most part, inherent in candidates; developmental programs have limited ability to impact them.

Typical Competencies for an FLM Success Profile

Figure 4-5 provides a representative list of competencies that can enable FLM success in each of the three roles. The list was compiled by looking at the FLM success profiles used by many different sales forces. Competencies can be learned or developed through training, mentoring, or other learning methods.

| | Importance for Success as a . . . | | |
Competency	People Manager	Customer Manager	Business Manager
Selling, Negotiation, and Relationship-Building Skills	★★	★★★	★
People Management Skills • Selecting and recruiting the team • Coaching and developing the team • Managing and directing the team • Motivating the team • Managing team performance • Valuing diversity and inclusion	★★★		
Financial and Business Acumen • Understanding business concepts • Understanding industry and company • Managing change	★	★★	★★★
Functional Skills and Knowledge • Using tools and technology • Understanding products • Writing and presenting • Planning, organizing, and managing time	★★	★★	★★★

Figure 4-5 Sample Competencies in FLM Success Profiles and Their Importance for Different Sales Management Roles

Tailoring the Characteristics and Competencies for Your FLM Role

The lists in Figures 4-4 and 4-5 are illustrative. Your profile should include only the criteria relevant to the FLM role in your organization, and you may need additional criteria besides those listed. The categorization of items as characteristics versus competencies can at times vary with the role requirements as well. For example, conceptual abilities (such as problem solving or strategic thinking) are characteristics in many sales contexts because they require an inherent intellectual ability. Yet some would argue that certain conceptual abilities can be developed by teaching candidates specific problem-solving approaches and strategies. The best success profiles tailor the characteristics and competencies appropriately for the FLM role.

Focuses on the Most Critical Characteristics and Competencies

"One of the most common mistakes that companies make is to include too many characteristics and competencies in their success profiles," says Linda Vogel, a Principal at ZS Associates. "Generally, the key requirements of most sales management jobs can be captured in a dozen or fewer dimensions. If you include more than that, you'll lose focus on what's most important for success in the role." When we asked sales leaders from different companies and industries about their FLM success profiles, they reported models with anywhere from 10 to 35 different characteristics and competencies. These leaders generally agreed that just 10 to 15 competencies can capture the most important success dimensions for the FLM role. The Korn/Ferry Institute, a developer and publisher of research on how organizational leadership and talent development advance business strategy, suggests selecting 10 or fewer core competencies that create focus for the entire organization, and another 5 to 15 competencies that are specific to the job role.

Is Forward-Looking

At GE, sales leaders review the sales manager success profile in the Sales Leader Capability Guide periodically to ensure alignment with current and evolving business needs. "Typically, we focus 75 percent on what the best FLMs do today (based on input from sales directors) and 25 percent on looking ahead towards future sales force needs (based on input from senior sales executives)," says Conrad Zils, Global Director, Commercial Center of Excellence for GE Healthcare.

Fred Wagner says that a forward-looking view was also important for competency model development at Ethicon Endo-Surgery. "We learned that the necessary FLM competencies were changing as the focus on relationship selling diminished and the need for salespeople and FLMs to understand the customer's business increased," he says.

As business needs change and the FLM role evolves, the FLM success profile must also adapt. Sometimes the change is dramatic—for example, when an industry is deregulated and the sales force needs to sell competitively for the first time. Other times, the change is more subtle—for example, when the sales process becomes more consultative and the sales force needs to change its approach with customers, requiring sales managers to take on new responsibilities, such as coaching salespeople on consultative selling skills or spending more time securing resources from other company departments on behalf of customers.

Changes in the FLM success profile can require changes in the makeup of the FLM team. If the success profile includes new competencies, training and development programs can help current FLMs acquire the needed skills and knowledge. If the success profile includes new characteristics, however, sales leaders need to determine which current FLMs possess the needed characteristics. At United Airlines, for example, a transformation from a relationship-based selling approach to a value-based approach led to new success profiles for all sales roles. Every sales force member had to reinterview for the job. Through this process, leaders discovered that approximately 30 percent of current sales force members lacked the necessary characteristics required to adapt to the new selling model, so they replaced these sales force members. Sales managers who possessed the needed characteristics received training on the new sales process and how to effectively coach salespeople in the new environment.

At temporary housing provider Oakwood, the FLM success profile changed as customer expectations of the sales force increased. According to Chris Ahearn, former Senior Vice President of Corporate Sales and Marketing, "FLMs needed a broader skill set so they could coach and teach salespeople how to execute a new sales process that engaged customers in a more powerful and consultative dialogue about how Oakwood products and services impacted the customer's business." Oakwood created training programs to help existing FLMs and salespeople gain the necessary business skills needed to execute the new sales process, but not all FLMs and salespeople had the abilities and personal characteristics needed for success in the new environment. In the end, the company changed out a large percentage of its FLMs and salespeople, keeping those who matched well with the new success profile.

FLM success profiles change as business needs evolve. Consequently, successful FLMs must possess characteristics that enable them to adapt (for example, *ability to learn and innovate*) as well as competency in *change management*. "Change orientation is an important competency for all FLMs," says Liza Clechenko, a former Vice President of Sales, East/Gulf Coast, at BP. "Our profile is very specific in defining this competency. We expect FLMs to recognize the need for change by focusing on how business is changing, learning from both happy and unhappy customers, and understanding what the competition does better. We expect FLMs to develop and seek out solutions, enlist and motivate others around change, and drive change programs to successful conclusions."

Identifying the Right Characteristics and Competencies for the Sales Manager Success Profile

When developing an FLM success profile for your organization, you can tap multiple sources of input, including your company's current FLMs, experts from your company or industry, and existing research on leadership competencies.

Case Study: Identifying Seven FLM Success Principles at Novartis

In 2003, sales leaders at global healthcare company Novartis launched an initiative aimed at improving the effectiveness of first-line sales managers. Recognizing that the FLM role is critical to sales force success, sales leaders sought to understand the characteristics and competencies that drive exceptional FLM performance. They identified top-performing FLMs—those who had the best sales results (after accounting for differences in opportunity across sales districts) and who had consistently outstanding performance reviews based on competency assessments by their supervisors and upward feedback from their salespeople. For comparison, sales leaders also identified a group of FLMs who were average performers.

An analysis team studied the behaviors of FLMs in both groups. They observed FLMs on the job, surveyed FLMs and the salespeople they managed, and conducted focus groups with FLMs and their supervisors. The goal was to understand what FLM behaviors contributed to company success. The analysis team developed a set of 39 hypotheses about what made Novartis FLMs successful. Some of the hypotheses focused on FLM competencies—for example, in the hiring and coaching of salespeople, the use of personalized rewards, and the sharing of team vision. Other hypotheses focused on the personal characteristics of the FLMs—for example, decisiveness, ability to adapt to change, willingness to admit mistakes, and the will to win. The project team compared the competencies and characteristics of FLMs in the two groups and identified a proprietary list of seven success principles that differentiated the truly outstanding Novartis managers.

"Almost all of our managers were already using the seven Novartis success principles to some degree, but the best ones used the principles very frequently and executed them with higher quality," explains Greg Schofield, a former Executive Vice President and Head of Global Sales for Novartis. "We wanted to propagate these success principles throughout the management ranks, with a goal of boosting the performance of all managers to reach the performance levels that had already been achieved by our best managers—what we called the 'performance frontier.'"

Sales leaders set out to enhance the sales manager success profile to align with the seven success principles. "We identified which of the principles reflected competencies that you could train for, and these became the basis for a new FLM training program," says Greg. "We modified the existing training curriculum for new FLMs and adapted the performance management resource guide to align more closely with these competencies. Success principles that we believed were inherent characteristics of individuals were added to the FLM recruiting profile to improve screening of FLM candidates."

Learning from Your Current FLMs

Members of a company's own FLM team possess the characteristics and competencies that belong in the FLM success profile. Novartis discovered FLM success principles by studying its FLMs and contrasting the behaviors of superior and typical performers. Learning from your best performers involves two steps.

Step 1: Identify the Best Performers

A first step in using your FLM team to identify success behaviors is to isolate "superior" from "typical" performers. Several approaches can work:

- Look at district performance rankings on metrics such as sales growth, market share, and quota attainment to identify top and average performers among the FLM group. Confirm the names with sales leaders to ensure that top producers are also role models of appropriate behavior.

- Ask sales leaders to identify a list of top- and average-performing FLMs, based on their own observation. Or conduct a survey of sales leaders asking them to rate FLMs on relevant capabilities and performance dimensions.

- Use input from the FLM performance management process (for example, competency model assessments) to differentiate top- and average-performing FLMs.

- Use analytical approaches that separate the impact of district factors (market potential, competitive intensity) from the impact of the FLM's ability and hard work. In larger sales organizations with 20 or more FLMs, data-based techniques such as performance frontier analysis (described in the box) are useful for identifying FLMs who truly deserve to be in the top group because of their effort, not their luck.

Performance Frontier Analysis for Identifying Top-Performing FLMs

Performance frontier analysis uses historical district-level data to evaluate FLM performance. The technique isolates the impact of the FLM on district sales performance by accounting for district differences that are outside the FLM's control — such as district market potential, starting customer base, competitive intensity, and length of time the FLM has been managing the district.

The approach can include multiple dimensions of district differences, but for simplicity, we show an example here in two dimensions (see Figure 4-6). Each dot in the plot represents a sales district (with a number identifying the district next to the dot; those highlighted in italics are referenced later in the text in this box). District sales are influenced by district market potential, which this company measured using an index (100 = the average district). The market potential index reflects a combination of account-level estimates provided by salespeople and business demographic data. The best-performing districts are those with the highest sales relative to their market potential index.

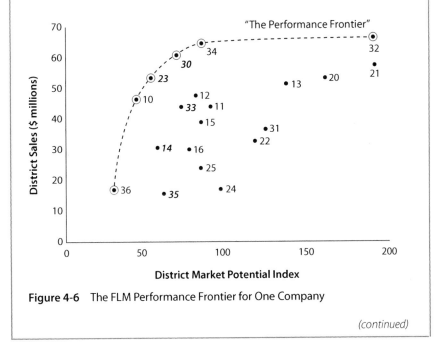

Figure 4-6   The FLM Performance Frontier for One Company

(continued)

(continued)

The dotted curve connecting the best-performing districts at the top of the plot represents the performance frontier. The frontier predicts the sales that are possible for districts with different amounts of potential. Why? Because an FLM in the sales force has already demonstrated that it is possible to achieve this level of performance. For example, by looking at the range of sales between two districts that are on the frontier — 23 and 30 — we can see that it is possible for districts with similar potential (in the range of 50 to 75 percent of average) to produce sales in the $52–60 million range. Yet some districts in this range — for example, districts 35, 14, and 33 — are producing sales that are well below this benchmark level. Performance frontier FLMs are those who are on or close to the performance frontier curve. Many companies use a range, such as within 10 percent of frontier performance, to define this group.

When the number of FLMs is large enough to enable valid results, performance frontier analysis enhances traditional methods of identifying the FLMs who comprise the group of best performers.

Step 2: Isolate Performance Frontier FLM Behaviors

Once you have identified top- and average-performing FLMs, the next step is to identify and contrast the competencies and characteristics of individuals in the two groups. Information about competencies can be gathered in several ways. Some competencies can be gleaned through direct observation of FLMs on the job; however, observation alone may be insufficient because the FLM job requires many diverse responsibilities, and all critical behaviors are unlikely to occur during the observation period. Additionally, the presence of an observer sometimes influences the behavior of the individuals being observed. Techniques that can enhance the learning that occurs through observation include interviews with individual FLMs as well as focus group and panel discussions with groups of FLMs. These techniques work best when there is a structured process for asking questions and probing for detailed examples of what superior and average FLMs do in specific sales management situations. Information about competencies can also come through in FLM evaluations provided by superiors, subordinates, and peers.

Information about the characteristics of top- and average-performing FLMs is best gathered by looking at ratings for FLMs by their superiors on personal characteristics (for example, integrity or drive for results). Information about characteristics such as interpersonal abilities can also come through in salespeople's upward evaluations of their managers and from input from peers and others with whom FLMs interact (for example, people in Sales Operations or Human Resources). In some cases, the recruiting process includes assessments that measure characteristics, and these tools can provide inputs to the process as well.

Learning from Experts and from Existing Research

"Learning from current FLMs is most effective when sales leaders want to fine-tune and incrementally improve an existing FLM success profile," says Kelly Tousi, a Principal at ZS Associates. "But it is not always the best approach in cases where the sales management job is changing." When a sales force goes through a selling process transformation, what has worked for managers in the past may not work in the future. In such cases, it is important to supplement the input of current FLMs with input from industry experts, consultants, or sales leaders who may have a broader perspective on what will be required for future success in the FLM role. In cases where FLMs have a large customer management role, customers can be a good source of input as well. Not only can customers enhance your understanding about the effective behaviors of your own FLMs, but they may also provide insights about success behaviors of FLMs at competing companies.

Many consultants and research-based organizations specialize in talent management and job profiling. These organizations can help you develop a success profile for your FLMs, as well as for other sales force positions. They can provide lists of core leadership competencies and characteristics (based on observational research) and can suggest the capabilities required for different types of jobs. It is also useful to review models used by other companies that have similar job roles and to look at the competencies and characteristics listed in Figures 4-4 and 4-5. "Often at larger companies, the human resources function will weigh in heavily on competencies and characteristics," says Sandy Cantwell, Vice President of Sales Operations at Cardinal Health. "Supplementing HR input with learning from outside experts is the best route when specific sales role profiling work is needed."

Using a Framework

The framework described in this chapter helps you break the task of developing an FLM success profile into manageable pieces that reflect research-based thinking about the dimensions of FLM success. Use the example in Figure 4-7 as a template for identifying the characteristics and competencies that your FLMs need to execute the three FLM roles—people manager, customer manager, and business manager—successfully.

	People Manager	Customer Manager	Business Manager
Characteristics (innate to the individual)	Customer focus		
	Problem solving and decision making		
	Listening	Listening	Strategic thinking
Competencies (can be learned and developed)	Industry, company, and product knowledge		
	Time management skills		
	Presentation and written skills		
	Team management skills: coaching, recruiting, managing remotely, motivation	Customer planning skills Commercial skills Negotiation and influence	Sales force effectiveness tools and skills Financial and risk acumen Internal selling skills

To illustrate the framework, we have suggested possible categories for the characteristics and competencies in the GE success profile.

Figure 4-7 A Framework and Example to Help You Develop an FLM Success Profile

Conclusion

The FLM success profile provides a template for aligning the other FLM success drivers. The success profile helps you with

- *FLM selection* by defining the characteristics and competencies to look for when evaluating candidates for FLM positions, thus improving the odds of selecting the best candidates.
- *FLM development* by suggesting the competencies to emphasize in FLM training, apprenticeship programs, and other development programs that help managers acquire the skills and knowledge they need to succeed in the job.
- *FLM support* by outlining the competencies you'll need to support with the processes, systems, and other resources that FLMs need to excel in their role.
- *FLM performance management* by telling you what skills and knowledge to include in the competency model that sets expectations and standards for

FLM performance. This reduces bias and unfairness in the FLM performance management process and thus delivers higher levels of performance.

- *FLM motivation* by defining what competencies to reward and recognize. Although FLM incentive compensation is typically tied to results metrics (for example, sales, profits, or market share), competency assessment often plays a large role in determining career advancement and salary increases and has impact on many FLM recognition programs.

By aligning the FLM success drivers with your sales manager success profile, you can build a potent sales management team that enables execution of your sales force strategy.

Creating a Strong First-Line Sales Management Team

I Defining the FLM job	II Creating a strong FLM team	III Enabling the right FLM activity

The Focus of Section II

Creating a strong team of first-line sales managers (FLMs) requires selecting and nurturing sales management talent to encourage sales team retention and to produce financial results. Two FLM success drivers, discussed in Chapters 5 and 6, help you create a strong sales management team that enables high performance.

Selecting the Best Sales Management Talent (Chapter 5)

You can't win unless you have the right players on the team—players who have the managerial characteristics defined in your FLM success profile. To get the best management talent, you need to start with an applicant pool of candidates who possess these characteristics, not simply those who are the best salespeople. Choosing the best management talent from the applicant pool requires selection techniques that allow you to observe the candidates' work, evaluate their past behaviors, and assess the candidates using tools that test for success characteristics. With a thorough and cogent selection process in place, you can select the best prospective FLMs and convince them to join your team.

Enhancing Sales Management Competencies (Chapter 6)

With the right talent on the team, you need to nurture that talent so that FLMs constantly learn and stay engaged in their jobs. Training and development are essential for FLMs who are new to the job and need to make the critical transition from salesperson to manager. They are also important for FLMs who are new to the company and need to develop company-specific competencies and assimilate company culture. Finally, training and development help FLMs who have been on the job to refresh their skills and adapt to a constantly changing environment. By blending high-touch learning methods (for example, personal coaching and customized classroom learning) with more efficient methods (for example, peer-to-peer best-practice sharing and online resources), you can make appropriate investments to fill critical FLM competency gaps, thereby impacting the performance not only of FLMs, but also of every salesperson.

What Sales Leaders Say About Creating a Strong FLM Team

Lance Osborne   Vice President, Pacific Territory Director, AFLAC

"We promote salespeople from within to the FLM position. Those who perform well in sales become part of a bench and are considered for management positions. Most of our salespeople want to become managers and move up in the company. The challenge is to select the right ones." Lance has held several sales leadership positions at AFLAC.

Chris Hartman   Vice President, Central Zone, Cardiology, Rhythm and Vascular Group, Boston Scientific

"By providing training and testing of FLM candidates over a period of time, and by allowing many opportunities for both the candidate and the company to evaluate fit with the FLM job, [our Momentum program helps us] . . . select the best internal FLM talent." Chris has served in many sales and marketing leadership roles at Boston Scientific, where he approaches the complexities of managing FLM team performance by making constant improvement an integral part of how his team works.

Quinton Oswald   CEO, SARcode BioScience

"FLMs are enrollers of culture, up and down the organization. Be sure that the individuals that you select for the FLM team exemplify the culture you want for the sales organization." Prior to his CEO role with SARcode BioScience, Quinton was a Vice President and business unit leader for Tissue Growth and Repair at Genentech, and Senior Vice President for Global Marketing and Sales Effectiveness at Novartis.

Conrad Zils   Global Director, Commercial Center of Excellence,
GE Healthcare

 *"Combining world-class training with in-the-field coaching programs helps us institutionalize new behaviors and drive positive change more effectively throughout the organization."* Conrad leads the Commercial Center of Excellence, established to improve direct and indirect go-to market strategies across GE Healthcare. In a previous role as Global Director of Sales Programs and Sales Force Effectiveness, he was responsible for improving GE's sales leadership expertise and driving a global portfolio of sales force effectiveness programs.

Linda Vogel   Principal, ZS Associates

 *"By providing training in integrated, bite-size nuggets and by allowing FLMs time to practice new skills on the job and reflect on the learning before moving on, [an FLM development program] has greater impact."* As a leader in the Sales Force Effectiveness Practice at ZS, Linda helps her clients measure the effectiveness of their sales organizations and align talent management, coaching, and learning curriculums to propagate best practices and enhance overall effectiveness.

CHAPTER 5

Selecting the Best Sales Management Talent

First-Line Sales Manager Selection: A High-Impact Decision

Promoting or hiring the wrong person for a first-line sales manager (FLM) job can have serious and long-lasting consequences. When you hire the wrong salesperson, performance suffers in one territory. But when you promote or hire the wrong person for a sales manager position, performance is compromised across an entire district or region.

What Happens When You Hire the Wrong Salesperson?

When Jerry, the Vice President of Sales for a building products manufacturer, had a sales position open up, he was thrilled to learn that his acquaintance Bill (who worked for a competitor) was looking to make a career move. Jerry had always been favorably impressed with Bill when the two met up at industry meetings. And Bill lived in the perfect location to work the territory. Jerry was anxious to fill the vacancy quickly, so he hired Bill. One year later, it was evident that Bill was not the right person for the job. He did an adequate job of supporting current customers, but he was not good at driving new sales. After a year in the job, Bill had made only a handful of sales to new customers. Meanwhile, the company was losing opportunity in the territory, and many prospects had signed on with competitors. It took Jerry two years to recover from the hiring error: one year to discover and document Bill's performance problem, six months to try to fix the problem with coaching and performance management, and another six months to replace Bill. The error cost the company many times Bill's annual salary.

What Happens When You Hire the Wrong Sales Manager?

When Jane, the Vice President of Sales for a medical products company, needed to fill a sales management position, she agreed to hire Ted, an MBA who had been successful working in the company's finance department and needed a stint in sales to stay on the fast track to top management. It soon became clear that Ted's unwillingness to ask for help, combined with his lack of sales experience, made him a poor candidate for the job. Ted spent a lot of time in his office sending emails, and too little time working personally with his salespeople and customers. He pretended to be a sales expert in front of his team, even though he was not. Within a matter of months, Ted had destroyed his credibility with the team.

It took Jane two years to replace Ted, but that was not the end of the story. By the time Ted was replaced, many of the talented salespeople on his team had left the company because they felt that Ted was holding them back. Ted had replaced some of them, but because he was not very good at recognizing sales talent, his replacements were weak performers. Jane estimated that it took more than three years for sales in Ted's district to recover from the hiring error, as both the manager and three-quarters of the salespeople on the team had to be replaced. The real and opportunity costs to the company were many times Ted's annual salary and many times the annual salary of every salesperson who had to be replaced.

Although hiring the wrong salesperson is a costly error, selecting the wrong FLM is even more costly and usually has a longer-lasting negative impact on sales.

The Focus of This Chapter

Although many sales leaders feel that their own experience and intuition make them good at identifying candidates who will be successful FLMs, intuition alone is not enough to ensure consistently strong results when recruiting sales managers. The best companies choose FLMs through a three-step selection process that is part of a larger ongoing process for selecting and nurturing talent to drive FLM retention and performance (see Figure 5-1).

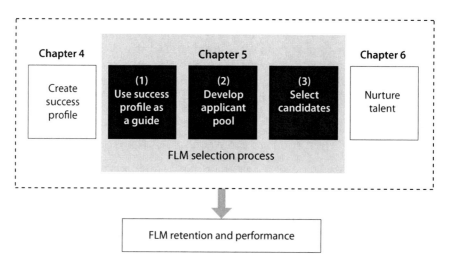

Figure 5-1 A Process for Selecting and Nurturing Talent to Drive FLM Retention and Performance

This chapter is organized around the three steps in the FLM selection process:

- Using the characteristics in the success profile to guide FLM selection
- Developing a promising pool of internal and external applicants
- Selecting the best candidates and convincing them to join the FLM team

The chapter concludes with some insights for selecting and sustaining an exceptional sales management team.

Selecting the talent for your sales management team is a key FLM success driver and a critical first step in creating a strong sales management team (see Figure 5-2).

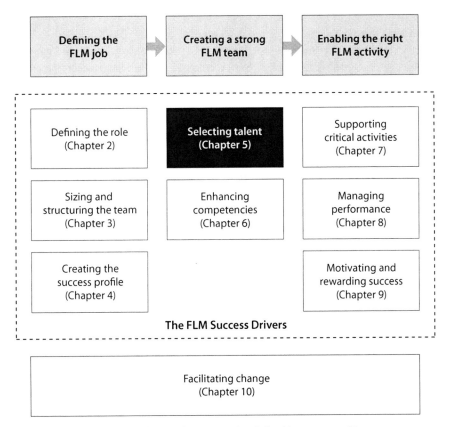

Figure 5-2 An Approach for Building a Winning Sales Management Team

Using the Success Profile to Guide FLM Selection

Selecting excellent FLMs starts with understanding what you are looking for in candidates. As described in Chapter 4, a success profile specifies the personal characteristics and competencies that are required of a successful sales manager. Characteristics (for example, empathy, ambition, and strategic thinking) are traits that are inherent in a candidate's personality, character, and aptitude. Competencies (for example, coaching skills, product knowledge, and technology usage) are skills and knowledge that candidates can learn and develop, provided they have the right personal characteristics to enable their success.

See Chapter 4 for a list of additional characteristics and competencies that companies include in their FLM success profiles.

Screen for Characteristics, Train for Competencies

"You can't send a duck to eagle school," says one sales leader. "You can teach a turkey to climb a tree, but it's easier to hire a squirrel," says another. Individuals will only be successful in the FLM role if they have the right personal characteristics for the job. Consequently, when it comes to FLM selection, the characteristics in your success profile are "knockouts" for choosing candidates. It is critical to screen for characteristics because they are inherent in a candidate; training has limited ability to affect them. If the job requires someone with a strong drive for results, for example, you'll need to find FLMs who are self-motivated and goal-oriented; it is unlikely that training can develop these characteristics. It is critically important to develop solid approaches for screening FLM candidates on the characteristics in the success profile.

The role of competencies in the success profile for candidate selection depends on whether you plan to "buy" the skills and knowledge required to do the FLM job or to "build" the competencies through training and development programs after candidates are selected. Companies have different philosophies about hiring experienced managers (see the discussion later in this chapter about applicant pool strategies). Yet regardless of your strategy about buying or building competencies, what is most important is that candidates have the innate personal characteristics required for job success. For example, if the FLM job requires coaching skills, you can hire candidates who learned these skills in their previous job, or you can train and mentor candidates to develop these skills after they are hired. But if candidates lack the innate personal characteristics required for good coaching—for example, empathy and leadership abilities—they are unlikely to succeed whether or not they have prior coaching experience. You can use experience as a screen for narrowing down your pool of candidates, but it is critical to test all candidates—experienced and inexperienced—for the personal characteristics in the success profile.

Use Characteristics as Knockouts, Not Selectors

Profiles provide useful guidelines for FLM selection, but it is impossible to create a list of truly discriminating characteristics that can accurately predict success each and every time. There are bright people who are average managers and people with average intelligence who are great managers. There are experienced people who are good managers and experienced people who are poor managers. There are extroverted people who are good managers and introverted people who are good managers.

Usually, FLM candidates cannot be successful unless they possess at least a minimum level of each of the personal characteristics listed in the success profile. For example, suppose a sales leader screens FLM candidates on three personal characteristics: interpersonal abilities, results-drive, and conceptual abilities. A candidate who demonstrates very high results-drive but has very poor conceptual abilities should be eliminated. At the same time, candidates should not be selected simply because they are very strong in a single competency or characteristic. For example, exceptional interpersonal abilities in a candidate cannot make up for a lack of the other two dimensions. The best candidates possess a baseline level of every important personal characteristic. Use the screening characteristics as knockouts, not as selectors, in your FLM selection process.

Developing a Pool of Promising Applicants Who Fit the Success Profile

The quality of the candidates who are offered FLM positions depends on the quality of the applicant pool. Although there can be exceptions, in most situations, sales experience is a requirement for inclusion in the applicant pool. It is hard for managers to gain the respect of their salespeople if they have never worked as salespeople.

Looking Internally Versus Externally for Candidates

Most companies look primarily at internal candidates for FLM positions, but there are situations where it makes sense to recruit experienced managers from other companies. Several sales leaders reflect on the views within their companies regarding internal versus external FLM candidates:

- "We promote salespeople from within to the FLM position," says Lance Osborne, Vice President, Pacific Territory Director at AFLAC. "Those who perform well in sales become part of a bench and are considered for management positions. Most of our salespeople want to become managers and move up in the company. The challenge is to select the right ones."

- "In our industry, many FLMs were former successful salespeople for their companies, but there is also a desire to get headquarters people who have potential to advance within the company to get field experience by doing a rotation as a sales manager," says Quinton Oswald, CEO of SARcode Bio-Science and a longtime sales leader in the pharmaceutical industry.

- "Many of our tenured salespeople are not interested in becoming managers, but many of our newer salespeople do aspire to have career paths that lead to sales management," says Sandy Cantwell, Vice President of Sales Operations for Cardinal Health. "Historically, most of our FLMs started as salespeople and were promoted from within through the ranks, but recently we have started hiring more FLMs from outside the company—both from within the industry and from other industries."

- "FLM selection strategies were different at two companies I've worked for," says Helmut Wilke, a high-tech industry sales leader who is currently a Vice President of Sales at Microsoft. "Sun Microsystems had several hundred FLMs in the U.S. and extensive internal support resources. Consequently, the company promoted salespeople from within and developed their management skills internally. Extreme Networks had just 15 FLMs in the U.S. With fewer internal resources for developing managers, the company hired FLMs with a track record of success with other companies. We looked for quality: the right attitude, the right ethics, and evidence of management experience that demonstrated integrity and fairness."

Applicant Pool Strategies for Internal Candidates

Internal applicant pools have many advantages. You (or others within the company) know internal candidates and have had the opportunity to observe and evaluate their work. Internal candidates know the company, its products, and company culture and likely already have some of the internal and customer connections they will need to be successful as FLMs. Using internal applicant pools is also likely to be viewed positively by salespeople who will see opportunity for advancement within the sales organization and company. Salespeople may like working for someone who was a former peer whom they respected, and they may feel motivated to be successful if they aspire to be promoted in the future. However, there is also a flip side to promoting from within. In the words of one sales leader, "Every time I promote a salesperson to manager of a district I make one salesperson happy and nine salespeople unhappy." So internal promotions need to be managed thoughtfully and carefully.

Selecting internal candidates can also help minimize short-term compensation costs, as it often takes a substantial pay boost to lure the best management talent away from other companies. However, because internal candidates usually lack management experience, they require management development—an investment a company must make in order for an internal applicant pool strategy to be successful. (See Chapter 6 for more on sales manager training and development.)

Finding the Right Salespeople for the Applicant Pool

In many companies, it's easy to attract internal candidates to the FLM applicant pool. For most salespeople, this is their first potential career promotion, and they greet the possibility with excitement. There are many rewards associated with the new job, including management perks, greater power, recognition of achievement and success, and (often) higher pay. Many companies consider sales management to be the next logical career step for salespeople who are succeeding. Salespeople want to move up within the company and want to be viewed as successful; a promotion to management is a visible sign of their success.

"GE has a strong history and culture of developing managerial talent. A side effect of this can be that sometimes great GE salespeople pursue sales management roles instead of bigger, more strategic selling roles where they'll be more successful," says Conrad Zils, Global Director of the Commercial Center of Excellence for GE Healthcare. "Identifying and grooming those salespeople who have strong managerial skills, in addition to respectable sales skills, to take the FLM position is critical to keeping salespeople engaged and motivated."

Not every successful salesperson is a good candidate for FLM. In fact, during a recent session of our Accelerating Sales Force Performance executive education course, we asked the sales leaders in attendance, "Do you think that most good salespeople make good sales managers?" Almost unanimously, the class agreed that no, the best salespeople are frequently not the best managers. Yet these leaders also agreed that within their companies, top-performing salespeople get promoted to sales manager all the time.

Case Study: Creating a Strong Applicant Pool of Internal Talent for the FLM Position at Boston Scientific

Medical device manufacturer Boston Scientific has a defined process for identifying potential management talent within the sales organization to create a strong internal applicant pool. "Sales leaders are constantly on the lookout for new talent, and the process of identifying internal candidates for FLM positions is embedded in the annual performance review process," says Chris Hartman, Vice President, Central Zone, for Boston Scientific's Cardiology, Rhythm and Vascular Group. "We have tools for rating salesperson performance that predict future leadership potential. We identify salespeople with high leadership potential early in their careers—sometimes as early as when they are first selected for a salesperson role. Those with the right profile and interest receive further opportunities to demonstrate their management abilities and skills." (Read more about how Boston Scientific selects the right internal candidates for FLM positions later in this chapter.)

When the Internal Applicant Pool Is Too Small

In some selling environments, few salespeople have an interest in being considered for promotion to manager. In some industries, successful salespeople outearn their managers, making it difficult for companies to attract competent sales managers, especially from the ranks of salespeople who have several years of experience in a sales role and earn substantial commissions or bonuses. In addition, some sales environments have many salespeople who enjoy working independently and are reluctant to manage others. In such environments, the long-term solution is to build a culture that values people management so that more salespeople aspire to be part of the management team. But this takes time and can be challenging. And regardless of the culture, there are always some candidates who are unwilling to relocate to take on a management role. Attracting internal candidates to the sales manager applicant pool can require helping candidates work through these issues. If the issues cannot be addressed sufficiently, consider looking externally for management talent.

Applicant Pool Strategies for External Candidates

If too few candidates within the sales force have the necessary qualifications for, or interest in, becoming sales managers, you'll need to look externally for management talent. Limited resources for training salespeople to develop managerial competencies can also suggest that the best strategy is to look at external candidates who have prior management experience. If management skills gained at other companies are highly transferable and you can pay to lure strong, experienced sales managers from their current jobs, external sources may be a good place to look for talent for your applicant pool.

External candidates have some advantages. They already have management skills and experience, enabling them to become productive quickly. Such candidates often bring in a fresh perspective and have new skills or knowledge that can help the company succeed, particularly in a rapidly changing marketplace. If they come from a company that competes with yours, they may bring customer contacts. Sometimes they bring sales talent as well if they can convince their best-performing salespeople to make the move with them.

External candidates do create some risks that need to be dealt with. They don't know your products, people, and culture. And they can bring baggage in the form of incompatible work styles and attitudes that need to be managed. Careful screening to avoid incompatibilities, and a thoughtful on-boarding process to immerse experienced hires in the company culture and processes can mitigate these risks.

Attracting good external candidates to the applicant pool starts with a job posting that accurately describes and "sells" the job to prospective candidates without overselling it. Companies use numerous sources for finding applicants from outside the company: referrals, agencies, company recruiting web sites, headhunters, Internet job boards, unsolicited write-ins, former employees, customers, competitors, advertisements, and trade shows. Referrals from current employees, customers, or others with personal connections to those making hiring decisions are consistently ranked by sales leaders as a good source of sales management talent. In fact, numerous surveys (including several we have conducted with sales leaders in our executive education courses) reveal that companies have the most success in developing a strong external applicant pool when they favor trusted sources that can provide reliable information about candidates and their likelihood of success. Good referrers have observed the candidate's past behavior, are familiar with the job requirements, and are well suited to match the candidate's skills and experiences to the job requirements. Good referrers with a personal connection to someone at the company also want to make a quality recommendation so they don't jeopardize their relationship with their contact. Referrers who are company employees don't want to jeopardize their career. Most companies offer prizes or cash awards to employees who provide referrals of candidates who are hired and stay with the company for a period of time, usually at least six months. Companies can also encourage referrals by publicly recognizing employees who bring in candidates.

Internal Versus External Candidates for the Applicant Pool: A Summary of Benefits

Figure 5-3 summarizes the advantages of building an applicant pool of internal versus external candidates for the FLM job. Of course, sometimes the best strategy is to include both internal and external candidates in the pool.

Advantage	Internal Candidates	External Candidates
Selection	Candidates' work can be observed and evaluated directly.	
Training and development	Candidates know the company and its products.	Candidates usually have prior management experience.
Sales force morale	Strong performers are rewarded with career progression.	Candidates are viewed as a "boss" from the start, and there is no jealousy about the selection.
Culture	Candidates know and fit with the company culture.	Candidates bring in outside perspective.
Connections to enable success	Candidates have internal connections with others on the sales team or in other company departments.	Candidates have external connections with prospective customers and new sales talent.
New skills and knowledge		Candidates can bring in skills and knowledge the company lacks, especially in a changing market.
Cost	Compensation cost is usually lower in the short term (less need to pay to attract talent).	Development time and cost are usually lower in the short term if candidates have strong managerial experience.

Figure 5-3 Advantages of Internal Versus External Candidates for the FLM Position

Selecting the Best Candidates and Convincing Them to Join Your Team

Selection requires gathering information about all of the candidates in the applicant pool—both internal and external—and sifting through it to determine which candidate is best.

The Best Selection Techniques

A meta-analysis by American psychologists Frank L. Schmidt and John E. Hunter[1] looked at the effectiveness of different employee-selection techniques across a variety of jobs. The analysis revealed that the best ways for companies to predict job success in the recruiting process included work sample tests (such as putting candidates in a hands-on situation or presenting them with a case study that simulates important parts of the job); structured behavioral interviews (that ask questions about past behaviors or experiences that relate to success profile characteristics and competencies); and job-tryout procedures. Yet even companies that utilize all of these techniques often make mistakes in selecting candidates. The study found that unstructured employment interviews, résumé screens, and reference checks—techniques that are used quite commonly by companies to select job candidates—are, in fact, poor predictors of job success.

The best FLM selection processes use multiple predictive techniques as part of a thorough and cogent selection process. This process should provide opportunities for those making selection decisions to observe the candidate's work (using techniques such as work sample tests and job-tryout procedures) and to evaluate candidates through structured interviews. Online assessment techniques have also been used successfully at many companies as an input for FLM selection.

Observations of the Candidate's Work

When selecting among internal candidates, it is relatively easy to find opportunities to observe candidates' work, both by watching them in their current job and by giving them special assignments that test their suitability for the FLM position. With external candidates, work observation requires creativity during the recruiting process. You'll need to test candidates for the characteristics and competencies in your success profile. Figure 5-4 shows several examples of effective work sample tests that can be built around a business case study. Figure 5-5 provides examples adapted from case studies used at Boston Scientific for selecting FLMs.

---

[1] Frank L. Schmidt and John E. Hunter, "The Validity and Utility of Selection Methods in Personnel Psychology: Practical and Theoretical Implications of 85 Years of Research Findings," *Psychological Bulletin* 124, no. 2 (1998): 262–74.

To develop a business case study as an FLM selection tool, develop a short description of a fictitious sales district, including the following:

- Background on performance issues/opportunities for some of the salespeople
- Description of key issues/opportunities with some key customers or prospects
- Summary of major external business challenges facing the district (for example, changes in customer needs, the competition, or the environment) as well as changes in company strategies and priorities that impact the sales force
- Data on sales performance trends, market potential, and sales activity—by salesperson or major customer or for the whole district

Give the candidates time to review the case materials, and then engage them in discussion and role-playing exercises that test them on job characteristics and competencies. Some examples follow.

FLM Role	Assessment Description	Sample Characteristics and Competencies
People Manager	Ask the candidates to assess the performance of each salesperson and to explain what management actions they would take to address issues and capitalize on opportunities.	Conceptual abilities Management competency
	Ask the candidates to role-play (the candidate is the FLM; the interviewer is a salesperson). Select a specific performance issue, and ask the candidates to demonstrate how they would coach the salesperson to improve on that issue.	Interpersonal abilities Coaching competency
Customer Manager	Ask the candidates to develop and present a plan for increasing business with a specific customer. Focus on what role the manager would play in helping the salesperson.	Customer focus Conceptual abilities Planning skills
	Ask the candidates to role-play (the candidate is the FLM; the interviewer is a customer). Describe a challenge to the company's relationship with the customer, and ask the candidates to demonstrate how they would address the issue.	Interpersonal abilities Selling competency
Business Manager	Ask the candidates to assess district performance and to role-play how they would bring their boss up to speed on current performance, issues, and opportunities (the candidate is the FLM; the interviewer is the FLM's boss).	Conceptual abilities Business acumen

Figure 5-4   Using a Business Case Study to Evaluate FLM Candidates

Advanced Technologies (AT) is your largest account, with $5 million in annual sales. Mary Thompson is the senior buyer and decision maker in the Purchasing Department. Your salesperson, Alex Perez, has a strong, long-standing relationship with Mary and enjoys nearly 100 percent of her business. Mary likes to use the latest technology, appreciates the quality of your product, and has never received complaints from those who use your products. You are aware, however, that your competitors have been aggressively pursuing all angles to get an "in" at this important and large customer.

Alex has let you know that he has received an open bid "opportunity" from AT's CFO. The "suggested target" prices on the bid document are far lower than any prices you have offered in your district, and you suspect that your largest competitor is behind the request. Moreover, according to the CFO, that competitor has already agreed to the prices. The CFO says you have one week to respond to his pricing demands and suggests that any supplier who does not meet the price targets jeopardizes all business with AT. The AT account represents a significant percentage of your district's sales and would have a major impact on Alex's viability with the company if it were lost.

What will you do?

Case Study 2

You are diligently thinking through your response to the Advanced Technologies contracting dilemma when you receive a phone call from your sales technical trainer. The new salesperson that you hired three months ago has just failed his initial training exam. The trainer says that it is not a complete surprise, as the new hire often comes ill prepared to his training sessions. The sales trainer wants to know what you want to do.

What do you want to do?

Case Study 3

You receive a text from your second-highest-volume senior salesperson requesting that you meet him for lunch. He has been with your company for six years and has been a key part of the district's success. He is generally very personable, but you are concerned because he seemed disengaged at your sales meeting last week. You assumed that he just had a tough day. At the restaurant, he tells you that he has a job offer from your main competitor that pays "significantly more." He plans to sign the offer tomorrow.

How do you reply?

(continued)

Figure 5-5 Examples Adapted from Case Studies Used at Boston Scientific for Selecting FLMs

---

Case Study 4

It's been a busy day. You have received an aggressive contract request from your largest account, heard that one of your "star" new hires is failing, and learned that one of your top salespeople is ready to jump to your main competitor. As you ponder how to break all of this news to your boss, you receive an email from another one of your salespeople. The message reads:

"Good news! Triangle Design just signed the three-year 80 percent deal that we proposed last week." You smile, knowing that she has worked incredibly hard to earn this business—and it represents $2 million in upside for the district.

How do you respond to this news?

Note: Advanced Technologies (AT) and Triangle Design do not refer to actual companies and are used for illustrative purposes only.

Figure 5-5 *(continued)* Examples Adapted from Case Studies Used at Boston Scientific for Selecting FLMs

When possible, job tryouts are another technique for observing candidate behaviors. Some companies require that candidates undergo training before a final offer is extended (an approach that is easier to implement with internal candidates than with external ones). More commonly, companies will allow candidates who have received an FLM job offer to shadow someone in the job for a period of time. This helps with selection from the candidate's point of view: candidates who discover that the job is not for them may decline the offer. That way, the candidate avoids taking a job he or she may not be suited for, and the company doesn't invest time training someone who won't last. A challenge in making job shadowing effective for those candidates who are unfamiliar with the diversity of the FLM job is that the candidate may need to follow someone on the job over a period of time to get enough perspective to assess the job accurately.

Structured Interviews

Most companies use interviewing as a means of screening FLM candidates. When interviewing is not structured (in other words, interviewers create their own questions and agenda) and when questions are not specifically tied to the FLM success profile, selection results are typically not good. Interview-based candidate selection is improved significantly when structured interviewing approaches are used.

The best structured interviews use questions that are predetermined based on the success profile. Interviewers employ a consistent method for scoring candidates' answers to these questions. A technique called behavioral interviewing builds on the observation that a candidate's past behavior is a good predictor of future behavior. Interviewers ask candidates to recount experiences in their lives in which they have demonstrated characteristics or competencies that are part of the success profile. An interviewer can ask questions that relate to specific competencies in the success profile that the candidate developed and utilized in the prior job. But most important, interviewers should seek to discover whether candidates have the right personal characteristics that can enable their success. By designing questions that probe for personal characteristics, the interviewer can evaluate whether a candidate is likely to be successful at developing the needed competencies on the job (see Figure 5-6 for some sample questions).

Many interviewees are aware of behavioral interviewing techniques and arrive at the interview prepared to answer these types of questions. Interviewers must ask probing follow-up questions to ensure that candidates are not being superficial and to be sure that they are not misrepresenting their experience. Still, effective structured interviewing is much better at predicting job success than informal, ad hoc interviewing.

Online Assessment Tests

Many companies use online assessment tools as one input in the FLM selection process. There are many assessment tests, including ones that measure abilities and aptitude, knowledge and skills, situational judgment, personality, and behaviors. Candidates answer questions or participate in simulation exercises, and their answers and performance are compared against a database of responses from people who have been successful in similar jobs. The tools can be customized to test for the characteristics and competencies that are important for a specific FLM job. Testing advocates claim that the tests have high ability to predict job performance and thus help you pinpoint the best people for the FLM job. The tests also enable you to assess the characteristics of candidates without creating legal risk for the company.

Selecting the Right Internal Candidates

When selecting internal candidates for FLM positions, both the candidate and the company have access to considerable information for making an informed decision. Internal candidates know the company and its culture and can easily get an inside perspective on what the FLM position is really like. The company has a job performance history for the candidate. Because past performance is a good predictor of future performance, this history should get significant weight in the selection process. Past sales success is an indicator of results-drive, a characteristic that is important for both salespeople and sales managers. And sales managers who are successful as salespeople make good role models for the sales force.

FLM Role	Candidates with Prior Management Experience	Candidates Without Prior Management Experience
People Manager	**Selecting and recruiting:** Talk about a specific occasion when you made a mistake in hiring someone. How did you deal with the situation? **Coaching:** Describe a time when you coached an employee to overcome a selling obstacle. **Managing performance:** Describe a time when you had to tell a subordinate that you were dissatisfied with his or her work.	**Interpersonal abilities:** Talk about a difficult individual that you've had to work with and how you managed to work with that person. **Empathy:** Describe a situation in which you were able to effectively "read" another person and guide your actions by understanding the person's needs. **Leadership:** Give an example of your ability to build motivation in your coworkers or on a volunteer committee.
Business Manager	**Strategic thinking:** Describe the methods you have used to define a vision for your team. **Planning and organizing skills:** Tell us about a time when you organized an event for your team that was successful. **Ethics:** Talk about a time when a subordinate submitted an expense report with some questionable expenses. How did you handle the situation?	**Conceptual abilities:** Give an example of a time you used judgment/logic to solve a problem. **Organizational savvy:** Talk about a politically complex work situation and how you dealt with it. **Time management skills:** Describe a time when you had too many things to do and had to prioritize your tasks.
Customer Manager	**Selling skills:** Describe how you prepare for a sales call for a new client. **Relationship-building skills:** Give an example of a time when you had to address an upset customer. What was the outcome? What was your role in defusing the situation? **Negotiating skills:** Describe the last time you had to negotiate with a difficult customer. **Influencing others:** Talk about a time when you had to use your communication skills to influence someone's opinion. **Listening:** Give an example of a time when you made a mistake because you did not listen well to what someone had to say.	

Figure 5-6   Sample Behavioral Interview Questions for Selecting Candidates for Different FLM Roles

From the perspective of career progression, you'll want to promote your best people. But not everyone who is successful as a salesperson will be successful as a manager. When selecting internal candidates, look at the relevant skills and abilities acquired from the candidate's previous job, but also test for the additional skills and abilities required to be successful in the new job. The best candidates have a proven track record of success but also have a strong desire and ability to win through others.

What to Do When a Good Salesperson Lacks Managerial Characteristics But Wants to Be an FLM

Too often, the practice of selecting the best salesperson to become sales manager results in a mediocre sales management team and at the same time wastes the talent of excellent salespeople. Once promoted, a good salesperson who is not suited to a managerial role is likely to miss the freedom and excitement (and sometimes the money) of her former sales job, and quickly becomes frustrated by the multitude of people management and administrative issues that she has to deal with. Eventually, she leaves her position and the company. For many excellent salespeople, a promotion into management is not the right career move.

So what should you do if an excellent salesperson wants to become an FLM, but you don't think he has the characteristics to be successful in the role? As a first step, talk to the individual about what the role entails, sharing candidly the frustrations that many successful salespeople have felt after taking an FLM job. In some cases, particularly when salespeople have been in their jobs for a while and earn large commissions or bonuses tied to sales performance, a move from salesperson to manager also involves a pay cut. If the salesperson understands what he's getting into, he may realize that he is not cut out to do the job and may withdraw from consideration on his own.

If the salesperson still insists that he wants to be an FLM, a good selection process will test him in the role. For example, by giving the individual a role as a mentor or field trainer, in addition to his sales responsibilities, he gets a chance to try out a people management role and see how he likes it, and you get a chance to see how well the individual performs. You may find out that your initial assessment of the candidate was wrong.

"Dual career paths have enabled our sales organization to keep many of the best and brightest salespeople who are most valuable as individual contributors," says Sandy Cantwell of Cardinal Health. "You can succeed by becoming a manager or by becoming a 'super salesperson.' We have a formal career roadmap for both management and individual contributor roles. Our top sales role, the Strategic Account Vice President, is roughly equivalent in level to a Regional Vice President on the managerial side."

Case Study: Selecting and Developing Internal Talent for the FLM Position

Boston Scientific has a formalized corporate program that helps sales leaders select and develop the right internal candidates for the FLM job. "When considering employees for FLM development, sales leaders generally seek those who have demonstrated excellence in three competencies," says Chris Hartman. These are the three competencies:

1. *Selling* by generating strong sales results in the territory. At a minimum, candidates must have hit their sales plan in two of the previous three years to be considered.

2. *Teaching others to sell* by acting as a mentor to a new salesperson. "Mentors are responsible for helping new salespeople get off to a good start. There is a formal schedule of responsibilities for mentors that dictates what support the mentor should provide during the new salesperson's first six months on the job. In addition to helping the new salesperson get acclimated, the mentorship program is an excellent way for sales leaders to evaluate a candidate's potential as a coach. It also allows the candidates to evaluate how much they enjoy being in a coaching role," explains Chris.

3. *Managing* through exposure to leadership roles that test the candidate's ability to perform managerial functions. "This can include serving in a field training role or on a sales advisory board, product launch task force, or local steering committee (for example, that helps guide sales force direction in high-impact areas such as improving talent management, developing a positive sales culture, and enabling more effective sales execution). These opportunities give candidates a chance to demonstrate skills and capabilities while giving exposure to higher-level decision making and/or to other internal departments, such as Sales Operations or HR."

Every year, sales leaders identify 10 to 20 salespeople who have demonstrated the ability to sell, teach, and manage and who have expressed a desire to pursue sales management as part of their individual career plans. Interested employees complete a formal application and selection process that culminates with senior leadership interviews. The actual number of employees selected annually is determined by the readiness of the individuals and the anticipated needs of the Boston Scientific sales organization. Those who are selected enter a company management assessment and development program called Momentum. To be eligible for Momentum, candidates must also be willing to relocate. "Momentum candidates participate in a range of general leadership and practical tool training that prepares them for the FLM role," says Chris. "They get exposure to topics such as coaching, performance management, interviewing, and negotiation. Candidates also participate in 360-degree evaluations to discover more about their own leadership styles and to learn strategies for becoming an effective manager."

During the final element of the program, participants are given a mock region with a description of the personality styles and sales performance of mock salespeople. They are asked to prepare a 90-day plan as if they were accepting a manager position in that region, and the plans are presented to the class and to sales leadership. This ensures that the candidates are ready to take on a real region when they are called to action.

Momentum candidates keep their sales responsibilities while they participate in the program. "Participation typically adds 10 to 20 percent to a candidate's workload, but it can be a big intrinsic motivator for the right person. And usually because participants have a few years of experience under their belt, they have mastered their territory, and they have capacity to take on additional work," says Chris. "In its simplest form, the candidates should be practicing many of the competencies we expect from a manager as a peer leader *before* they get the FLM role.

"Sometimes, candidates will pull out of the program by their own choice after seeing firsthand what a manager does. And occasionally, sales leaders will pull a candidate out if they feel that the candidate and company are best served by keeping the person in an individual contributor role. By providing training and testing of candidates over a period of time and by allowing many opportunities for both the candidate and the company to evaluate fit with the FLM job, the program has been very valuable for helping Boston Scientific select the best internal FLM talent," says Chris.

Selecting and Developing Internal Talent for the FLM Position in Smaller Sales Forces

Although smaller sales forces may not have sufficient scale to run formal FLM selection and development programs like Momentum, they can realize many of the benefits that such programs provide by using informal and inexpensive methods of evaluating and developing candidates for the FLM job. Salespeople with management potential can act as peer mentors to new salespeople or can get exposure to leadership roles by helping plan sales meetings, filling in for FLMs on temporary leave, or taking on roles such as local trainer or interviewer. Some companies seek to give salespeople with managerial potential "milestone experiences," such as opportunities to participate on special task forces or to solve specific customer challenges. Participation in these types of leadership activities gives sales leaders and the candidates themselves an opportunity to evaluate fit with the FLM job. At the same time, such roles allow FLM candidates to broaden their experience and gain some initial on-the-job training, making them better prepared to jump into the FLM role if they are selected. External, general-enrollment management courses at universities or sales-training organizations are also an inexpensive and effective way for smaller sales forces to develop managerial talent. (See Chapter 6 for a list of some programs.)

Best Practices for Selecting FLM Talent

Adapt the Selection Criteria to the Situation, But Also Think Long-Term

Sometimes the situation in a particular sales district or region influences what characteristics and competencies are the most important selection criteria. "When I'm hiring an experienced FLM from outside the company to manage a low-performing sales district, I emphasize competencies such as a demonstrated ability to assess talent and upgrade the team, as well as experience in hiring, firing, and managing performance-improvement plans," says Amy Davalle, Vice President of Sales—West for medical device company Smith & Nephew. "With internal candidates, on the other hand, promotions can be especially tricky when a new FLM is required to manage former colleagues. It is important for the new FLM to transition into a position of authority quickly so he is viewed by current peers as a boss. If the transition takes too long, authority may never get established. I look for characteristics such as trust, respect of others, and demonstrated leadership beyond just sales numbers, as well as resilience to address jealousies from people who may try to undermine the new FLM. But in all FLM hiring situations, I look for competencies and characteristics that will be required for long-term success in the district."

Sell as You Select, But Describe the Job Accurately

Selling the advantages of the FLM job is a key part of the selection process for both internal and external candidates. Interviewers and other evaluators should provide candidates with a solid sense of the benefits as well as the challenges of the job (and the company for external candidates), in addition to assessing applicants' personal characteristics and competencies. Every person who is involved in the recruiting process should sell (but not oversell) strong candidates on the opportunity, while making sure that prospective FLMs develop an accurate picture of what the job is really like.

One of the best ways to ensure you retain FLM candidates, particularly those who are moving up from a sales role, is to make sure candidates know what the job is really like before they accept it. The role of sales manager is very different from the role of salesperson, and if the job has been oversold or if its negative aspects have been downplayed, new FLMs are bound to be dissatisfied down the road. Lance Osborne from AFLAC lets FLM candidates know that they'll need to make sacrifices when they move from salesperson to manager. "You have to go from managing clients to managing people; this is a big change, and FLM candidates need to understand both the positive and negative aspects of the role change."

Close Effectively

After applicants have passed the necessary hurdles, the process of convincing candidates who have offers to take the job kicks into high gear. After so much hard work to find the right candidates, it is frustrating to lose them after an offer has been made. Obviously, a very attractive offer makes it more likely that the candidate will accept, but effective follow-up does not cost much and can also make a big difference. Let candidates know that you want them. Have several people call to show interest, including the vice president of sales and possibly even the CEO. Take candidates out to dinner to meet the people they will be working with in a more casual environment. Consider inviting candidates to a company meeting, send them company press releases, and follow up with them appropriately to see how the decision process is progressing.

Insights for Selecting and Sustaining an Exceptional Sales Management Team

Assign the Best People to Recruiting

People tend to promote or hire individuals they are comfortable with and who often are similar to themselves. Successful people will not be intimidated by successful job applicants — in fact, they look for people they think will be successful. If you want excellent sales managers, make sure that those who make promotion and hiring decisions are excellent managers themselves. If the recruiting and selection team is weak, it is highly likely that the candidates they select will be weak as well.

The sales leaders who make FLM hiring and selection decisions are typically high up in the organizational hierarchy. They have high-pressure jobs with responsibility for many decisions that impact company strategy and profitability. Yet selecting the right FLMs is one of the most important responsibilities these leaders have. A sales force that does not put its best people in charge of the FLM recruiting process, or does not give sufficient attention to the critical decision of whom to promote or hire for the FLM team, can never be excellent.

Constantly Be on the Lookout for FLM Talent

Even with the best efforts at retaining FLMs, turnover in the position is inevitable and needs to be planned for. Vacancies in the FLM position create risk. Without leadership, a district of salespeople can veer off course quickly. Salespeople won't get the coaching and support they need, good salespeople may leave, salesperson recruiting slows down, and over time, district or regional performance may suffer. The risk of sales loss can be immediate in cases where the departing manager has a significant role as a customer manager or where the departing manager has the power to take the best-performing salespeople along to a competitor.

As a result of these risks, some sales leaders rush to fill FLM vacancies. This is a mistake. Rush to hire a star candidate, but never rush to fill a position. A vacant district can create temporary setbacks, but a poor "warm body" hire to fill the position places sales in jeopardy for a much longer period of time. Always be on the lookout for new FLM talent. "If you go grocery shopping when you're hungry, most likely, you'll come out with junk food," says Chris Hartman. By recruiting before a position becomes available, an empty position can be filled right away — with an excellent candidate. Effective FLM recruiting programs — such as the Momentum program at Boston Scientific — provide a "bench" of worthy candidates, so that when a vacancy occurs, sales leaders can go to the bench and staff the position quickly. This is especially effective in situations where new FLMs need considerable training before they can take on their new role; candidates can complete the training while they are on the bench.

Bench programs work best for large sales organizations that select several to many new FLMs each year, but sales leaders of smaller organizations can also take steps to prepare for future FLM vacancies. Always keep a list of potential FLM candidates — employee referrals, candidates who rejected offers in the past, candidates who were an excellent second choice on a prior recruiting foray, customer employees, former employees, employees in other functions, or even someone the manager met on an airplane. You never know when you'll need to fill an FLM position.

Manage Turnover in the FLM Position

Recruiting a talented group of FLMs is a critical step in building a winning sales management team. However, a strong FLM recruiting program does little without the right programs, processes, and systems in place for nurturing and retaining FLM talent and continuously managing the inevitable turnover that occurs in the position.

A modest amount of FLM turnover is normal and even healthy. As FLMs with strong leadership potential get promoted and as weaker performers leave, new FLMs bring in fresh ideas, approaches, abilities, and attitudes that help members of the FLM team continue to advance their capabilities. But too much turnover in the FLM position is costly. There are many direct costs associated with FLM turnover, including termination and severance expenses, as well as the cost of recruiting, on-boarding, and training new talent. But even more significant is the indirect cost of lost productivity as sales districts or regions operate without leadership until FLM vacancies are filled.

At most companies, the FLM position includes individuals in different stages of their careers. Once promoted, some FLMs will stay in the job until they retire. Others view the job as a stepping-stone on a career path to the top. At Microsoft, for example, "the position of FLM is a critical engagement for some high-potential employees who are rising up through the ranks," observes Jay Sampson, former General Manager, U.S. Emerging Media Sales at Microsoft. "We typically see a rotation of two to three years, but of course we foster an environment where other FLMs can stay in the job for 10-plus years, potentially taking on larger teams to manage as their experience grows."

The best sales leaders use a flexible management approach that meets the career needs of the diverse group of individuals on the FLM team.

Conclusion

By continuously selecting and nurturing FLM talent, sales leaders can create and retain a strong team of sales managers who will drive sales force performance. Selecting the best FLM team requires identifying the characteristics that individuals need to be successful in the FLM role, creating a strong applicant pool of candidates who possess those characteristics, and then using proven selection techniques to choose the best candidates for the job.

With the right talent on the team, sales leaders must nurture that talent so that FLMs constantly learn new skills and stay engaged in their jobs. The next chapter of this book shows how another key FLM success driver—enhancing competencies through training and development—contributes to FLM retention and engagement and helps drive sales team success.

CHAPTER 6

Enhancing Sales Management Competencies

First-Line Sales Manager Development: A Key Sales Force Effectiveness Driver

Companies spend more than $20 billion in the United States alone on training their sales forces, according to the American Society of Training and Development. Yet too few of these resources are directed toward a key participant in driving sales force success: the first-line sales manager (FLM). When one salesperson's skills and knowledge are enhanced through training and coaching, performance improves in a single territory. When one FLM's skills and knowledge are improved through training and development, performance improves across an entire district. Very often, companies can leverage investments in FLM development to produce considerable effectiveness gains at a relatively small cost. Yet too many companies do not have adequate or ongoing development programs for their sales managers. The right investments in FLM development can enable both small and large sales organizations to enhance sales effectiveness significantly.

"If you rely on raw talent to drive FLM success, maybe the top 20 percent of your managers can be successful. To help the other 80 percent be successful, too, you need to establish sales management programs, processes, and systems and develop FLMs around them," says a sales leader who leads the corporate leadership development program for a large global sales organization.

Most FLMs are former salespeople and do not come into their jobs knowing how to manage. Without training and development, they have to improvise. The right development prepares all FLMs to take on their new and evolving responsibilities and creates stronger and more consistent results across the FLM team. At the same time, the learning helps new managers achieve the confidence and the shift in mind-set they'll need to make the critical transition from salesperson to manager.

Many sales leaders tell us that their companies don't provide enough development opportunities for FLMs. Often, the programs that do exist focus primarily on coaching. Coaching is clearly an important part of the job; however, training on how to coach, by itself, is not enough to prepare most FLMs for the diverse range of people, customer, and business management responsibilities they are expected to perform. When budgets get tight, management development programs are often one of the first things that get slashed. As a result, too many companies underinvest in formally developing their FLMs. And regrettably, most FLMs also get too little informal coaching and advice from their bosses. Salespeople almost always have a first-line sales manager they can go to for guidance—someone who has clear responsibility for coaching and developing them. Yet FLMs likely report to someone whose duties may include managing a regional office or other physical assets and contributing to corporate strategies and initiatives. Too often, these individuals don't spend enough time developing the FLMs who report to them.

The Focus of This Chapter

The talent that you select for your winning sales management team needs to be developed so that all team members acquire and continuously improve the necessary success competencies. This chapter focuses on building a good program for training and developing your FLM team. The chapter is organized into two sections:

- Development *content*—how to identify the critical gaps in FLM skills and knowledge that need to be filled
- Development *methods*—how to combine classroom training, learning from colleagues, and other learning resources in enhancing the FLM competencies

Developing critical success competencies is a key FLM success driver and an important component of creating a strong FLM team (see Figure 6-1).

Designing FLM Development Content Around Success Competencies

The best FLM training and development content focuses on the success competencies that new and current FLMs need to develop to carry out their role. It is important to differentiate between the *characteristics* and the *competencies* required for FLM success (see Chapter 4). Characteristics are inherent traits, such as empathy, integrity, and drive for results. Development programs have limited ability to impact characteristics. To get the right characteristics, you need to hire and retain the right people (see Chapter 5). Competencies, however, are learned skills (for example, skills in coaching or in business planning) and knowledge (for example, knowledge of the performance management process or of customer needs). Competencies—and the gap between current and desired FLM proficiency on the competencies—influence content for FLM development programs.

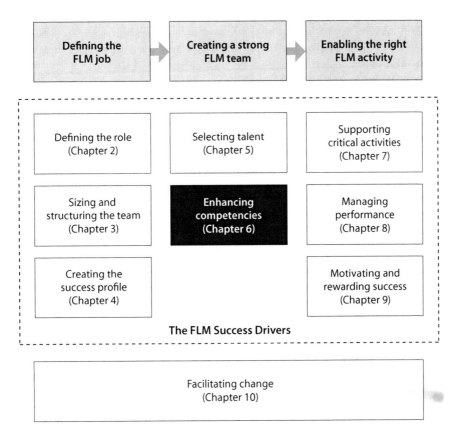

Figure 6-1   An Approach for Building a Winning Sales Management Team

"At GE, our leadership competencies—as defined in the GE Sales Leader Capability Guide—drive training and development needs across our global sales organizations," says Conrad Zils, Global Director of the Commercial Center of Excellence for GE Healthcare. (See Figure 4-2 in Chapter 4 for a list of the competencies.) "When making decisions about sales manager development programs, we always start with the leadership competencies and how they are changing and evolving. A steering committee of senior sales executives works with our training and development experts to profile what the next generation of best-in-class GE sales managers should look like. Then we update the competencies, identify gaps in FLM skills and knowledge, and fill in those gaps by providing new courses, coaching programs, and development resources. As a result of this process, we have added training programs in several high-priority areas recently, including enhancing sales force effectiveness and improving sales manager coaching." GE also has an online system that links competency development to specific learning resources, including articles, books, internal and external courses, and web sites.

Development Content for New FLMs

"When you become an FLM, the first 90 days are critical, particularly for earning the respect of the salespeople you manage," observes Lance Osborne, Vice President, Pacific Territory Director at AFLAC. "If you mess up in the first 90 days, it can be really hard to get back your team's support." Strong programs for bringing FLMs on board and developing them to excel at critical success competencies can help new managers rapidly become fully engaged and productive members of the sales organization.

Development content for FLMs who are new to the job or company should link to competency gaps. These gaps are largely determined by your FLM applicant pool strategy. If your new FLMs come from inside the company, they likely have company experience but not sales management experience. If your new FLMs come from outside the company, they likely have sales management experience but lack company experience. Figure 6-2 lists the competencies that are most important to develop in FLMs who come into the job with different combinations of company and sales management experience. The four situations shown are numbered in sequence from the most basic to the most extensive development needs.

Situation 1: If a New FLM Knows the Company and Knows How to Manage Salespeople, Focus on Job-Specific Requirements

Situation 1 of Figure 6-2 might occur when an FLM transfers from one sales division within the company to another. Such individuals have to get up to speed on job-specific requirements. They need to learn about the people they will manage, the geographic area or major accounts they will be responsible for, and the tools and resources that can help them do their job. These job-specific requirements are an important part of development for FLMs in all four situations. But the other three situations go beyond these basics.

Situation 2: If You Hire Experience from Outside, Focus on Company and Product Knowledge and Culture

Situation 2 of Figure 6-2 is typical for companies that hire FLMs who have sales management experience with other companies. A good hiring process screens for managerial competencies and the right personal characteristics. New managers need to focus most on developing product and other company-specific skills and knowledge.

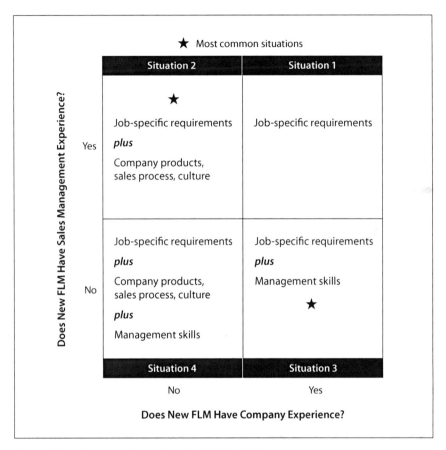

Figure 6-2 Competencies to Develop in New FLMs

"At Extreme Networks, we only hired FLMs who had a track record of managerial success with other companies," said Helmut Wilke, former Senior Vice President of Worldwide Sales for the network solutions provider. "The people we hired already knew how to manage, coach, and interview. New manager development focused on product and other company-specific skills and knowledge."

Although hiring FLMs with prior management experience reduces the need for managerial skills development, keep in mind that experienced hires may not have received excellent or recent training in critical areas such as hiring, coaching, and managing performance. They'll need to refresh or update their skills, break bad habits, or at a minimum familiarize themselves with the specific approaches that your company uses. In addition, new FLMs from outside the company don't know your people and culture. Sometimes, they bring baggage in the form of incompatible work styles and attitudes that will need to be managed.

Immerse experienced hires in the company culture right away to help them assimilate. Begin indoctrination through an orientation session on their first day on the job. Have company leaders communicate preferred culture choices and share stories of company heroes and legends that communicate desired culture choices. Engage new managers early on in meetings or other less-formal events in which they can interact with peers, superiors, and subordinates who are already part of the culture.

Situation 3: If You Promote from Inside, Focus on Management Skills

Situation 3 of Figure 6-2 is typical for companies that promote salespeople from within to the FLM position. New FLMs are already familiar with the company and its products, sales process, and culture; they need to develop their managerial skills.

Medical device company Boston Scientific promotes salespeople from within to the FLM position. New manager development content focuses on competencies such as coaching, managing performance, and interviewing. (See Chapter 5 for more information on Boston Scientific's Momentum program.) The goal is to help successful salespeople become excellent sales managers by fostering skills that in many cases may be new to them. "FLM training is critical to getting FLMs out of their comfort zone (selling) and into leading and managing high-performance sales teams," says Chris Hartman, Vice President, Central Zone, for Boston Scientific's Cardiology, Rhythm and Vascular Group.

In addition to learning management skills, salespeople who are making the transition into sales management need to learn how to navigate the administrative side of the job. "New managers need to learn the operational processes required to run a sales team—for example, how to approve large orders or reassign accounts," says Alysa Parks, Global Director of Learning and Expertise Development at consulting firm ZS Associates. "Simple tools and resources for on-the-job support—plus assigning each new FLM a mentor—can help newly promoted FLMs get up to speed on 'small stuff' that can derail their ability to succeed."

All new FLMs who are former salespeople can benefit from advice from those who have been in their shoes before. Andy Anderson, a former President of U.S. Operations at pharmaceutical maker Searle (now part of Pfizer), would tell newly promoted FLMs: "When I got my first promotion to FLM, I walked around with a swagger and thought, 'Finally, I get to be the boss and tell people what to do.' But quickly, I discovered that being an FLM isn't about being a boss—it's about being a coach." Another sales leader shared the following advice with new FLMs: "The day you become a manager, it becomes about them. Your job is to help your people grow. Walk around with a watering can in one hand and a bag of fertilizer in the other hand."

At one company, a camcorder is used to capture lessons learned and best-practice advice from high-performing, experienced FLMs. New FLMs can access an online podcast library to hear timely advice from experienced peers anytime and anywhere. Informal advice from those who have been there is important for helping salespeople make a successful transition into the FLM job.

Situation 4: If You Hire People from Outside Without Management Experience, Focus on Company Knowledge and Management Skills

Situation 4 of Figure 6-2 happens rarely, but it is possible, especially in rapidly growing sales organizations. Individuals who come into the FLM job lacking both company and sales management experience will have to learn all aspects of the company, management, and the job.

Topics to Include in a Development Program for New FLMs

Development content for new FLMs varies with the relative importance of the three FLM roles: people manager, business manager, and customer manager. Several topics that are important for new managers are listed in Figure 6-3. The time allocated to each topic depends both on the FLM role and on whether an individual was promoted from within or hired with experience from outside the company.

The topics to emphasize can also vary with a sales leader's management philosophy. Many new FLM training programs emphasize leadership development in the curriculum, but some sales leaders, such as Fred Wagner, a former Vice President of Sales at J&J's Ethicon Endo-Surgery division, feel that leadership gets too much emphasis. "What new FLMs really need to be successful is day-to-day guidance on how to manage their people and their team. We expect people to jump into being 'leaders' before they have mastered the fundamentals of management. Good FLM training programs focus on building a strong management foundation first and foremost."

The Importance of a Strong On-boarding Program

A strong on-boarding program helps all new FLMs (whether new to the company or just new to the job) acquire a level of knowledge and skill that enables them to be effective in their jobs and "in the know" about how to get things done in the FLM role. On-boarding helps new FLMs make connections with people who can help them succeed and helps them get up and running quickly with information about the salespeople and customers in their districts. On-boarding also

FLM Role	Common Topics in the New FLM Development Curriculum	For FLMs Promoted from a Company Salesperson Role	For Experienced FLMs Hired from Outside the Company
People Manager	**Interviewing skills:** company recruiting process, interview guides and cases, behavioral interviewing, what to ask and what not to ask	Full training on all topics, plus company-specific approaches ★★★★	Refresher training with emphasis on company-specific approaches ★★
	Coaching: company process, effective field visits, overcoming coaching fears, diverse communication styles, using coaching tools and dashboards		
	Performance management: company process, goal setting, performance appraisals, having difficult conversations		
	Leadership: principles of leadership, team building, establishing a success culture		
Business Manager	Forecasting, budgeting, business planning, sales pipeline management	Full training on all topics, plus company-specific approaches ★★★★	Refresher training with emphasis on company-specific approaches ★★
	Optimal sales resource allocation		
	Time allocation strategies		
Customer Manager	Manager's role in the sales process	Refresher training on the sales process with emphasis on manager's role ★★★	Full training on the company's sales process, plus manager's role ★★★★
All Roles	Company and product knowledge	Refresher training—from a manager's perspective ★	Full training on all topics, plus a manager's perspective ★★★★
	Company culture		
	Management systems and tools		

Note: The number of stars reflects the most likely relative importance of the development topics.

Figure 6-3   Common Topics in Development Programs for New FLMs

familiarizes new FLMs with the tools that can enable their productivity—for example, laptops, handheld devices, and software.

A formal on-boarding process especially helps FLMs who are new to the company. It helps new employees learn about company history and values so they can begin to assimilate into the culture. On-boarding also introduces FLMs who are new to the company to people at headquarters and on the sales team who can help them. Finally, it enables them to get up to speed with corporate policies and take care of administrative matters (for example, tax, insurance, and other employment forms).

Mentors can add value as part of the FLM on-boarding process. At a novelty gift company, each new FLM gets two mentors: one who started in the job recently and can relate to the challenges of being new, and another who has experience and can share wisdom.

Development Content for Current FLMs

Development content for current FLMs should focus on the areas in which there are competency gaps in the FLM team. There are many ways to identify the most important gaps.

Linking to the Performance Management Process

You can identify competency gaps through observation and insights that emerge during the performance management process (see Chapter 8). When FLM performance reviews are based on competency models, sales leaders will identify competency deficiencies directly through performance management and can address the deficiencies with appropriate training and development. Results metrics, too, can signal a need to look for development remedies for performance issues (see Figure 6-4).

Consider a Development Solution If FLMs . . .

- Consistently do not make their numbers
- Have high variability in salesperson performance across their districts
- Were previously strong performers but are no longer doing well
- Have consistently high turnover of salespeople in their districts
- Hire many new salespeople who never make it out of the box and leave the company within their first year

---

Figure 6-4 Signs That Your FLM Team May Need Additional Development

"Too often sales leaders use training as a quick fix when performance gaps are, in reality, more complex and caused by other variables," warns Alysa Parks of ZS Associates. "Warning signs that show up in results can sometimes be addressed with training and development; however, studies have shown that training alone is a solution only 15 to 20 percent of the time. Usually, performance deficiencies result from other causes besides knowledge and skill gaps."

Before jumping to a training and development solution, ask yourself if any of the following factors might be contributing to performance issues:

- External factors, such as unfavorable market dynamics, uncompetitive products, or a flawed go-to-market strategy
- Factors within other sales force programs, such as unreasonable sales force goals, inappropriate incentives, or inadequate sales force tools and resources
- Deficiencies in personal characteristics of FLMs, such as a lack of integrity or drive for results

If performance issues are largely the result of any of these factors, then development will have little impact on the problem. However, if a careful diagnosis of the situation suggests that performance issues result from *competency* deficiencies (for example, a lack of understanding of the best way to coach or manage), FLM development can be an effective solution.

Building Development Programs Around the Competencies of Your Best-Performing FLMs

By identifying the competencies that differentiate your top-performing FLMs from your average-performing FLMs, it's possible to create powerful FLM development content. Training and development were important components of the FLM performance frontier study at Novartis (see Chapter 4). In the study, members of an analysis team used performance frontier analysis, along with sales force observation, to identify a set of seven proprietary FLM success principles: specific characteristics and competencies that differentiated Novartis's best FLMs. Sales leaders believed that some of the success principles were characteristics that had to be hired for. Most of the success principles, however, they believed were competencies that could be trained for. The "train for" competencies became the basis for a new FLM training program and for modifications to the existing training curriculum. The training helped propagate the trainable FLM success principles to Novartis FLMs all over the globe.

Assessing How Your Selling Environment Is Changing

FLMs need to continually develop new skills and knowledge as the FLM role changes and as the competencies necessary to succeed in the role evolve. Consider some examples of how companies have changed their development content for FLMs in response to business changes.

- At GE: "As we were rebounding from the global financial crisis, we added training courses and coaching programs for FLMs to improve retention and engagement of our salespeople. Similarly, in a move to create stronger customer relationships, we began building global/strategic account management capabilities in many disparate businesses. We facilitated best-practice sharing sessions that enabled global GE sales organizations from across the business to learn from each other and share ideas on the topic," says Conrad Zils.

- At Genentech: "As changes in the U.S. healthcare environment led to increased variation in local needs across the country, we developed new training programs for FLMs to help them adapt sales strategies and allocate resources to the unique needs of local markets. These were supported by an evolving CRM platform to assist resource decision making and entrench the learning," says Quinton Oswald, former Vice President and Business Unit leader for Tissue Growth & Repair at Genentech.

Prioritizing FLM Development Needs Based on Performance and Impact

With limited time and budget available for FLM training and development resources, companies need to prioritize the investments that will have the greatest impact on the bottom line. A global medical products company created a performance/impact scorecard that it used to prioritize FLM development initiatives (see Figure 6-5). Company leaders suspected that the company's FLMs were not consistently performing at exceptional levels, as evidenced by high salesperson turnover in some districts and high variance in FLM performance. Improved FLM development was an important first step for enhancing sales force effectiveness. The company did not have a standard approach to developing its FLMs, and in some cases it provided no formal training at all.

Sales leaders at the company wanted to design an FLM development program that would have the highest impact on sales force performance. Focusing on nine important FLM success competencies, the company surveyed salespeople, first-line sales managers, second-line sales managers, and HR and training personnel to gain insight about two aspects of each competency:

- **Performance.** How effective was the FLM team at each competency?
- **Impact.** How important was each FLM competency for driving sales force success?

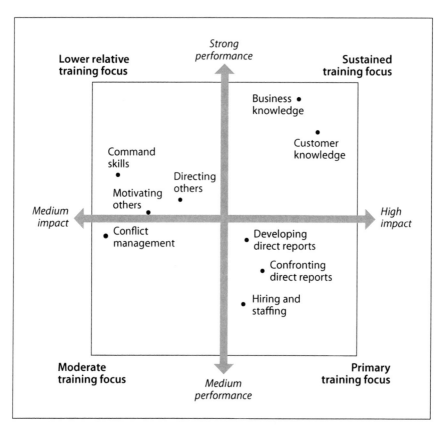

Figure 6-5 A Performance/Impact Scorecard for Setting FLM Development Priorities at a Global Medical Products Company

The results of the survey provide a snapshot of the FLM team's current performance and the impact of each competency. The position of each competency on the scorecard suggests an action. Competencies with strong performance and high impact, such as *business knowledge* and *customer knowledge*, should be monitored closely to ensure that FLM performance remains high. Competencies with medium impact and strong performance, such as *command skills*, should be monitored to see if performance shifts with time. The competencies that present the greatest opportunity for FLM improvement through training and development are those that have high impact but inadequate current performance — especially if those competencies are required frequently for success in the FLM job. The company focused its initial FLM development investment around three critical people-management competencies:

- **Hiring and staffing.** Inconsistent interviewing practices among FLMs led to missed opportunities to acquire the best talent. The company created a well-defined interviewing process, educated all FLMs on that process, and began requiring new managers to sit in on interviews conducted by experienced managers. It also educated the entire FLM team on the availability of HR resources to support recruiting efforts, and enabled idea sharing among FLMs on recruiting best practices.

- **Developing direct reports.** Insufficient coaching by some FLMs led to underdeveloped selling skills in many salespeople. In addition, managers used inconsistent metrics to evaluate salesperson performance. The company defined and communicated the percentage of FLM time that should be dedicated to coaching and provided training to all FLMs on effective coaching techniques. It identified FLMs who were doing a good job of coaching their people and had them contribute to the training program development.

- **Confronting direct reports.** Many managers were not well prepared to deal with a range of personnel issues and conflicts, particularly when confronting poor performers. The company provided training on specific strategies and techniques for dealing with these issues and enabled FLMs to share best practices. It also educated managers on legal, ethical, and business issues and processes for underperforming salespeople. Legal and HR managers were brought in to help with the training.

The performance/impact scorecard helped sales leaders at the global medical products company identify the training and development investments that would close the most important FLM performance gaps that were impacting the bottom line.

Using Multiple Learning Methods for the Highest Impact

FLM development can be accomplished through many different methods—it's not just about classroom learning. The best sales organizations select methods that involve blended learning approaches, adult learning models, and repeated reinforcement.

Blending Learning Approaches for Effectiveness and Efficiency

"In traditional learning models, learning and work are separate. You're either working or attending a class. In reality, learning takes place through a blend of both, and organizations will want their skill development programs to reflect this," says Alysa Parks.

A popular best-practice model for workplace learning and development is the 70-20-10 formula, a concept developed by the Human Resources Learning and Development Team at Princeton University's Center for Creative Leadership. According to the formula, 70 percent of learning and development takes place from real-life and on-the-job experiences, 20 percent comes from feedback and from observing and working with role models, and just 10 percent comes from formal training. Consequently, the best development programs provide support for learning beyond formal training. Blended learning approaches rely on a planned combination of learning methods, including those listed in Figure 6-6.

The right combination of methods depends on your objectives, your situation, the preferences of individual learners, the information to be shared, and time and budget constraints. A thoughtful and purposeful selection of methods allows FLMs to draw on multiple resources (including classroom training) to gain and reinforce the skills and knowledge they will need to be successful. It enables you to blend highly effective methods (such as job shadowing or coaching by supervisors) with more efficient methods (such as online courses or business books) to accomplish FLM learning objectives at a reasonable cost.

GE uses the concept of blended learning by providing a variety of resources to help all 5,800 FLMs worldwide accomplish their learning objectives. A three-day

Using Structured Learning Opportunities	Learning from Colleagues	Leveraging Learning Resources
Classroom training • Corporate training courses • External seminars and workshops • University-sponsored courses **Self-directed training** • Self-paced reading and workbooks • Video-based courses • Online courses **Experiential training** • Case studies • Role-playing exercises • Board games • Structured field experiences • Job shadowing	**Coaching by supervisors** **Mentorship programs** **Structured learning communities** • Online communities • Best-practice sharing sessions • Industry conferences **Informal learning channels** • Collaborating with peers • Informal chats with colleagues	**Personal reading** • Current business journals • Business books (like this one!) • Internet blogs and resources **Company learning resources** • Company library • Company intranet • Company CRM system

Figure 6-6   Examples of Learning Methods for a Blended Learning Approach

Essentials of Sales Management course focuses on critical leadership competencies and provides a strong foundation for successful sales management that is rooted in improving sales force effectiveness. The course is designed around GE's Sales Leader Capability Guide, an online resource that defines the set of global GE sales leadership competencies. The guide links competencies to specific learning opportunities. These opportunities include articles, white papers, books, seminars, internal and external courses, video clips, and webinars. All GE FLMs have access to this information and are encouraged to utilize these learning tools to enhance their development, particularly in areas where they need to enhance competency.

As part of a blended learning approach, many companies emphasize real-life and on-the-job experiential learning through coaching and mentorship programs for FLMs. "Our new managers get assigned mentors who can give peer-to-peer encouragement and guidance," says Sandy Cantwell, Vice President of Sales Operations at Cardinal Health. Some companies assign mentors from outside the sales department to FLMs to broaden their exposure and help them develop skills that are not sales-specific. At many companies, second-line sales managers (the FLMs' immediate superiors) play a large role in developing FLMs and can spend as much as 50 percent of their time coaching their FLMs for success.

Companies that embrace the concept of blended learning embed the process of continuous learning into their culture. Members of the sales force (including FLMs) become responsible for their own development and seek out ways to constantly improve their skills and knowledge. Sales leaders continuously encourage the sharing of knowledge, using both formal and informal means to capture and propagate learning across the sales force. The sales organization becomes a "learning organization" in which the development and exchange of knowledge become inseparable from the work environment.

Making Skills and Knowledge Stick with Adult Learning Models

Research-based models of how adults learn can help you choose the most effective learning methods for your FLM team. Educator Malcolm Knowles, a pioneer in the field of adult learning, developed a theory of adult education called *andragogy*. Researchers and consultants Harold Stolovitch and Erica Keeps outline four key principles of andragogy that they believe are most applicable for adult learning in the work setting:[1]

1. **Readiness.** Adults learn best when they are ready and motivated to learn the information. By focusing on learner needs and by continually reinforcing meaningful benefits to learners, trainers enhance learner readiness and thus improve learning and retention.

---

[1]Harold D. Stolovitch and Erica J. Keeps, *Telling Ain't Training* (Alexandra, VA: ASTD Press, 2002).

2. **Experience.** Training is more effective when trainers draw from and speak to the learners' experience. If trainers present information that is either too high or too low for the learners' experience level, learners will tune out. By getting to know the background of learners, trainers can pitch training appropriately to enhance its impact.

3. **Autonomy.** Adults become better engaged in learning when they decide what to learn and when they actively contribute during training. When learners participate in discussion and problem solving, they learn and retain more than when they simply listen passively.

4. **Action.** Adults learn best when they need new information or a new skill now; unless they apply it right away and see results, they rapidly lose the learning. Focus new learning on skills and knowledge that can be used right away on the job, and engage the FLMs' boss in encouraging and supporting the learning.

Build on these observations about adult learning when designing FLM training and development programs for high impact. Focus content around what FLMs want to learn, what is appropriate for their experience level, and what is most immediately relevant to their job. Methods that encourage autonomy in how adults learn—for example, case studies, role-playing exercises, on-the-job train-ing experiences, and discussions—can be very effective.

Printing, packaging, and facilities products distributor xpedx (a division of International Paper) built on concepts of adult learning when it used a simulation technique to help FLMs learn how to improve sales pipeline management. "The simulation exercise presented FLMs with typical dilemmas," explains John Barb, a former Vice President of Sales. "For example, one of your salespeople has submit-ted a large proposal to a prospective customer, but the customer keeps delaying a decision. What should you do? Should you do nothing and give the salesperson more time to handle the situation himself? Should you jump in and contact the prospect directly, knowing that your sales skills will likely seal the deal? Or should you make a joint call with the salesperson to learn more about the situation, enabling you to coach the salesperson on the best next step? FLMs choose their course of action, and the simulation predicts the impact of their decision on key success metrics, such as sales, customer satisfaction, and long-term engagement." Simulation exercises like this can be very effective at getting learners immersed in the content and making learning memorable.

Increasing Training Impact by Reinforcing Learning

People typically soon forget much of what they learn in the classroom unless the learning is continuously reinforced. Many companies sequence their training programs, enabling managers to learn what to do, apply what they have learned in the field, and then come back to the classroom after some time has passed to take their learning to the next level. GE sequences many of its FLM training and coaching programs so that in the first level, FLMs learn basic coaching techniques, the expected value of good coaching, and ways to build these activities into their regular operating rhythms. Then after applying their skills in the field using the coaching guidelines and scorecards, FLMs come back for second-level training to further enhance their coaching skills. "Combining world-class training with in-the-field coaching programs helps us institutionalize new behaviors and drive positive change more effectively throughout the organization," says Conrad Zils.

Microsoft offers a large number of internal courses for sales managers in a prescribed sequence. "New FLMs have required courses to complete in their first year of people management. After that, there is an academy of courses to complete in order to continue to progress. Our training program is linked to the performance management process, where we track participation in training and look for specific improvement in skills after training," says Jay Sampson, former General Manager of U.S. Emerging Media Sales.

"Sometimes a modular training program that is rolled out in a series of one-hour calls or meetings is more effective than a multiday session," says Linda Vogel, a Principal in ZS Associates' Sales Force Effectiveness practice area. "Day-long sessions often result in 'drinking from the fire hose.' By providing training in integrated, bite-sized nuggets and by allowing FLMs time to practice new skills on the job and reflect on the learning before moving on, the overall program has greater impact."

In addition to reinforcement through the sequencing of formal training programs, the impact of training can be increased by providing specific opportunities and resources for FLMs to strengthen their skills and knowledge on the job. Here are examples of effective follow-up actions:

- After new FLMs complete their training on interviewing skills, allow them to observe experienced interviewers in live recruiting situations—for example, by participating on an interview panel with an experienced FLM and an HR representative.

- Conduct refresher training on performance management just before the annual review cycle, so that the content is very relevant and FLMs can put their skills to work right away.

- Provide paper-based or electronic job aids ("cheat sheets") for FLMs to access when they need them, or provide mini cases that they can use with their salespeople as a coaching tool.

- Consider creating an online community or discussion board that helps FLMs collaborate and share best practices. Manage the content to avoid the spread of misinformation and to keep the site current and productively focused.

The FLM's supervisor plays an important role in reinforcing learning. The best individuals in this role consider FLM learning and development to be an important job responsibility. They set an example by participating in training with their people, rather than simply giving an introduction and then leaving. They seek out specific opportunities to help FLMs strengthen their skills and knowledge on an ongoing basis. For example, at Boston Scientific, senior sales leaders often survey FLMs to understand which skills need attention, and they organize skills development sessions in conjunction with regularly scheduled management team meetings or as part of the company's Regional Management University (RMU) Program. RMU development programs are conducted at Boston Scientific's corporate office as well as at regional locations across the country to ensure that managers are able to take advantage of the education. Current offerings include Leading High Performance Teams, Managing Self, and Developing and Retaining Top Talent. In many instances, content needs are driven by changing market conditions. "Much of the learning in these training programs is peer driven. For example, we asked a sales manager who excelled at contracting to lead a session on the topic and share best practices with his peers," explains Chris Hartman. He adds, "People appreciate learning from their peers because of the 'real world' credibility that they possess. Also, the experience of being recognized as an expert in front of the manager team is viewed as a perk for the person selected as the trainer. That is always a plus!"

At BP, Liza Clechenko, a former Vice President of Sales, East/Gulf Coast, would encourage her FLM team to share ideas on the phone every two weeks. She scheduled regular phone calls so that team members could talk about successes and share strategies for dealing with day-to-day issues. The phone calls also provided Liza with the opportunity to disseminate information to keep everyone aligned around the sales strategy.

Selecting Methods Appropriate for the Size of the Organization

Development methods that work well in larger sales forces are not always appropriate for smaller sales forces.

Efficient Development Methods and External Resources for Smaller Sales Organizations

Smaller sales forces may not have sufficient scale to run internal sales manager development programs. Because there are a limited number of sales manager vacancies in any one year, internal sales manager training and development tend to be one-on-one, with new managers learning from other managers or through guided self-study. "At BP, with only five FLMs on my team, it didn't make good business sense to have a formal internal FLM training program," says Liza Clechenko. Liza would do some internal training when there was a significant change affecting the sales organization (for example, when the company revamped its sales process), but most FLM learning was accomplished using methods such as the biweekly conference calls.

In addition, Liza would occasionally send her FLMs to outside courses. Several universities and sales-training organizations offer general-enrollment programs on sales management (see Figure 6-7 for examples). FLMs in smaller sales

Program*	Select the Team	Build the Team	Lead the Team	Manage the Team	Reward the Team	Manage the Business
TopLine Leadership: Sales Management Leadership in the 21st Century	★	★	★	★		★
Resolution Systems: Sales Management Summit Training Program	★	★	★	★★		★
The Kahle Way: Sales Management Training System	★	★★		★★		
Sales Leadership, Inc.: Take the Lead	★	★	★	★★		★
University of Wisconsin — Madison: Effective Sales Management	★	★		★★	★	★
University of Chicago Booth School of Business: Fundamentals of Effective Sales Management	★	★		★	★	★
American Management Association: Fundamentals of Sales Management for the Newly Appointed Sales Manager			★	★★★	★	

Note: The number of stars reflects the focus of the course agenda across topics.

*List compiled January 2012.

Figure 6-7 Examples of General-Enrollment Programs for FLMs and Their Focus Across Aspects of the Sales Manager's Role

organizations can benefit from these programs, provided that the agenda is well matched to the specific FLM role and success competencies. Many training organizations will customize their programs at additional cost to increase the impact of the program and to better align it with the company's culture and sales process. But small sales forces usually have insufficient scale to justify the cost of a custom program.

Regular conference calls with your FLM team are an effective and inexpensive way to encourage ongoing learning and development, especially in smaller, geographically distributed sales organizations. The calls provide a good forum for discussing hot topics and sharing best practices. During calls, ask FLMs for their input on which topics or "difficult situations" they'd like to discuss, maintain a list, and choose one to include on the agenda for each call. If appropriate, assign one FLM as the topic leader, and ask that person to research the topic in advance and share the findings during the call.

At Extreme Networks, Helmut Wilke preferred face-to-face meetings to teleconferences for developing his sales management team: "With only a few dozen FLMs globally, we didn't have the scale to provide a large internal training resource. I met with my team once a quarter, and those individuals would meet with their teams quarterly and in person as well. I planned the meetings meticulously, went for attractive locations, and always led the meetings in person. The cost was high, but a live meeting helped to build the culture, made people feel part of the company, and created team bonding that led to low sales force turnover. With today's globally distributed workforce, working for another company is only a mouse click away. It is crucial to invest in old-fashioned personal relationships; sufficient face-to-face time builds loyalty."

By following best practices for development (see Figure 6-8), smaller sales organizations can establish an effective FLM team without creating overhead.

Best Practices for Small Sales Forces

- Use custom-developed classroom training rarely and only for significant events (for example, when the sales process changes).
- Leverage low-cost training methods, such as best-practice sharing with peers, online resources, and books and articles.
- Send FLMs to outside general-enrollment courses with an agenda well matched to your needs.
- Select FLM candidates based on both characteristics and competencies to limit the need for extensive management training for new FLMs.
- Make FLMs responsible for their own development, and create a culture that values and encourages constant learning and improvement.

Figure 6-8 Some FLM Development Program Guidelines

Formal, Custom Programs for Larger Sales Organizations

For large sales organizations, the number of managers often justifies investment in formal FLM development programs, such as GE's Essentials of Sales Management course. These programs are customized around the sales organization's specific needs. Region Manager Camp at Cardinal Health is built around a common training platform that provides general grounding for FLMs across the company's multiple divisions. "In a one-week session, FLMs learn critical success competencies, including extensive coaching and feedback, goal setting, financial reporting, HR best practices, and leadership capabilities. Most Cardinal Health divisions follow up Region Manager Camp with deeper dive training specific to their own needs. The program is designed primarily for newly appointed managers, but many experienced Cardinal Health FLMs have attended the course as well, finding the program to be a useful refresher of their skills and knowledge," says Sandy Cantwell.

FLM development programs like these often include internally developed materials and modules as well as materials created by working with outside partners, such as universities and training companies.

A challenge for large companies that have their own internal sales management development programs is to keep the programs fresh and adapt them continuously as needs change. This takes time, resources, and a commitment to constant innovation. By following best practices (see Figure 6-9), companies with large sales organizations can maximize the return on their investments in FLM development.

Best Practices for Large Sales Forces

- Develop your own FLM training and development programs tailored to your needs.
- Partner with outside training companies or universities that offer sales programs, but customize their approach to your situation.
- Partner with your company's training department to ensure that programs stay fresh, improve constantly, and adapt as needs change.
- Respect the time of your FLMs by focusing programs on the most critical competencies; eliminate programs that no longer add value.
- Supplement and reinforce learning from formal training with low-cost training methods, such as best-practice sharing with peers, online resources, and books and articles.
- Select FLM candidates based on their personal characteristics; develop the necessary management competencies through training.
- Make FLMs responsible for their own development, and create a culture that values and encourages constant learning and improvement.

Figure 6-9 Some FLM Development Program Guidelines

Conclusion

Finding or developing the right development resources for FLMs is difficult. FLMs have a complex role in which they have to wear multiple hats: people manager, business manager, and customer manager. The role is specific to the selling environment, and many of the responsibilities are difficult to do well. And because many companies have only a handful of FLMs, it is often hard for them to justify significant investments in customized training. Busy sales executives who feel pressure to deliver short-term results too often neglect the development of their FLM teams, leaving sales managers to acquire on their own the critical competencies—for example, recruiting and performance management skills and business knowledge—that can drive long-term success.

The best sales organizations use creative approaches to overcome these challenges. They invest in developing their FLMs—both those who are new to the job or company and those who have been on the job and need to refresh their skills and adapt to a constantly changing environment. The best sales organizations seek to continuously fill critical FLM competency gaps through learning approaches that blend effective high-touch methods (for example, personal coaching and customized classroom learning) with more efficient methods (for example, peer-to-peer sharing of best practices, online resources, or other written materials). By making appropriate investments in FLM development, every sales organization can increase the effectiveness of its FLM team, thereby impacting the performance not only of the FLM team, but also of every salesperson.

Enabling the Right First-Line Sales Management Activity

| **I**
Defining the FLM job | **II**
Creating a strong FLM team | **III**
Enabling the right FLM activity |

The Focus of Section III

Enabling the right activity for first-line sales managers (FLMs) requires providing the support that FLMs need to accomplish important job tasks effectively and efficiently, managing performance so that FLM activity stays aligned with company goals, and motivating the right management activity for driving sales team success. These three FLM success drivers, discussed in Chapters 7 through 9, help you enable the right sales management activity for creating strong results.

Supporting Critical Sales Management Activities (Chapter 7)

First-line sales managers need support to get their job done well. Good support includes business processes and systems, access to support personnel and resources, and the right data and tools for helping FLMs make better decisions, reduce workload, and achieve stronger bottom-line results. The right support programs produce a positive return on investment by creating value for the sales force, customers, and the company.

Managing Sales Management Performance (Chapter 8)

To keep sales force activity aligned with company goals, you need a process for managing ongoing FLM performance, based around metrics and frameworks that measure both inputs (FLM capabilities and activities) and outcomes (salesperson quality and activity, customer results, and contribution to company results). Good performance management allows consistent, effective, and timely evaluation of FLM performance, enabling you to respond quickly to performance issues and ensure that every individual in the FLM job is successful.

Motivating and Rewarding Sales Management Success (Chapter 9)

FLMs need motivation to engage in the activities required for achieving company goals. By using all of the FLM success drivers described in this book to create a motivating sales culture, and then reinforcing the culture with specific motivation and reward programs, you can appeal to three fundamental FLM motivators — achievement, social affiliation, and power — and thus encourage the right sales management activity to ultimately drive company results.

What Sales Leaders Say About Enabling the Right FLM Activity

Denise O'Brien   Vice President of Business Development, Global Sales and Client Development, ARAMARK

"Companies will invest in support for their salespeople, maximizing the investment by hitting a large number of people. Additionally, sales leaders get attention as executives. Middle managers fall between these two roles. Their needs are unique and warrant special focus." Denise has held several positions at ARAMARK, giving her broad experience in areas such as operations, sales force effectiveness, and business development.

Chris Ahearn   Senior Advisor, TPG Capital

"Many companies say they have a coaching process, but often the process is not thorough or . . . nobody's helped sales managers learn how to use it." As part of TPG's operations team, Chris leads sales effectiveness initiatives for the private equity firm's portfolio companies. Prior to joining TPG, he held executive sales and marketing roles at Oakwood Worldwide and FedExKinko's. Chris believes that the FLM is the cornerstone and key point of leverage of a high-performance sales force.

Tony Yeung   Associate Principal, ZS Associates

"Effective support for the FLM is critical but often lacking. Strong support processes, resources, and tools can dramatically increase the effectiveness and efficiency of an FLM group." Tony works in the business-to-business sales and marketing practice at ZS, where he focuses on go-to-market strategy and transformation. He works with companies to drive sales manager effectiveness and engage sales managers as key facilitators of change.

Greg Schofield Former Executive Vice President and Head of Global
Sales, Novartis

"Recognition is . . . a huge part of building culture. Who wins the awards and what you put on the scoreboard tells managers what's important." Greg's experience in the healthcare industry includes sales and marketing leadership positions at Novartis, at Pharmacia & Upjohn, and most recently at Apria Healthcare.

Jay Sampson Executive Vice President, Global Sales, Marketing and
Advertising, Machinima Inc.

"Recognizing the exceptional performance of an FLM broadly within the organization can be a powerful motivator." Prior to joining Machinima, Jay was General Manager, U.S. Emerging Media Sales at Microsoft, where he defined the organization's go-to-market strategies and led sales teams responsible for new media offerings in gaming, mobile, and video.

Chad Albrecht Principal, ZS Associates

"Incentive compensation [IC] is a powerful tool for driving FLM motivation. But IC plan design for managers can be complicated as leaders strive to align FLM and salesperson incentives while taking into account the unique requirements of sales managers." Chad is a leader in the Sales Compensation Practice at ZS and works with clients to create and implement motivational sales incentive plans, set fair and challenging sales goals, and implement incentive administration systems.

CHAPTER 7

Supporting Critical Sales Management Activities

Enabling the Sales Management Team Through Excellent Support

"Support levels have direct impact on the quality of outcomes for first-line sales managers," says Marshall Solem, a Principal at sales and marketing consulting firm ZS Associates. "By providing managers with defined business processes and systems, access to support personnel and resources, and the right data and tools, sales leaders can help sales managers make better decisions, reduce workload, remove administrative roadblocks, increase time in the field, and achieve better bottom-line results."

First-line sales managers (FLMs) face a broad spectrum of demands. Caught in the middle between salespeople, customers, and top management, they are squeezed from all sides. Rarely do they have enough support resources for getting everything done—and done well.

"All too often, first-line sales managers don't get the support they need," says Jay Sampson, former General Manager, U.S. Emerging Media Sales at Microsoft. "It seems that all too frequently when it comes to prioritizing investments in sales force support, FLMs rank third, behind salespeople and senior sales leadership. Yet FLMs are in a critical role—where the rubber meets the road."

Denise O'Brien, Vice President of Business Development for Global Sales and Client Development at professional services company ARAMARK, agrees. "Companies will invest in support for their salespeople, maximizing the investment by hitting a large number of people. Additionally, sales leaders get attention as executives. Middle managers fall between these two roles. Their needs are unique and warrant special focus," she says.

Although FLMs in many companies don't get enough support for critical job functions, we also see situations where "support creep" results in excessive costs to sustain support programs that no longer add enough value.

The Focus of This Chapter

This chapter shows you how to put the right support resources in place for enabling your FLMs to maximize the effectiveness and efficiency of the most critical activities they engage in as people, business, and customer managers. The chapter is organized around four topics:

- The three forms of sales manager support: processes and systems, people, and data and tools
- Supporting FLMs in their roles as people, business, and customer managers
- Weighing the costs and benefits of FLM support programs
- Best practices for enhancing overall FLM team effectiveness through support

Providing sales managers with support for critical activities is a key FLM success driver and an important element of enabling the right sales management activity (see Figure 7-1).

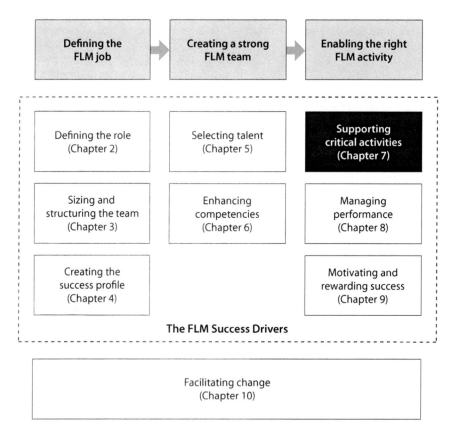

Figure 7-1   An Approach for Building a Winning Sales Management Team

Three Forms of Sales Manager Support

Support for the sales management team comes in three main forms:

- *Processes and systems* that guide the work to be accomplished, including methodologies, work steps, and thinking frameworks that facilitate important FLM tasks and decisions.
- *People* who can provide administrative, analytical, and advisory expertise and support to meet FLM needs.
- *Data and tools* that enable FLMs to carry out the activities that can drive sales force success. This category includes metrics, analytics, software tools (for example, incentive calculators), and reporting mechanisms (for example, dashboards and prospect lists).

FLMs can benefit from all of these forms of support when performing their roles as people manager, business manager, and customer manager (see Figure 7-2).

Processes and Systems

Many FLMs come from a front-line selling role, and they often have little management experience. "FLMs need a system that they can run with," says one sales

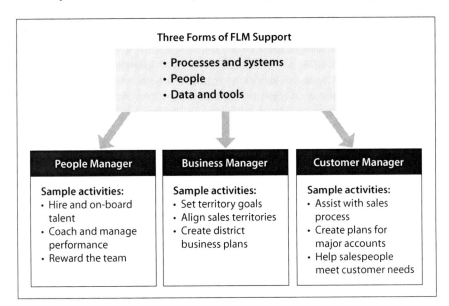

Figure 7-2 Supporting the Three FLM Roles

leader. Systems and processes help ensure high quality and consistency across the FLM team in performing critical tasks, ranging from managing salesperson performance to setting territory sales goals to developing major account plans.

The fact that FLMs typically work in a remote environment, with limited access to corporate office resources and day-to-day interactions that keep them connected to company business objectives, makes providing adequate support processes and systems for FLMs even more important. "It is critical to build bridges that keep FLMs in sync with other company functions, such as marketing and manufacturing," says Liza Clechenko, a former Vice President of Sales, East/Gulf Coast at BP.

People

FLMs also need access to the people who can support their needs and help them get tasks accomplished effectively and efficiently. An analyst has better skills than an FLM does for finding the right data, crunching numbers, and creating high-impact reports. An HR specialist is more efficient and knowledgeable than an FLM is at performing some people management tasks, ranging from designing the best job interview questions or structuring an effective performance review to ensuring that the right employment paperwork gets completed or a job posting gets entered correctly into an online system.

Companies often discover that FLMs spend too much time on activities that should be done by someone else in the company. For example, by surveying its FLM team, a distributor of hardware products for the construction industry discovered that sales managers spent over a third of their time performing service, support, and administrative activities. Many of these tasks could be delegated to the company's customer service team or to administrative support staff, thus enabling a higher span of control and freeing up time for FLMs to perform activities that were more central to their role.

Data and Tools

FLMs need the right data and tools to enable good decision making. For example, they need performance dashboards that support good coaching, data and tools that allow them to set fair and attainable territory goals, and current customer information to be effective enablers of the sales process.

A story demonstrates the impact that a lack of good data and tools can have on FLM effectiveness. Jack, an FLM for an office supply company, receives his quarterly regional sales quota from headquarters. The quota is 5 percent higher than it was last quarter, which is a considerable stretch. Each salesperson will have to increase sales by 5 percent (on average) before accelerated commissions will kick in. Jack expects pushback from every salesperson about the quota increase.

Yet the growth will have to come from somewhere. Jack wants to make the quota allocations fair, and he knows that growth opportunity is greater in some territories than in others. He identifies some large accounts that, in his mind, have unrealized potential. But as he approaches his salespeople about growth opportunities at these accounts, all he gets are excuses. "I can't increase sales at ABC. The buyers just signed a long-term contract with a competitor, and they won't even talk to me," says one salesperson. "I can't sell anymore to XYZ because we've already maxed out the potential," says another. The list of excuses grows as Jack approaches each of his salespeople.

Jack's gut feel is that there is more business to be captured at many accounts. But he has no data to refute what his salespeople are telling him. The salespeople know more than he does about what is going on with customers. "If only I had better information about what the real opportunity is in our accounts," thinks Jack. "If all I have to go on is what salespeople tell me, I'm never going to find the right places for getting the growth we have to deliver."

Supporting FLMs in Their Three Roles

FLMs need support to be successful as people, business, and customer managers. The right support enhances FLM decision making (increased effectiveness) and also helps FLMs complete time-consuming tasks in less time or enables them to delegate some tasks to cheaper resources (increased efficiency).

Supporting FLMs in Their People Manager Role

FLMs benefit from support in several aspects of people management. Some examples are provided here.

Hiring and On-boarding Talent

FLMs can't win unless they have the right players on their team. In most companies, although sales management has ultimate responsibility for hiring salespeople, Human Resources (HR) personnel are an important partner in the hiring and on-boarding process. Several sales leaders discuss how HR supports their sales forces in acquiring talent.

- "In our business, sales force hiring is relationship-driven, so success depends on an individual's own personal network. HR has partnered with us to help our FLMs leverage web sites such as LinkedIn to support more effective hiring," says a sales leader at a company in the online advertising business.

- "In our company, sales managers make the hiring decisions, but HR does most of the paperwork. By partnering with HR, we minimize FLMs' involvement in the administrative aspects of hiring (and firing)," says a sales leader at a uniform company.

- At xpedx (a distribution business within International Paper), a mix of regional and national recruiters help FLMs find good salespeople. "The recruiters help FLMs throughout the hiring process by locating sources for the best candidates and suggesting situational questions to use in interviews to help FLMs screen on specific capabilities that salespeople need to succeed in their first six months," says John Barb, a former Vice President of Sales.

- "HR supports our sales force by conducting online candidate assessments and doing background and reference checks. We have streamlined the process of working with HR so there is a healthy tension between the control and discipline that HR brings to the hiring process and the need to move quickly to attract top sales talent. If the process moves too slowly, you may lose great candidates to other opportunities," says a sales leader at a provider of business staffing services.

The right HR professional for supporting FLMs has expertise in the entire hiring process, knows the legal aspects of hiring, and understands the specific hiring goals and needs of the sales force.

Once hired, new salespeople must acquire a level of knowledge and skill that enables them to be effective in their jobs and "in the know" about how to get things done in the organization. The task of on-boarding new salespeople often falls on the FLM, and the responsibility can be quite time-consuming. "We put together a center of excellence for supporting our FLMs in on-boarding salespeople," says Sandy Cantwell, Vice President of Sales Operations at Cardinal Health. "Our on-boarding program for new salespeople provides a full day of orientation and gets new salespeople set up with their handhelds and laptops. New salespeople get a great first day experience and enter training ready to go and with a positive attitude. We also give FLMs a checklist of what they are expected to do for new salespeople during their first 30 days. Employee satisfaction went through the roof after we started this program. It saves managers time and frustration. We can support a significant number of new salespeople each year with very inexpensive, high-impact resources. It's been a huge win with a huge return."

Sales leaders at medical device company Boston Scientific also take on-boarding very seriously. "We have a 26-week on-boarding period in which corporate, the FLM, and a mentor all play a role," says Chris Hartman, Vice President, Central Zone, Cardiology, Rhythm and Vascular. "Mentors are experienced salespeople who have management interest and potential; serving as a mentor by helping new salespeople get up to speed is part of their management development process. There is a formal schedule of what corporate, the FLM, and the mentor should do to help a new salesperson on-board successfully."

Coaching Salespeople

Sales manager coaching is a high-impact area when it comes to providing FLMs with the right support. Many companies provide FLMs with a prescribed coaching process and tools for documenting expectations, observations, and performance objectives for salespeople. A multinational pharmaceutical company asks FLMs to complete field visit coaching reports. FLMs get guidance on salesperson behaviors that constitute "excellent" versus "average" performance and on how to assess and coach their people. FLMs are expected to complete coaching reports with each salesperson after every field visit, documenting what was discussed and identifying objectives for the next coaching session. The salesperson gets a copy and has to approve and agree with the report. Everything is handled electronically using tablet computers.

Tools for supporting coaching do not have to be high-tech to have impact. One sales leader in the construction business bought each of his FLMs spiral notebooks to use as coaching logs for their salespeople. The process was informal, as FLMs were simply asked to jot down highlights of their coaching sessions with each salesperson and to document the skills the salesperson should work on. Coaching effectiveness increased significantly as a result.

FLM coaching was a critical success factor when temporary housing provider Oakwood Worldwide transformed its sales process from a relationship-based approach to a consultative approach. The new sales process required salespeople to engage customers in a more powerful and consultative dialogue. Sales leaders recognized that strong FLM coaching would be essential to help salespeople excel in this new and more challenging role, and the change provided Oakwood with an opportunity to implement a new coaching process. Chris Ahearn, former Senior Vice President of Corporate Sales and Marketing, talks about the impact the new coaching process had on the Oakwood sales transformation:

> Many companies say they have a coaching process, but often the process is not thorough, or even if it is, nobody's helped sales managers learn how to use it. And worse yet, the process frequently is not adopted consistently. At Oakwood, we knew that coaching would be pivotal in driving cultural change. To develop our prescribed coaching process called Oakwood Associate Review (OAR), we observed and studied best practices of rock star sales managers, got input from a focus group of top-performing and core-performing salespeople, and looked at outside research on sales effectiveness. We based the process around a premise: plan, coach, execute, and win. We showed FLMs how to sit down with subordinates and engage

in a dialogue structured around a dashboard of key metrics. The metrics reflected results (for example, sales versus quota and top 10 wins or losses), potential (for example, how many prospects in the pipeline and top 10 active opportunities), and activity measures. Guided by the metrics, FLMs were expected to discuss with the salesperson what happened and work together to understand the cause and effect. We developed a guide that showed FLMs how to spend their time in order to have the most productive discussion. We gave FLMs an annual performance objective for the amount of coaching they should do. The entire organization was embedded in the OAR process. Surveys indicated that our salespeople got significantly more coaching by way of OAR than other companies studied, and our salespeople wanted *more*. Customers too said they observed a positive difference as a result of the process.

At xpedx, John Barb says, "the effectiveness of coaching improved when we began providing FLMs with a new sales coverage tool." The tool allows FLMs to compare performance of their salespeople on key metrics such as territory sales, gross profit, and number of customers. To prepare for coaching sessions, FLMs can drill down into the details of a salesperson's territory to look at a breakdown of the business by account, product, and industry. "The tool gives FLMs new visibility by providing access to data that measures account potential. Account potential was calculated based on factors such as industry, account size, and past sales," John says. "For the first time, FLMs have a benchmark for understanding account potential. This facilitates a more balanced discussion with their people about the best tactical territory plans and goals. The data help FLMs point salespeople toward the best prospects and help them coach salespeople on how to focus their time and energy against the best opportunities." Because the sales coverage tool presents information in a concise and visually friendly format, it is a powerful tool for enabling FLMs to communicate with their people and take action to improve performance.

Managing Performance

HR can be an important partner with the sales force in supporting FLMs through the performance management processes. At a multinational pharmaceutical company, each sales region has its own HR specialist. When performance issues arise with a salesperson, an FLM delivers the message to the salesperson, but HR is there as a resource to coach the FLM behind the scenes. HR also helps FLMs at Boston Scientific with performance management. "By engaging the HR team early in the performance management process, we save a lot of time on the back end," says Chris Hartman.

FLMs can benefit from a framework to use when evaluating salespeople. Many companies provide a salesperson competency model that defines competencies and performance expectations for salespeople (see Chapter 8 for an example of an FLM competency model). Such models encourage consistency across FLMs in evaluating salespeople and implementing consequences. The models also reduce bias and unfairness in the sales force performance management process.

Analytical tools can help FLMs discover the right strategies for enhancing district performance. For example, using a framework that compares salespeople's capability and motivation levels (see Figure 7-3), FLMs get insights into the performance management actions that are most appropriate for ensuring sustained success across their sales team.

FLMs will want to reward and learn from star salespeople who have both capability and motivation. By sharing their success strategies with other salespeople, FLMs can improve performance across the sales team. For salespeople who are capable but not motivated, FLMs can consider the right programs and incentives as possible motivators. For salespeople who are motivated but not capable, FLMs can consider a coaching remedy. For salespeople who lack both capabilities and motivation, FLMs can consider a performance improvement plan with an eye toward possibly moving the individual out of a sales role; even if the situation is remedial, the investment to improve both dimensions may be too great. If a motivation or capabilities deficiency stems from inherent characteristics of the

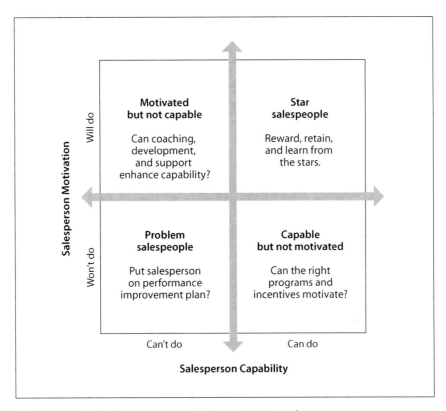

Figure 7-3   A Tool to Help FLMs Manage Salesperson Performance

individual, then the wrong individual is in the sales job, and it's best to move that individual into a different role in which he or she can succeed. (See Chapter 4 for a discussion about characteristics, which are inherent traits, versus competencies, which are learned behaviors.)

Rewarding the Sales Team

An important part of the FLM's people management role is rewarding salespeople for their commitment, hard work, and results. FLMs can impact sales team motivation by recognizing their salespeople for a job well done. They also play a key role as implementers of the sales force incentive compensation (IC) plan.

By consistently recognizing FLMs for their successes, sales leaders help create a motivating culture within the sales force (see Chapter 9). If an FLM receives a phone call from his boss with a simple "thank you" for a job well done, that FLM is more likely to make a similar call to one of his salespeople. Some companies give FLMs a small budget to spend on local contests, spiffs, or awards. Such programs do not have to be expensive to have great impact. Creative and inexpensive awards can be very effective motivators and can help reinforce a culture of respect and appreciation.

FLMs play an important role in maximizing the impact of the company's sales IC plan on salespeople's activities. "For an IC plan to motivate and direct sales force behavior, salespeople have to understand and embrace the plan. FLMs play a key role in this process," says Stephen Redden, the Managing Principal of ZS Associates' Sales Compensation Practice. "When a salesperson needs advice and direction about the IC plan, or wants to know 'is this a good deal for me?' the first place he goes is to his FLM. Companies need to support their FLMs so they are prepared."

The best companies support FLMs in implementing the sales IC plan by doing the following:

- Training their FLMs on the IC plan by taking time at sales meetings or conducting online sessions to show FLMs how the plan works.
- Providing materials to help FLMs explain the IC plan, sell its benefits, and coach their salespeople on a range of IC issues.
- Asking select FLMs for input before making IC plan changes. This provides perspective on how the field will perceive the change and helps ensure sales force acceptance.

Supporting FLMs as People Managers: A Summary

Figure 7-4 lists some examples of resources that companies have used to support FLMs in the role of people manager. Use the list as a starting point for ideas about the types of support that can help your FLM team excel in this role.

FLM Responsibility	Examples of Support Resources That Companies Can Provide
Developing an applicant pool of sales talent	• Analysis of what recruiting channels work best • LinkedIn support • HR management of recruiting channels (outside recruiters, college campuses, online sources, etc.) • HR management of the applicant pool
Selecting the best salespeople	• Structured interview and evaluation process • Interview and assessment guides and cases • Day in the field • Interviewers from HR or from sales leadership
On-boarding new talent	• Corporate on-boarding program • Checklist of on-boarding tasks for FLMs
Coaching	• Dashboard of metrics to guide the coaching process • Coaching process and expectations • Mentorship program
Managing salesperson performance	• Dashboard of metrics to guide the performance evaluation process • Competency model and evaluation framework • Metrics and dialogue for managing underperformers • HR advisory support
Recognizing salespeople	• Analytics that identify outstanding salesperson performance • Small budget to spend on local spiffs or rewards • Phone calls of appreciation from company leaders
Implementing the incentive compensation plan	• Incentive calculators • Incentive plan guidebooks • Advisory support from Sales Operations

Figure 7-4   Examples of Support Resources to Help FLMs in Their Role as People Managers

Supporting FLMs in Their Business Manager Role

FLMs benefit from support in several aspects of business management. Some examples are provided here.

Goal Setting

As part of the business manager role, many FLMs are responsible for allocating district or regional sales goals to their people. Goal allocation is required at least annually in almost every sales force, and it often occurs monthly or quarterly, depending on the sales force incentive compensation plan. Getting the goal allocation right is critical; goals that are fair, realistic, and motivational to all team members stimulate peak team performance. Companies can support FLMs in the goal-setting process by providing them with a good starting point for their goal allocations. Headquarters can create suggested goals based on formulas that are applied consistently across the sales force, taking into account territory factors such as historical sales, market potential, and growth projections. Then using computer-based systems and tools (often web-based), FLMs can review formula-suggested goals and make adjustments based on local knowledge. They can submit suggested changes to their supervisors (and ultimately back to headquarters) for review and approval. Goal-setting tools, coupled with structured processes for goal review and approval, enable fast turnaround, good accuracy, and detailed documentation of goal adjustments. (See Figure 7-5 for a sample goal-setting tool.)

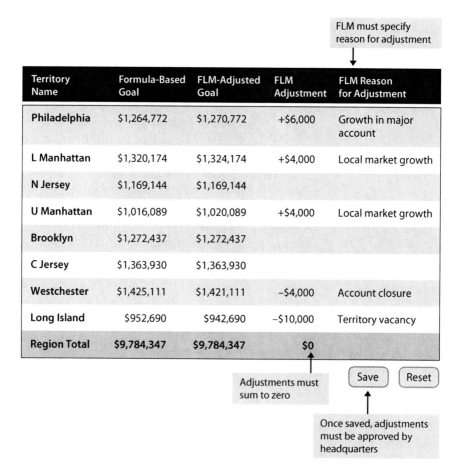

FLM must specify reason for adjustment ↓

Territory Name	Formula-Based Goal	FLM-Adjusted Goal	FLM Adjustment	FLM Reason for Adjustment
Philadelphia	$1,264,772	$1,270,772	+$6,000	Growth in major account
L Manhattan	$1,320,174	$1,324,174	+$4,000	Local market growth
N Jersey	$1,169,144	$1,169,144		
U Manhattan	$1,016,089	$1,020,089	+$4,000	Local market growth
Brooklyn	$1,272,437	$1,272,437		
C Jersey	$1,363,930	$1,363,930		
Westchester	$1,425,111	$1,421,111	−$4,000	Account closure
Long Island	$952,690	$942,690	−$10,000	Territory vacancy
Region Total	$9,784,347	$9,784,347	$0	

Adjustments must sum to zero

Save   Reset

Once saved, adjustments must be approved by headquarters

Figure 7-5 A Goal-Adjustment Tool That Helps FLMs Review and Adjust Territory Sales Goals

Territory Alignment

Another time-consuming, difficult, yet critical task for FLMs in the business manager role is aligning sales territories. Sometimes, territories need to be realigned in response to events, such as the expansion, downsizing, or restructuring of a sales force. Other triggers for realignment are less apparent—for example, evolving product lines, changing customer demographics, or a new sales process that impacts workload distribution across territories. Companies can provide easy-to-use mapping tools, coupled with structured processes, which help FLMs with realignments. FLMs can use these tools, but more often, an analyst at headquarters who is expert in using the tools acts as a resource to whom FLMs can turn for help with realignments. The tools allow FLMs to easily evaluate "what if" alignment scenarios and recommend salesperson-account assignment changes to sales leaders. Leaders can approve changes that adhere to company guidelines for metrics such as territory workload, potential, and travel requirements.

Business Planning

Companies can provide structured processes and thinking frameworks to help FLMs create better business plans. "An effective regional plan helps FLMs gain access to company resources, allocate those resources more effectively, create more realistic objectives and forecast targets, and make better business decisions for driving results," says Tony Yeung, an Associate Principal at sales and marketing consulting firm ZS Associates. For example, sales leaders at a medical device company provide FLMs with a framework for creating a regional business plan. They also provide salespeople with a framework for creating territory plans that align with the regional plan (see Figure 7-6). FLMs receive training around the framework and get online business-planning tools that support framework activities.

Relatively simple and easy-to-implement business-planning tools can also have a great impact on FLM efficiency. A template for preparing a quarterly business review, for example, can ensure consistency of planning across the FLM team while saving considerable time.

Case Study: Supporting FLMs with Sales Force Effectiveness Enhancement at GE

In 2006, GE launched a "commercial excellence" initiative that included a strong focus on improving global sales force effectiveness. A corporate position was established: director of global sales force effectiveness. The initiative helped to support GE's 5,800-plus FLMs in several important aspects of their business management role. Three targeted areas for sales force effectiveness improvement—customer potentialization and prioritization, territory alignment, and target setting—had direct impact on FLMs. The director of sales force effectiveness

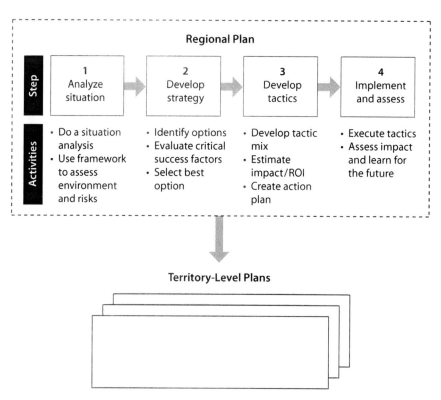

Figure 7-6 A Framework for Regional Business Planning by FLMs at a Medical Device Company

provides GE sales organizations across the globe with consulting resources to mentor, guide, and share company-wide frameworks, tools, and best practices in these three areas. The director is enabled by a team of future GE leaders participating in the company's prestigious Experienced Commercial Leadership Program (ECLP). The corporate team also developed a Sales Leader Capability Guide and a course in Essentials of Sales Management for FLMs. The guide and the course encouraged the effectiveness ideas to take root in the businesses and helped ensure that the concepts were implemented to produce tangible business results.

Supporting FLMs as Business Managers: A Summary

Figure 7-7 lists some examples of resources that companies have used to support FLMs in the role of business manager. Use the list as a starting point to identify resources for helping your FLMs excel in this role.

FLM Responsibility	Examples of Support Resources That Companies Can Provide
Goal setting	• Territory goal-setting process and tools • Advisory and analytic support from Sales Operations
Territory alignment	• Mapping and territory alignment tools • Territory alignment process • Advisory and analytic support from Sales Operations
Business planning	• Dashboards and metrics showing sales and market trends • Business planning templates • Advisory and analytic support from Sales Operations
Administration and communication	• Tools for budget and expense management • Processes for enabling communication between the field and headquarters

Figure 7-7 Examples of Resources That Can Support FLMs with Business Management

Supporting FLMs in Their Customer Manager Role

FLMs benefit from support in several aspects of customer management. Some examples are provided here.

Executing the Sales Process

As customer managers, FLMs are involved in a range of sales process activities. They may assist with critical sales process steps (for example, pricing or negotiating), participate in deals where manager involvement adds credibility for the customer, or maintain relationships with the company's most important customers or high-level decision makers within customer organizations.

Many companies support both their sales managers and their salespeople by providing a prescribed sales process that organizes the selling activities, enablers, participants, and tools that can successfully advance a prospect from a lead to a customer. The sales process specifies what the sales force and others in the company should do to develop, deliver, and reinforce long-term value for customers. Having a defined process helps keep the FLM's role in the sales process clear, thus avoiding role pollution and discouraging FLMs from getting involved in activities that salespeople should handle.

Good sales force support for customer management is organized around the steps of the sales process. For example, salespeople and sales managers at United Airlines (UA) used a suite of tools to add value to the sales process they used to build and manage relationships with corporate customers and travel agencies (see Figure 7-8). UA offered these customers a mix of consultative services, travel management and support programs, and comfort and productivity options for business travelers—all of which created business value beyond best-price alternatives. Beginning in 2005, the UA sales force used a suite of sales technology tools to help it demonstrate the value of UA solutions. The tools facilitated structured business discussions with customers that helped the sales force better understand customer needs, tailor the best solution, build the best deal, communicate the total business value of the deal, and review and reinforce the value that UA created for the customer on an ongoing basis.

A common role for FLMs in the sales process is to help with the design and negotiation of large deals. Computerized tools can help FLMs organize customer

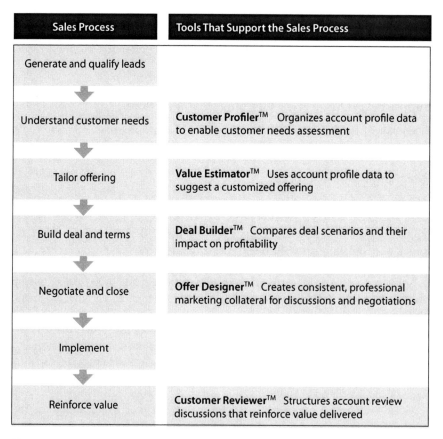

Sales Process	Tools That Support the Sales Process
Generate and qualify leads	
Understand customer needs	**Customer Profiler**™ Organizes account profile data to enable customer needs assessment
Tailor offering	**Value Estimator**™ Uses account profile data to suggest a customized offering
Build deal and terms	**Deal Builder**™ Compares deal scenarios and their impact on profitability
Negotiate and close	**Offer Designer**™ Creates consistent, professional marketing collateral for discussions and negotiations
Implement	
Reinforce value	**Customer Reviewer**™ Structures account review discussions that reinforce value delivered

Figure 7-8 Adding Value to the Sales Process for Corporate Customers and Travel Agents at United Airlines

information and create a compelling proposal for meeting customer needs. Although many customers need customized solutions, the core offering can usually be standardized by customer segment. A support person or group at headquarters can prepare standardized documents in response to a customer request for a proposal, while incorporating appropriate legal and financial controls.

Pricing guidelines from marketing and defined processes for gaining pricing approvals (dependent on deal size) encourage consistency across the sales force and save FLMs time. Some companies have pricing committees to handle very large deals. Standard contracts available on a company intranet and appropriate guidelines from legal encourage consistent and efficient contracting.

Planning for Major Accounts

The right information (for example, a comprehensive account plan, stakeholder map, sales history, sales potential estimate, and record of the company's past sales and service contacts with the customer) enables FLMs to gain customer insight to support strategic planning for major accounts. For example, GE Capital (a provider of financing to business customers who want to purchase, lease, or refinance capital equipment or other assets) has developed a lead-generation engine that uses algorithms to query customer and prospect data and predict a need for financing triggered by a specific event or situation. These leads are then funneled to salespeople through the CRM system, and follow-up actions are tracked by FLMs.

Helping Salespeople Meet Customer Needs

Salespeople often turn to their FLMs when they need information for their customers. For example, a customer requests a past purchase history, which the salesperson wants to enhance with an analysis of the cost savings that past purchases have produced for the customer. Without good information or analytic support, such requests can be overwhelming and frustrating for FLMs. One FLM notes, "Usually, the information is available somewhere among the dozens of sales reports I receive from headquarters, and often it's available in electronic format, but it's hard to remember which report or which system and what password I need to access the data. And often, the numbers in one system or report don't match the numbers in another. Some requests require complex calculations. Unfortunately, I don't have the time or the skills to provide my salespeople with all the information they need to have impact with customers." Good support—either through focused and consistent sales reports and tools, or through access to a support team of people with analytic or administrative skills—helps FLMs get information to help their salespeople help their customers.

A significant portion of FLM customer management time is often spent helping salespeople secure resources that customers need from other company departments. The right FLM support enables efficient and effective cross-functional interactions. At a novelty gift company, sales leaders meet quarterly with leaders from various departments that the sales force interacts with, such as Marketing, Accounting, and Customer Service. The goal of these meetings is to work through any frustrations that occur when FLMs or salespeople interact with these departments and to figure out ways to remove barriers to smooth interaction. At many companies, a company-wide CRM system provides a single source of customer information. This makes cross-functional interaction easier for all parties (including FLMs) and improves a customer's experience in doing business with the company.

Determining Whether FLMs Need Customer Management Support

Keep in mind that the role of "customer manager" is often the most comfortable role for FLMs. Most FLMs got promoted to the role because they were successful as salespeople. FLMs can benefit from support in their customer manager role, but as Amy Davalle, Vice President of Sales—West for medical device company Smith & Nephew, points out, "You need to be very clear on what you want your FLMs to focus on. They are likely to gravitate naturally to the role of customer manager. But is this where you want them to spend their time?"

Supporting FLMs as Customer Managers: A Summary

Figure 7-9 lists some examples of resources that companies have used to support FLMs in the role of customer manager. Use the list as a starting point for ideas of the types of support that can help your FLM team excel in this role.

Weighing the Costs and Benefits of FLM Support

Clearly, no sales force should implement every idea suggested in this chapter. The right support depends on the situation and what is most critical for the FLM role. Without clear advantages for customers, salespeople, and the bottom line, FLM support programs simply add overhead and drain profitability. This happens especially when new support programs are layered on over old programs over time.

Assessing FLM Support Needs Regularly

Ongoing FLM support needs change over time as the sales environment evolves, sales processes change, and company priorities shift. FLM support needs can also change temporarily in response to specific events. For example, a sales force expansion creates need for extra support in recruiting and on-boarding new salespeople and in realigning sales territories. Providing FLMs with the right kinds and

FLM Responsibility	Examples of Support Resources That Companies Can Provide
Sales process support	• A documented sales process with defined steps, enablers, participants, and tools • Data and tools that support sales process activities • Headquarters support for proposals and pricing on large deals • Lead generation and tracking systems
Major account planning	• Tools for accessing detailed and current account data — e.g., stakeholder maps, sales history, sales potential estimates, past customer contact
Helping salespeople meet customer needs	• Information and analytic support for meeting customer requests for information • Processes and systems that facilitate coordination and communication with other company functions

Figure 7-9   Examples of Resources That Can Support FLMs with Customer Management

right amount of support requires ongoing assessment of sales force needs and the value that different support programs create.

When looking to add an FLM support program, evaluate the potential impact on financial results (for example, higher sales), customer results (higher satisfaction levels), and FLM activities (more time for coaching). Implement only those programs that promise benefits that will justify their cost.

At the same time, when looking to cut sales force costs, consider the bottom-line impact of cutting FLM support. FLM support is often one of the first items to get slashed when sales forces feel pressure to reduce costs. We know of several companies that, when faced with slumping sales in a bad economy, cut administrative support for their FLMs. At the same time, at least one of these companies also increased sales management span of control, giving each manager more salespeople to supervise. Cuts like these should not be made indiscriminately. Although such moves cut costs in the short term, they increase FLM workload, leaving less time for FLMs to spend developing their people, customers, and business for the long term.

Testing the Value of FLM Support Programs

Although the impact of FLM support programs on costs is obvious and immediate, the impact on top-line results is complex and difficult to measure and takes longer to become apparent. Four simple tests can help you measure the value that FLM support programs create. Conduct these tests periodically to enable good decisions about which support programs to enhance, maintain, or eliminate to maximize sales force effectiveness.

- **The FLM usage test.** What do your FLMs say about specific support tools, programs, and resources? Which ones do they like and use regularly, and which are used sporadically or by only a handful of FLMs? Some support programs benefit all FLMs. Others will be used by some FLMs and not others. A good FLM support program provides a critical core of standard support that all FLMs use, plus a manageable set of options to address the needs of specific FLM subgroups. For example, analytically inclined FLMs may get value from a system that provides detailed performance data and analytic capabilities; other FLMs may prefer to use an administrative or analytic support team to prepare analyses or presentation materials. To conduct this test, track usage, conduct field surveys, or simply ask FLMs informally for input.

- **The FLM activities test.** Track FLM activity periodically through field surveys or observation. Compare activity before and after you implement a support program to assess the program's impact. For example, did coaching time increase when you improved the coaching methodology? Did time in the field increase after you provided FLMs with administrative support?

- **The sales force test.** Find out what impact FLM support programs have on salespeople's perceptions of their managers and on sales force activity. Conduct a sales force survey, for example, to find out how salespeople's opinion of FLM coaching effectiveness is impacted by a new FLM dashboard. Do salespeople say that their managers use the dashboard? Do salespeople perceive a benefit to the tool? Also track salespeople's activities, and look for improvement on the dimensions that coaching should impact.

- **The customer test.** Ask customers, either informally or through surveys, if they have observed a change in service levels, sales force knowledge, or responsiveness as a result of a new FLM support program. Has the program impacted customer satisfaction levels?

By establishing processes for conducting these tests every year or two, you can create metrics to help you estimate a return on investment for FLM support programs. At a minimum, you should conduct the tests before you add new FLM support programs. That way, you can eliminate programs that no longer add value and, at the same time, ensure that new programs get resources and attention for addressing new and emerging FLM needs. You have to be willing to clean out the closet periodically.

Implementing Effective FLM Support Programs for Large or Small Sales Forces

The challenges of providing FLMs with excellent support vary with the size of the sales force. Smaller sales forces often do not have the scale to invest in extensive processes, people resources, and data and tools for supporting FLMs. FLMs in small companies often have to figure things out on their own, and those who are resourceful seek outside resources to help them, such as existing software solutions, books, and peer advisers. Small companies can seek opportunities to provide FLM support that is informal and inexpensive — for example, opportunities to share best practices among FLM team members.

Larger sales forces are more likely to have enough scale to justify devoting company resources to developing custom processes, systems, data, and tools or to dedicating people to support a large FLM team. Often, the challenges for large companies are to provide valuable guidance (not just large amounts of data or overhead), to make support useful to a diverse group of FLMs with a range of needs and skills, to ensure that support resources focus on important aspects of the FLM role and continue to add value over time, and to stay flexible and responsive to changing business needs.

Best Practices for Enhancing Overall FLM Team Effectiveness Through Support

When it comes to supporting FLMs, sales leaders consistently share two areas of concern that cut across all three FLM roles:

- How to provide FLMs with powerful dashboards and analytic tools that focus attention on key metrics without overwhelming them with too much information
- How to help FLMs prioritize their time and avoid time traps that distract them from the most important aspects of their role

Here we discuss some strategies for addressing these concerns.

Providing FLMs with the Right Dashboards and Metrics While Avoiding Overload

FLMs benefit from access to accurate, current data about the activities of each salesperson, the potential of their accounts and territories, and the results achieved by account and salesperson. By using the framework shown in Figure 7-10 to integrate metrics from multiple sources, companies can create FLM

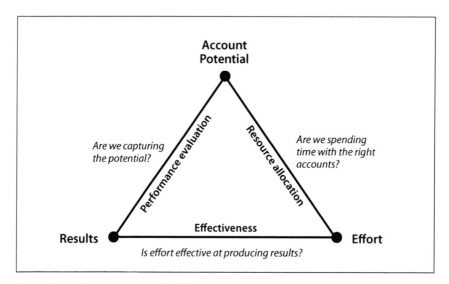

Figure 7-10 Integrating Results, Effort, and Account Potential Data in FLM Dashboards

dashboards that are insightful and actionable. FLMs can look at the relationships between results, potential, and effort to evaluate performance against opportunity, improve resource allocation, and increase the effectiveness of sales effort. Good dashboards and metrics enable FLMs to be better managers.

But it is important to avoid overloading FLMs with too many dashboards and tools. "We've taken a basically good concept and driven it to the point of overkill," says one sales leader about the proliferation of dashboards, reports, and sales force tools at his company. Many sales leaders tell us that their companies provide too much information to FLMs, often in difficult-to-manipulate formats. "Everyone wants the information in a different way," one sales leader says, "so we end up with multiple reports and individual tools with numbers that don't match. They all require a different password, they don't print to one page, and many are extremely slow to access. Some are used consistently, but I suspect that most are not."

GE's financial service business is a best-practice example of an organization that keeps its data for FLMs focused on business needs. "The marketing organization works very closely with sales to ensure that customer and prospect data are current, accurate, and complete," says Conrad Zils, Global Director of the Commercial Center of Excellence for GE Healthcare. "Instead of making unreasonable demands of our field sales teams to enter data, we try to manage most of the data entry behind the scenes by aggregating internal and external data sources. We minimize the time FLMs spend pulling reports by giving them real-time access to territory, salesperson, and account-level information. This frees up time for coaching and managing their teams."

Four strategies can help you avoid "information overload" in the dashboards and tools you provide for your FLMs:

1. **Pare down.** Stop producing the reports and tools that are rarely used. Look at current usage to determine what to eliminate, or delay sending out reports that you suspect have low value and see if anyone misses them. Don't say "yes" to every request for a new report. Instead, find out how the new report will be used and why it is needed. You'll often discover that the information already exists on another report.

2. **Pinpoint the most important metrics.** Include just a few metrics on each report or dashboard. (Select some that reflect effort, results, and account potential, as suggested in Figure 7-10.) Keep the metrics aligned with sales force goals and strategies and with the information you give salespeople. Include comparisons that make the metrics meaningful. For example, provide trends over time, comparisons to goals or other benchmarks, or status indicators (such as a red-yellow-green stoplight) that highlight extreme values. Decision-support analytics can help FLMs pinpoint anomalies and identify trends early so they can take appropriate action. Consider publishing a customized newsletter for each FLM or providing a "hot spot" analysis that identifies for FLMs which data is most important.

3. **Prioritize.** If you can't stop producing some reports altogether, provide the quickest access to the information that FLMs really need. For example, implement a "favorites" option that allows managers to easily access the reports they use frequently. Prioritization also helps address variance in data and analytic skills across members of the FLM team. Those who are less analytic can get to the most basic information easily, while those who are more data and computer savvy can dig deeper to take advantage of additional capabilities.

4. **Provide analytic support resources.** You can often make a strong business case for hiring a more cost-effective resource to help FLMs with data analytics: an administrative assistant to handle well-defined tasks or a regional analyst who will be more efficient and effective at providing creative decision support to FLMs. Some companies have established an analytic concierge service for their FLMs—a person or team that can respond to individual FLM requests for reports or analyses that address specific questions or needs. Many companies have offshored their standard report

production capabilities to reduce costs. Some have also offshored their sales force analytic capabilities for great impact at low cost. Others provide training to FLMs on how to use data and tools effectively, sometimes giving a tech-savvy FLM a peer leader role in the training or mentoring of others.

A "simplification" process that uses the four strategies above to reduce the number and complexity of sales force reports and tools can have a great impact on sales productivity. At one company, sales force scorecards had become excessively complex. Usage statistics indicated that two-thirds of salespeople and managers never opened their scorecards. After the company took some initial steps to improve and simplify the scorecards, usage improved from one-third to two-thirds of salespeople and managers. The company continues to pare down and simplify its scorecards, with a goal of increasing usage to close to 100 percent of the sales force.

Another caution about dashboards and tools is that to be successful in the long term, they need to be more than instruments of control for FLMs and sales leaders. Salespeople don't want to feel that their FLM uses a tool only to control their activities, just as FLMs don't want to feel that their boss uses a dashboard only to spy on them. The best dashboards are effective selling tools; they are value enhancers for salespeople and customers. They provide objective information for FLMs to use in coaching their salespeople on how to better meet customer needs, sell more business, increase effectiveness, make more incentive money, and be more successful. If a system's primary value is that of a sales force control device, not only can it undermine the sales culture, but the sales team will see little value in keeping the information in the system up to date. Without clear benefits for salespeople and customers, a system will quickly fall into disuse.

Helping Your FLMs Prioritize Their Time

"A hazard that can befall any sales organization is excessive or uncoordinated demands on the FLM's time from headquarters," says Chris Hartman of Boston Scientific. "Internal groups such as Marketing, Finance, and even Research and Development often depend on the FLM for information and insight to assist with their business functions. While valuable, meetings, conference calls, and even emails from these corporate departments can interfere with the primary activity of the FLM and ultimately adversely impact company sales performance." At Boston Scientific, internal groups are encouraged to schedule interactions with the FLMs on Mondays and Fridays only. "Tuesday, Wednesday, Thursday are considered dedicated field time for FLMs to devote to their salespeople and customers," Chris explains. "An important responsibility for any senior sales leader is to limit the amount of 'non-sales stuff' that gets to FLMs and to manage that which is necessary in a manner that doesn't disrupt the focus or flow of the time that FLMs must spend in the field."

When it comes to FLM time traps, such as email and meetings, most sales leaders concur that "less is more." Take a close look at the meetings that your FLMs attend and the value that those meeting have. Ask yourself, "Does time spent in meetings help customers or increase sales? Could a monthly meeting be held quarterly?" By eliminating or shortening some internal meetings, one company in Australia increased the time that FLMs spent in the field by almost 9 percent.

Some companies provide FLMs with administrative assistants. Sales leaders have different views about this practice. Some follow the philosophy of leaders at an online advertising company: "Top management would never let us hire administrative support for the sales force. They would say it was a complete waste of resources." Many believe that administrative assistants have value, but they have eliminated them when faced with pressure to cut costs. Of those companies that provide administrative support to their managers, the level of support varies. A food company provides one administrative assistant to handle data entry and paperwork for 24 managers. At the other end of the spectrum, at a medical device company, each administrative assistant supports just two managers. The assistants take responsibility for collecting purchase orders as well as handling travel arrangements and expense reports. A more typical ratio in sales forces is one administrative assistant for every seven or eight FLMs.

If you use administrative assistants to support your FLMs, expect variance in the extent to which different FLMs will use the resource. Some will take full advantage of the support, while others may prefer to do more on their own — for example, by making their own travel arrangements or managing their own expenses. Take this variance into account when determining the appropriate ratio of FLMs to administrative assistants. Track the usage of administrative support by FLMs on an ongoing basis to ensure that the resource continues to add value to justify the added cost. Usage tracking also helps you identify the best practice. For example, do FLMs who use administrative support effectively spend more time in the field? Does this translate to better results? Share what you learn about best practices in using a support resource with the entire FLM team, and eliminate support resources if usage is not contributing to better performance.

Conclusion

Good support is a key FLM success driver. Support for FLMs comes in many forms, including organizing systems and processes, access to people who provide administrative, analytic, and advisory services, and data and tools that enable

FLMs as people, customer, and business managers. The right support programs produce a positive return on investment by creating value for the sales force, customers, and the company.

FLM support enhances sales force effectiveness by helping FLMs do the most important aspects of their job better, while communicating to FLMs what the company wants them to do. The implementation of a new coaching tool, for example, tells FLMs that coaching is important and that the company is investing to help them become excellent coaches. At the same time, the right support increases FLM efficiency by enabling FLMs to take non-mission-critical activities off their plates—for example, through the automation of administrative tasks or through the off-loading of some tasks to less expensive resources.

With the right support resources in place, you can drive sales management team success by enabling the right FLM activity.

CHAPTER 8

Managing Sales Management Performance

Keeping the Sales Force on Course

As a salesperson, Jerry made President's Club every year. Since his promotion to first-line manager (FLM) just over a year ago, Jerry has struggled. He hasn't made a successful transition from doer to manager. He "helicopter manages" his people, hovering over them and getting involved in every deal. He gets frustrated with the work styles and performance of people who are not as driven as he is, and he's not good at giving salespeople constructive feedback. The turnover of good salespeople might be becoming a problem in Jerry's district, and his quota performance has declined each quarter.

Christine's success as an FLM is driven by her people management skills. She is a great motivator who receives consistently outstanding feedback on her management skills from the people she manages. But as customers become better informed and buying processes become more complex in Christine's business, the expectations placed on Christine are changing. The company wants her to develop a broader skill set that includes business acumen so she can lead her team to meet the evolving needs of customers. Christine struggles with meeting the new expectations; her strengths are in people management, not in running numbers and developing business strategies.

Hank, a successful FLM for 25 years, is frustrated by all the new technology the company expects him to use. He finally got comfortable using email and his laptop when the company launched a new web-based sales force automation system and adopted handheld devices. Some younger salespeople in Hank's district don't even bother to check voicemail and email regularly; they prefer to stay connected through texts and social media—something Hank has no interest in. Although effective when interacting with salespeople and customers face-to-face, Hank is challenged by the new high-tech world of sales.

Jerry, Christine, and Hank are struggling to be successful. And more than likely, as these FLMs struggle, the salespeople in their districts are not getting the guidance and leadership they need to perform to their potential, customers aren't getting the right level of attention, and sales results are less than what they could be.

All of these situations can be addressed with the right FLM performance management process. If Jerry is having trouble adapting to his new role as a manager, he can benefit from coaching and training that can help him start leading and stop doing. He can learn by observing the management approach of a colleague who is successful in this role. Christine, who is struggling to keep up with the business demands of the job, can get assistance from support tools and training that can help her develop the business skills she needs to adapt to the new sales approach. Hank needs a sympathetic helper and mentor who can show him how to incorporate the new technologies into his daily routine.

A good FLM performance management system enables and controls the sales organization. It not only benefits FLMs who are struggling; it also helps strong performers stay motivated and challenged. It enables all FLMs to learn, grow, and improve constantly. It provides direction and resources that help FLMs accomplish company and personal goals. It adapts to the needs of different FLMs, providing guidance to those who need it and empowering those who can be effective without close supervision. It tracks metrics that reflect important FLM capabilities, activities, and results and provides FLMs with feedback to keep their focus aligned with company goals. It allows sales leaders to evaluate the capabilities of the FLM team.

The Focus of This Chapter

This chapter helps you establish an effective process for managing the performance of FLMs so that sales force performance stays on course to achieve company goals. The chapter is organized around these four topics:

- Managing FLM performance by focusing on inputs and outcomes
- Understanding the steps in the performance management process and the critical role of second-line managers
- Using metrics and frameworks to enable the evaluation of FLM performance
- Improving FLM performance management

An effective performance management system is an essential FLM success driver that enables the right activity for the sales management team (see Figure 8-1).

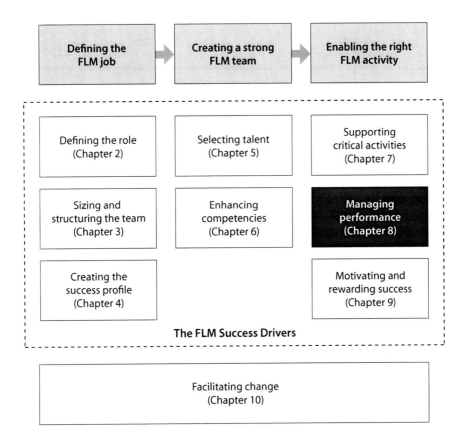

Figure 8-1   An Approach for Building a Winning Sales Management Team

Managing FLM Performance by Focusing on Inputs and Outcomes

Almost all organizations manage FLMs based on *what* they contribute to company financial results: outcomes such as district sales or profits. But good performance management also focuses on *how* an FLM contributes, as explained by a causal chain of five FLM performance categories (see Figure 8-2). The categories that sales leaders choose to focus on when managing FLM performance will affect the timing of impact on company results.

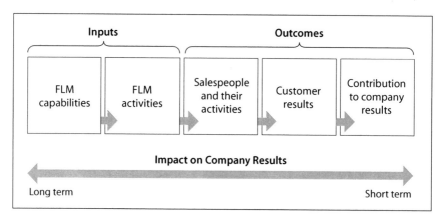

Figure 8-2   Five FLM Performance Categories and Their Impact on Company Results

A Causal Chain of Inputs and Outcomes

Excellent FLM performance starts with *FLM capabilities* (for example, strong people management, customer management, and business management skills). FLM capabilities enable high-impact *FLM activities* (for example, coaching salespeople in the field, spending quality time with key buying decision makers, and creating quality business plans). The FLM capability and activity categories are *input* measures. These categories focus on what FLMs do in their roles as people, customer, and business managers to create the outcomes.

The right FLM activities lead to positive outcomes for the three constituencies that FLMs impact: salespeople, customers, and the company. The causal chain of outcomes starts with excellence in *salespeople and their activities* (for example, high salesperson retention and satisfaction and quality salesperson activity), leading to *customer results* (for example, high customer satisfaction and repeat sales). Ultimately, all of the performance categories determine an FLM's *contribution to company results.*

A good FLM performance management process focuses on all five of the FLM performance categories. But the right emphasis across the categories depends on the situation. Considerations such as the nature of the sales process and the availability of good metrics influence what role each category plays in the performance management process. The experience of the FLM also plays a role. Inexperienced FLMs often benefit from management around capabilities and activities to help them learn the job. Experienced FLMs who already have the capabilities and know what activities are important may respond better to management around results. Sales culture and management philosophy also impact the right emphasis across the categories, and especially the focus on inputs versus outcomes. This is illustrated by the comments of sales leaders from two companies:

- A healthcare industry sales leader says, "We look at both lagging indicators and leading indicators in our FLM performance management process. We pay incentives on the lagging indicators (results), but we set goals, track, and evaluate on the leading indicators as well—for example, how skilled is an FLM at coaching, or how much time did the FLM spend in the field? The leading indicators enable us to learn what drives results so we can share FLM success capabilities and behaviors with the entire FLM team."

- A professional services industry sales leader says, "Managing FLMs on activities would hurt the culture of our sales organization. We treat people as professionals and want to encourage an entrepreneurial spirit. If we ask managers to spend 60 percent of their time in the field, and then we track whether or not they are actually doing that, managers will perceive sales leaders as untrusting. We evaluate on results and expect that FLMs will engage in the right behaviors to drive those results."

The Timing of Impact on Company Results

Managing different FLM performance categories affects the timing of impact on company results. Managing on the company results category has short-term impact. For example, if you manage FLM performance by asking FLMs to "achieve quota this quarter," the impact on company results will be almost immediate. Managing on other performance categories has longer-term impact, as the time it takes for performance improvements to show up in company results is greater for categories that are further upstream (to the left) in the causal chain. Management around a capability—such as people management—may not produce measurable results for a year or more, although the outcome can have a greater impact and last longer.

Understanding the Process of FLM Performance Management

Through performance management, sales leaders can effect change in FLM capabilities and activities in order to drive performance in the output categories and ultimately create company results. Second-line sales managers (SLMs)—the supervisors to whom FLMs report—are the leaders in this process. In large sales forces, SLMs are often regional or area directors or vice presidents; in smaller sales forces, the SLM may be a national sales director or vice president. In either case, SLMs have primary accountability for managing the performance of the FLMs who report to them.

The Steps in the Performance Management Process

Performance management involves the active and directive series of the prescribed steps shown in Figure 8-3.

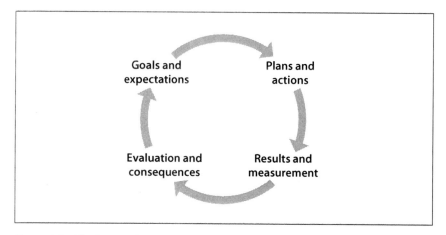

Figure 8-3   The FLM Performance Management Process

Through this process, FLMs and SLMs work together to set goals and expectations for FLMs in the five performance categories and to plan how to achieve them. It's up to FLMs to take action to carry out the plans, with appropriate help and guidance from SLMs and other sales leaders or company resources. Measurement is used to evaluate how well the goals and expectations are being met. Evaluation forms the basis for constructive feedback for FLMs and for determining consequences—ways to correct weaknesses and reward success. Consequences range from a reward and a revised goal for strong-performing FLMs to an improvement plan or redirection to a different career path for FLMs who are consistently not performing to expectations. Evaluation and consequences also lead to new goals and expectations for FLMs, as the performance management process begins a new cycle.

Figure 8-4 provides examples illustrating how the performance management process plays out, focusing on all five FLM performance categories. As stated already, the relative emphasis across the categories depends on the situation.

The Role of SLMs in the FLM Performance Management Process

"Given the long-distance relationship that most FLMs have with their boss and the organization, the performance management process—particularly the setting of goals and expectations—takes on greater significance in the sales area than in other functions," says Liza Clechenko, former Vice President of Sales, East/Gulf

	Set Goals and Expectations	Develop Plans and Take Action	Measure Progress	Evaluate and Implement Consequences
FLM Capability	Improve leadership skills	Attend leadership training Work with a mentor	Assess leadership competency (SLM assesses each FLM)	Annual review • Discuss progress vs. goals • Identify opportunities • Set new goals • Implement rewards (salary boost or promotion) • Implement consequences for shortfalls (performance improvement plan)
FLM Activity	Spend 2 days per week in the field coaching	Follow coaching schedule, and complete coaching log	Track and report coaching time (FLMs self-report) Collect upward feedback from salespeople	
Salespeople and Their Activities	Retain 90% of good performers	Create and implement development and career plan for each salesperson	Track salesperson retention Collect upward feedback from salespeople	
Customer Results	Retain 95% of top 150 customers	Help salespeople develop and implement retention and growth strategy for top 150 customers	Track customer retention Conduct customer satisfaction surveys	
Company Results	Achieve district sales quota	Develop and implement district sales plan	Track sales vs. quota	Quarterly review • Discuss progress vs. goals • Reward with incentive compensation

Figure 8-4 The Performance Management Process with Examples for the Five FLM Performance Categories

Coast at BP. "It is absolutely critical for SLMs to work with FLMs to establish a shared purpose and mind-set linked to business strategy. FLMs will make many independent decisions out in the field, and if they are disconnected from the business strategy, activities can get off track very quickly. FLMs need frequent touch points with their bosses to ensure ongoing alignment."

There is high variability in the amount of attention that SLMs give to the important responsibility of FLM performance management. Although some SLMs dedicate substantial time and effort to their role as coach and manager of FLMs, regrettably many SLMs give the role too little attention. SLMs have many responsibilities, some of which get significant attention from company leadership—for example, managing a regional office or other costly physical assets or contributing to corporate strategies and initiatives. SLMs can get drawn into these high-profile activities, leaving them too little time to spend managing and developing the FLMs who report to them. FLMs usually have clear responsibility for coaching the salespeople who report to them; in fact, FLMs often have specific objectives for frequency of coaching sessions or for spending a certain number of days in the field. Yet for SLMs, the coaching of FLMs, although expected, may not be a primary job focus.

The best SLMs take their role as coach and manager of FLMs seriously. They spend time with the FLMs they manage and develop a strong understanding of their performance. Given the inherent independence of the FLM job and the natural variation in the situations and opportunities that FLMs face, an involved SLM will see many different scenarios play out. Sales in one district exceed expectations, while sales in another are below expectations. Customer satisfaction is stronger in one district than another. One FLM has little turnover among good salespeople, while another struggles to attract and retain talent. As SLMs work with individual FLMs to help them improve, they are constantly observing what FLMs do right. Over time, an astute SLM develops a menu of behaviors that drive FLM success and, through ongoing interactions with FLMs and with peer SLMs, propagates these behaviors across the sales management team.

FLMs are more likely to get the performance management attention they need from SLMs when discussion, feedback, coaching, and guidance of FLMs are supported by a defined and recurring FLM review process (see Figure 8-5).

A good review process asks SLMs to meet monthly or quarterly with FLMs to discuss progress against goals and to make appropriate adjustments to business plans. Here are three examples:

- "At Cardinal Health, we have a monthly cadence in place for FLMs to review their business pipeline with SLMs," says Sandy Cantwell, Vice President of Sales Operations. "The process is supported by an internally developed forecasting tool that tracks opportunities. Through repetition and consistency, and with the support of senior sales leaders, the process has become part of our culture."

- "At Ethicon, regional sales directors sit down with their FLMs to discuss performance four times a year," says Fred Wagner, former Vice President of Sales for Johnson & Johnson's Ethicon Endo-Surgery division.

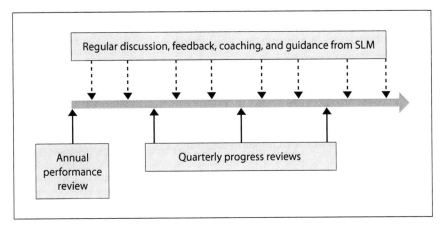

Figure 8-5   Engaging SLMs in FLM Performance Management

- "At Boston Scientific, we do a quarterly discussion with FLMs using a balanced scorecard," says Chris Hartman, Vice President, Central Zone, Cardiology, Rhythm and Vascular Group. "The balanced scorecard is also used as input for an annual performance appraisal and succession planning discussion." (Learn more about the balanced scorecard later in this chapter.)

A good review process also includes an annual discussion between FLMs and their SLMs to focus on a more comprehensive evaluation of overall performance and career planning. For example, Microsoft has a process for annual performance review and career planning discussions between FLMs and SLMs. "FLMs complete a career stage profile and meet with their SLM to agree on a plan," says Jay Sampson, former General Manager, U.S. Emerging Media Sales. "Working together, the FLM and SLM identify competency gaps and find training courses or development opportunities to help the FLM improve and grow. The conversation focuses 25 percent of the time on what has happened in the past and 75 percent of the time on what should happen in the future. This keeps FLMs focused on moving forward."

Using Metrics and Frameworks to Enable the Evaluation of FLM Performance

"You can't manage what you don't measure." As the old management adage suggests, the right metrics are a critical element of the FLM performance management process.

Characteristics of Good Metrics

Good metrics share some important characteristics.

Alignment with Strategy and the FLM Role

The right metrics encourage FLMs to engage in activities that are consistent with the role that sales leaders expect them to carry out to support the execution of the company's sales strategy. Appropriate metrics for an FLM who is primarily a people manager, for example, might include salesperson retention or time in the field coaching. An FLM who has customer management responsibility might be evaluated on customer retention or sales results for the customers that he or she is responsible for.

"FLMs have an important role as a conduit for communications between the field and headquarters departments such as Marketing and Supply Chain," says BP's Liza Clechenko. "This role pulls FLMs away from the field and can impact short-term results. It's important to align performance objectives and metrics with the desired focus of FLM activity."

Metrics and relative weightings should adapt as strategic priorities change. "We changed the metrics that we use for managing the performance of FLMs as the dynamics of our business evolved and the focus changed from growth to profitability," Liza says. "Instead of tracking volume delivery and new volume, we began to track the profitability of the volume that was delivered as well as the steps in the sales process."

Measurability

Financial metrics (for example, district sales and profits) are usually more measurable than are input metrics that drive the outcomes (for example, FLM people management skills or coaching time). But good performance management requires sales leaders to measure all important dimensions to the extent possible. When measurement isn't perfect, sales leaders should seek creative ways to capture the needed information. "Territory gross profit goal achievement is quantifiable, but measuring achievement of FLM activity goals involves shades of gray," says John Barb, former Vice President of Sales at xpedx, a distribution business within International Paper. "I get insight on how effective a manager is at an important task—say, tactical planning—by riding with one of the FLM's salespeople and reviewing the call plan. If the salesperson doesn't have a good call plan for the day, then that tells me a lot about how that salesperson is being managed."

Greg Schofield, former Executive Vice President and Head of Global Sales at Novartis, suggests, "By looking at field coaching reports for an FLM's salespeople, you can get a sense for how much time the FLM is spending coaching and the quality of that time. You can also ask salespeople to tell you about the time they spend with their manager."

FLM Control

Good metrics are impacted by an FLM's hard work and abilities, not by factors that are beyond the FLM's control. External market factors often affect results metrics. For example, an FLM in a district with above-average market growth will have an easier time increasing sales than an FLM in a district where the market is stagnant. An FLM in a small district with weak competition will be able to increase market share more easily than an FLM in a large district with significant opportunity and strong competition. Good metrics account for external factors so that FLMs are not penalized for district characteristics that they cannot impact. Good metrics also acknowledge what FLMs control within their defined role. For example, district profitability is an appropriate metric only if FLMs have the authority to affect profits by controlling district resource levels or by influencing pricing decisions.

Metrics for the Five FLM Performance Categories

Figure 8-6 provides some examples of metrics, organized into the five FLM performance categories. By measuring every category of the causal chain — starting with company results and working backward to determine how those results came about — sales leaders get insights for managing and improving performance. If

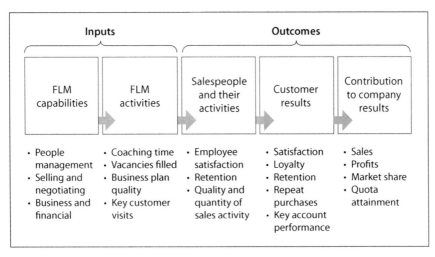

Figure 8-6 Examples of Metrics for Measuring the Five FLM Performance Categories

sales leaders can identify the people, customer, and business management capabilities and activities that lead to desired outcomes, they can share these insights with the FLM team. By propagating FLM success activities and capabilities, they boost performance of the entire sales force.

Frameworks for Encouraging Consistency in Managing FLM Performance

The best companies provide frameworks that encourage consistency of metrics and evaluation across FLMs and over time. Here we discuss some popular frameworks that are useful for managing FLM performance across different performance categories in the causal chain (see Figure 8-7).

Competency Models for Managing FLM Capability and Activity

FLM capability and activity—the inputs that ultimately determine company results—are perhaps the most difficult performance categories to measure objectively. Assessing FLM capability and activity requires SLM observation and judgment. SLM assessments can be supplemented with input from the salespeople each FLM manages; they can provide perspective on the FLM's abilities in areas

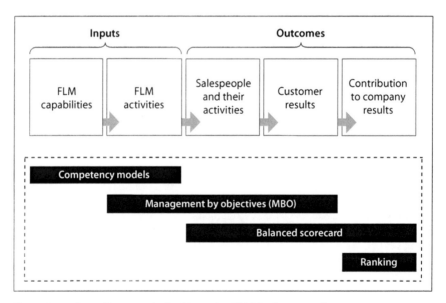

Figure 8-7   Some Frameworks for Managing FLM Performance Across the Five Categories

such as coaching and managerial effectiveness. SLMs need guidance to encourage objectivity and consistency in their assessments and managerial courage to provide honest feedback differentiating strong and weak performance.

To guide FLM capability and activity assessment, many sales organizations use competency models that define the level of skill and knowledge needed for success in an FLM role. Competency models provide a blueprint for managing performance and also can guide FLM selection, learning and development, support, and motivation programs.

Competency models should focus on FLM competencies (skills and knowledge), not characteristics (personal qualities). Job competencies (for example, coaching skills or market/company knowledge) can be learned and developed through the performance management process by providing FLMs with programs that train, mentor, support, and motivate around those competencies. Characteristics are inherent in a person's personality, character, and aptitude. To get the right characteristics (for example, empathy or integrity), you have to hire the right people. See Chapter 4 for a more detailed discussion contrasting characteristics and competencies.

Figure 8-8 shows one page of a 10-page FLM competency model used by a sales organization. The page provides a detailed description of three competencies that this organization considers important for FLM success in a people management role. The capability category *developing the sales team* is one of 10 capability categories that this company includes in its FLM competency model.

The top half of Figure 8-8 shows that in this organization, FLMs must have competency in field coaching, team improvement, and recognition to be successful at developing the sales team. The number and type of competencies are linked to the FLM role and to the profile of competencies that FLMs need for success, as well as to the culture and values of the organization. This company has identified specific FLM behaviors that define three levels of achievement for each of the three competencies.

The bottom half of Figure 8-8 shows how the company uses the competency model to guide the FLM performance management process. For two levels at the FLM position, there is an expected range of achievement on each competency. As part of an annual performance review, FLMs evaluate their own achievement on each competency while their managers (SLMs) make their evaluations. The grid helps guide the discussion between the SLM and the FLM during the review, where discussion centers on deficiencies in competencies and learning and development opportunities to help the FLM improve.

"Good competency models are quite specific," say Liza Clechenko. "It's important to define what low, medium, and high competence looks like, and to spend time discussing this with the management team. This helps to build a common language and understanding and helps FLMs understand what the organization expects of them."

	Basic	Skilled	Expert
Coaching the Team	• Recognizes the importance of coaching • Occasionally discusses skill development with team members and adapts coaching style to situation • Spends equal time in field with all performers	• Is a knowledgeable coach who provides feedback to facilitate behavioral change • Usually adapts coaching style to situation • On field visits, lets salesperson do majority of talking and probes to gain understanding • Spends more time with coachable low performers	• Is viewed by team members as a coach and mentor • Consistently adapts coaching style to situation • Engages team members in dialogue about business goals • Consistently asks questions that guide learning • Spends less time with high performers but keeps them engaged
Improving the Team	• Occasionally uncovers improvement opportunities for team members based on development plans and interests	• Regularly identifies improvement opportunities for all team members • Works with team members to align opportunities with development plans and interests • Follows up with team members to measure progress	• Encourages excellence by sharing and recognizing achievements of team members • Proactively works with team to develop relationships with key stakeholders • Has track record of leading others to sales success
Recognizing the Team	• Generally consistent in celebrating successes of team members	• Consistently recognizes and rewards team members	• Recognizes and rewards team members appropriately within the team as well as across the organization

Competency Expectation by Position, and Supervisor and Self-Assessment of Current Competency for One Salesperson

	Basic	Skilled	Expert
Coaching			O ◆
Improving			◆ O
Recognizing	O	◆	

Expected range for FLM (Level 1) Expected range for FLM (Level 2) ◆ Supervisor assessment O Self-assessment

Figure 8-8 An Excerpt from an FLM Competency Model Used by One Sales Organization

Management by Objectives for Evaluating Intermediate Inputs and Outcomes

Management by objectives (MBO) is a process through which managers work with their subordinates to jointly identify common goals, to define responsibilities and expected results, and to evaluate activities and results relative to goals as a basis for assessing each subordinate's performance.

Many sales organizations use management by objectives, especially for assessing FLM performance in categories in the middle of the causal chain. Here are a few examples:

- **MBOs for FLM activities.** Many FLMs have MBOs for coaching time with their salespeople. Or "an MBO might ask an FLM to meet with specific important customers a prescribed number of times per year," says Conrad Zils, Global Director of the Commercial Center of Excellence for GE Healthcare.

- **MBOs for salespeople and their activities.** Many FLMs have MBOs for employee satisfaction of their salespeople. "We have MBOs based around formal measures of salesperson retention," says a sales leader at a professional services company that was struggling with salesperson turnover.

- **MBOs for customer results.** Many FLMs have MBOs for customer loyalty and retention metrics. "The GE Capital sales force and many other sales forces use quantifiable MBOs for metrics such as customer satisfaction scores and coverage rates," says Conrad.

In most sales environments, it is harder to measure performance in these intermediate input and output categories than it is to measure financial results (for example, district sales and profits). MBOs provide a framework for establishing performance standards and then measuring and comparing FLM performance with those standards. Typically, FLMs and SLMs work together to set goals and plans for achieving MBOs. Through their involvement in the process, FLMs increase their commitment to objectives and are therefore more likely to achieve them.

MBO achievement should always be evaluated over a time period that is long enough to allow an FLM to affect the outcome; an annual evaluation period is typical.

The issue of whether to link MBO achievement to FLM incentive pay is controversial. Some sales organizations pay FLMs incentives for MBO achievement, usually by splitting incentive earnings into a larger portion tied to financial metrics (for example, district revenue or margin) and a smaller portion tied to quantified MBO achievement (for example, achievement of customer satisfaction or salesperson retention objectives). Because it can be difficult to measure MBO achievement objectively, many sales forces choose to decouple MBO achievement and incentive pay. "Without a rigorous MBO criteria and/or oversight process, it can be tough to get consistency of MBOs and ratings across the country," says Chris Hartman of Boston Scientific. "Too often as a result, incentives for MBO achievement end up paying out at almost 100 percent across the sales force."

A best practice for sales organizations: If financial results are objectively measurable, tie all or almost all incentives to financial metrics. If you tie a portion of incentives to MBO achievement, keep that portion small (not more than 20 percent). Focus on MBO achievement during the performance evaluation process by reviewing progress at quarterly reviews and in the annual evaluation that determines salary increases and career progression.

A Balanced Scorecard for Managing Outcomes

A balanced scorecard organizes metrics across multiple categories to provide a consistent framework for evaluating FLM performance. Good scorecards can include metrics from all of the performance categories, but they usually emphasize the outcome categories that sales leaders feel are most important for FLM success.

"At Cardinal Health, our scorecard includes many metrics but focuses on three major areas: financial results (region revenue and profit), voice of the employee (based on employee engagement surveys and ongoing feedback), and customer loyalty (based on customer engagement and satisfaction surveys)," says Sandy Cantwell.

"At Boston Scientific, we have four quadrants of scorecard criteria: financial metrics (e.g., sales growth; percent to plan), customer metrics (e.g., number of new customers; customer retention), people metrics (e.g., voluntary turnover; retention), and compliance metrics that ensure adherence with FDA guidelines," says Chris Hartman. "We track these metrics on a quarterly basis and use the scorecard as input to the performance appraisal process."

By combining financial measures of past performance with the determinants of future performance, a balanced scorecard focuses managers' attention on tangible and objective metrics that align with strategy and are used consistently across the FLM team.

Ranking (with Caution) for Managing Company Results

As part of the performance management process, many companies will rank all their FLMs on results metrics such as sales, sales growth, gross margin, quota achievement, and market share. Some sales leaders like to make ranked lists available to all, while others feel it is best to tell each FLM his or her rank but publish only the top of the list. Still others use rankings to determine promotions and other FLM rewards but keep all rankings confidential.

Most advocates of publishing forced rankings are firm believers in the motivational power of their approach. We hear comments like these:

- "Sales managers are motivated by competition. Ranking drives their competitive juices."
- "FLMs will work harder because they want to move up in the rankings."
- "The ranking helps us differentiate between excellent, average, and poor-performing FLMs."
- "We don't have to deliver the bad news. FLMs at the bottom get embarrassed and leave."

Sales leaders should use caution in publishing forced ranking of all FLMs, for several reasons.

- Because by definition there will be winners and losers, a forced ranking system can generate a lot of internally focused competition. For one person to move up in the rankings, another has to move down. FLMs may become more concerned with how they compare to their peers than they are with serving customers, beating competitors, or helping other FLMs succeed.
- Because many managers will not feel successful unless they are ranked at or near the top, forced ranking tells a large number of FLMs in a very visible way that they are "losers." This risks alienating the "middle" performers (75th to 25th percentile) — a large group that is likely important to company success.
- Forced ranking runs counter to the supportive culture that many sales forces want to create, particularly if published rankings are used as a substitute for ongoing performance feedback from SLMs. Published rankings can make FLMs feel undervalued and afraid to take risks.
- Rankings can be demotivating when there are only small performance differences between managers across a large range of rankings. Say that quota achievement for the top five managers ranges between 110 and 108 percent. The perceived difference between the #1-ranked FLM versus the #5-ranked FLM exaggerates a very small actual difference in performance.
- Published forced rankings can diminish the importance of SLMs in the performance management process. Weak SLMs can allow rankings to deliver the bad news to underperforming FLMs, instead of summoning the managerial courage to have honest and frank discussions that can help those managers improve.

These downsides to forced ranking are mostly eliminated when companies publish only the list of top performers and ask SLMs to privately share individual ranking information with the FLMs who report to them. When SLMs relay ranking information face-to-face, they can work with individuals to develop strategies for improving their rankings. At the same time, a published list of top performers publicly acknowledges the outstanding performance of top-ranked FLMs, who then become models for the rest of the FLM team, as others aspire to become part of the select group.

If sales leaders feel strongly that forced rankings of the entire FLM team should be published, the downsides of doing so can be managed in two ways. First, if the company keeps the time period for the ranking short, FLMs can recover quickly from a low ranking. Second, when the ranking is done using multiple criteria, FLMs have many ways to win. For example, a ranking on *total sales* favors the large sales district, *sales growth* favors the small sales district, and *market share* rewards the best performance relative to the competition. By ranking on a variety of metrics, it is possible to highlight the success of FLMs with different strengths and different types of districts.

Forced ranking, whether published or not, should always be based on clearly articulated objective criteria and should be contemplated only when the measures used as the basis for ranking are accurate and fair to all FLMs. A forced ranking based on unfair or inaccurate measures can make a satisfactory employee appear to be underperforming or can make an average performer appear excellent. A ranking that does not reflect true performance differences will be demotivating to many FLMs.

Improving FLM Performance Management

Excellent FLM performance management requires sales leaders to act quickly to remedy performance issues while leveraging the power of culture to direct FLM activity.

Act Quickly When an FLM Is Performing Poorly

Too often, sales leaders retain poorly performing FLMs for too long. With a weak manager in charge, salespeople disengage, and an entire district can spin out of control quickly. As soon as sales leaders recognize that an individual does not have the characteristics required for success as an FLM—a problem that cannot be corrected through training, development, and support—it's best to act quickly to move that individual into a role in which he or she can be successful, thus avoiding long-term damage to the district.

Early signs that an FLM is not cut out for the job can show up in any of the five FLM performance categories (see Figure 8-9).

The dilemma of whether to manage a problematic FLM *up* (try to improve the situation through feedback and coaching) or to manage the individual *out* (move the FLM out of the company, back to an individual contributor role, or into another more suitable position) is challenging. FLM capability and motivation are

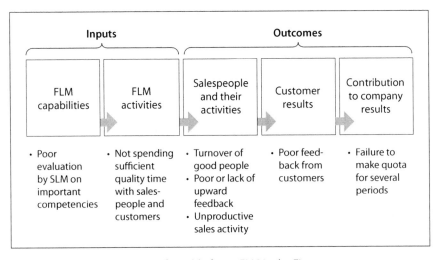

Figure 8-9   Some Early Signs of Trouble for an FLM in the Five Performance Categories

important factors influencing this decision. The framework shown in Figure 8-10 is a useful diagnostic tool. It draws on the same "can do/will do" framework as a tool described in Chapter 7 for helping FLMs manage the performance of their salespeople.

One of the situations shown in Figure 8-10 suggests clear action. FLMs who have both capability and motivation are "stars" you'll want to reward, retain, and learn from so you can share their success strategies with the entire FLM team. The other three situations require asking and answering some questions to determine the best course of action. The questions focus on whether it's possible to remedy the situation through management actions. For a problem that is primarily motivation-driven, look to FLM motivation programs and incentives as possible solutions (see Chapter 9). For a problem that is primarily capabilities-driven, look to remedies such as training and development programs that enhance FLM capabilities (see Chapter 6) and improved support for FLMs around job competencies (see Chapter 7). For an FLM who lacks both capabilities and motivation, consider moving the individual out of the FLM role; even if the situation is remedial, the investment required to improve both dimensions may be too great.

In some cases, a motivation or capabilities deficiency stems from inherent characteristics of the individual. (See Chapter 4 for a discussion about characteristics versus competencies.) If the problem is with characteristics rather than competencies, then the wrong individual is in the job, and it's best to move that individual into a different role.

If an individual will be most successful in a role other than FLM, look for ways to enable the individual to bow out gracefully—for example, by emphasizing

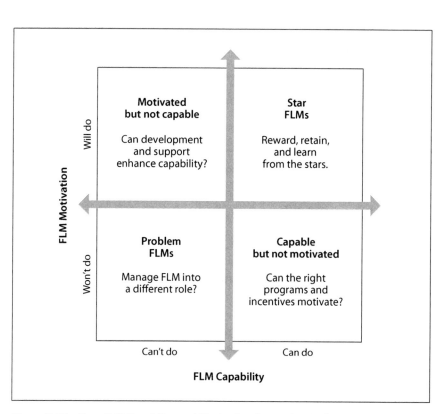

Figure 8-10 How FLM Capability and Motivation Determine Performance Management Consequences

the opportunity to reduce job stress and improve lifestyle by moving back into an individual contributor role. Careful attention to the communication can ensure that individuals understand their true core competencies, that they are mismatched to the FLM job, and that when slotted into the right place they can be successful. Typically, reassignments are more easily accepted during times of change or sales force reorganization, when FLM job skills are changing, and many FLMs are switching roles. But SLMs need to summon the managerial courage to make needed changes even when the sales force is not reorganizing. Retain one poor salesperson and you lose a territory; retain one poor manager and you lose an entire district.

When FLMs leave their position, either voluntarily or involuntarily, expect a transition period for the sales team. SLMs can step in and help FLMs who are taking over a new district to ensure a smooth transition and to help them gain the confidence of the district sales team.

Recognize the Power of Culture in Managing FLM Performance

"The sales force culture flows from sales force members' experiences and from leadership," says Chris Hartman. Sales force culture is defined by shared beliefs, values, and attitudes. Culture creates an unwritten set of rules that guide the way FLMs and other sales force members interact with one another and with customers.

Culture plays a powerful role in the performance management process. FLMs spend most of their time working in the field with limited supervision. It's not possible to provide continuous oversight of what FLMs do day to day, nor is it possible to capture metrics for every important FLM behavior or result. The sales culture provides direction to help FLMs make choices about how to handle the difficult situations that they face. A good culture encourages FLMs to "do the right thing" even when an SLM is not there to observe or when metrics cannot capture what is happening. The right culture can encourage desired behaviors—integrity, responsibility, and customer focus, for example—and thus is a powerful driver of FLM performance.

Sales leaders should not underestimate the importance of culture in managing sales team performance. "Culture comes from the top," says Greg Schofield of Novartis. Sales leaders can proactively encourage a positive sales culture in three ways:

- **Engage key culture influencers.** "Peer influence is perhaps the most powerful driver of culture," says Quinton Oswald, CEO of SARcode BioScience. "Find out who the key influencers of culture are in your organization—the people others routinely go to for answers and advice. Bring them into the process of creating the culture. Consider establishing a culture committee."

- **Communicate culture constantly.** "If you're not good at marketing the culture, it won't get implemented," says Greg Schofield. "Create a proactive plan for communicating the culture. Recognition is also a huge part of building culture. Who wins the awards and what you put on the scoreboard tells managers what's important. Propagate the culture by giving winners a chance to share what they are good at."

- **Select FLMs who embody the culture.** "FLMs are enrollers of culture, up and down the organization," says Quinton. "Be sure that the individuals that you select for the FLM team exemplify the culture you want for the sales organization." Chris Hartman notes, "It's important to bring in the FLMs first and get their buy-in to the culture; then you can bring in the salespeople."

A positive sales culture supports and enables the performance management process. At the same time, strong performance management is an important part of a positive sales culture. By doing a good job of managing FLM performance, sales leaders help establish a culture that in turn encourages FLMs to take their role as coaches and performance managers for their sales teams seriously. Investments to provide FLMs with the training and tools they need to be effective performance managers contribute to a positive culture and can lead to considerable improvements in sales force performance.

Conclusion

To keep sales force activity aligned with company goals, sales leaders need an effective process for managing ongoing FLM performance. A good FLM performance management process has four characteristics:

- It focuses on both the inputs and outcomes that FLMs can influence to drive company results.
- It includes a prescribed series of steps with strong involvement by second-line managers.
- It uses metrics and frameworks that encourage consistent and effective evaluation of FLM performance.
- It enables sales leaders to respond quickly to performance issues to ensure that every individual in the FLM job is successful.

Good performance management, aligned around a positive sales culture, is a key FLM success driver. It helps create a strong FLM team that engages in the right activity—key elements of a winning sales force.

CHAPTER 9

Motivating and Rewarding Sales Management Success

What Motivates First-Line Sales Managers?

We asked three first-line sales managers (FLMs) who work in the same sales organization, "What motivates you in your job?"

1. Anna, who has been in the FLM role for 10 years, has a strong desire to accomplish goals and be successful. "I want to lead a winning team," she says. "My goal is to go on the incentive trip every year, so I set challenging objectives for myself. This means I have to push my salespeople hard to achieve difficult goals as well." Anna is motivated by *achievement*.

2. Ben, who is in his eighth year in the FLM role, looks forward to the annual golf outing and national sales meeting. "I love being out in the field, interacting with my salespeople and their customers," he says. "We have a great group of first-line managers as well, and we get together often to share best practices. I take many of the ideas back and share them with my salespeople." Ben is motivated by *social affiliation*.

3. Charles, who has been a successful FLM for five years, values the autonomy and control he gets in his job. "I'm in charge of the West Region," he says. "I enjoy the freedom I have to lead and direct my team of salespeople. I also like participating in meetings at headquarters where company leaders seek my input about company strategy." Charles is motivated by *power*.

What each of these three FLMs finds most satisfying about the job, and what motivates each to succeed, is somewhat different. The achievement, social affiliation, and power motivators are all important for success as an FLM. Yet the relative importance of each motivator varies by person, depending on characteristics inherent in the individual's personality and character, as well as on the person's career stage and life goals. Figure 9-1 shows how the relevance of these three motivators varies for Anna, Ben, and Charles.

The motivators in Figure 9-1 are fundamental needs within individuals; they are the drivers that move them to act. Because the motivators are largely inherent within individuals (not competencies that can be learned), it is important to include characteristics that embody these motivators in your FLM success profile

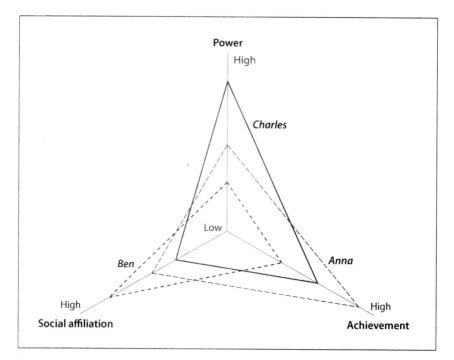

Figure 9-1   Importance of Power, Achievement, and Social Affiliation Motivators for Three FLMs

(see Chapter 4) and to screen for these characteristics during the FLM selection process (see Chapter 5).

We observe that successful FLMs are motivated by all three motivators to some degree at least and that a minimum level of each motivator is required for success. FLMs need an achievement motivator that drives them to attain challenging goals. They need a social affiliation motivator to build good relationships with their colleagues, customers, and salespeople. And they need a power motivator that enables them to take charge and get things done.

Understanding the three motivators helps sales leaders manage the FLM success drivers—the decisions, programs, systems, processes, and tools described throughout this book—to create a motivating sales culture. Motivation programs, including recognition and financial reward programs, further contribute to a culture in which FLMs are driven to engage in activities that align with company goals.

The right mix of motivation programs appeals to all three of the motivators and thus influences a diverse group of FLMs. To appeal to the achievement motivator,

Is Power the Great Motivator?

Researchers David C. McClelland and David H. Burnham investigated the impor- tance of achievement, social affiliation, and power as motivators for managers.[1] Interestingly, the researchers discovered that managers who are highly motivated by power are the most successful. Managers motivated mostly by social affiliation have a strong need to be liked, and this can interfere with their ability to get things done. Managers motivated mostly by achievement are likely to get things done, but they too often take credit for success at the expense of their team. Managers motivated mostly by power get things done by influencing the people around them and therefore are most effective at building a strong team that achieves organizational goals.

sales leaders can offer recognition programs. For example, they can publish a list of sales districts ranked by quota achievement or provide the opportunity to earn a spot in a prestigious and highly selective group, such as the President's Club. Financial rewards, such as sales contests or new incentive programs, also appeal to FLMs' desire to achieve. To appeal to the social affiliation motivator, sales lead- ers can share words of appreciation or can offer FLMs opportunities to interact with others—for example, occasions to attend meetings with their peers or to lead workshops for new salespeople. To appeal to the power motivator, sales lead- ers can offer FLMs opportunities for influence within the company—for exam- ple, occasions to share ideas with company leaders or to participate on task forces charged with responsibilities such as redesigning the sales process. Sales leaders appeal to FLMs' desire for achievement, social affiliation, and power by offering a diverse set of motivation programs, while at the same time, managing the FLM success drivers to build and sustain a culture of high achievement, teamwork, and trust and empowerment.

The Focus of This Chapter

This chapter is organized into two major sections that focus on how sales leaders can positively impact FLM motivation:

[1]David C. McClelland and David H. Burnham, "Power Is the Great Motivator," *Harvard Business Review* 54, no. 2 (1976): 100–110.

- By managing the seven *FLM success drivers* discussed so far in this book to create a motivating sales culture
- By providing an array of motivation programs that use recognition and financial rewards to further enhance FLM team motivation

In addition, an appendix to the chapter highlights some key decisions for designing incentive plans that motivate and direct FLM behavior.

Motivating and rewarding success is a key FLM success driver and an important component for enabling the right sales management activity to ultimately drive company results (see Figure 9-2).

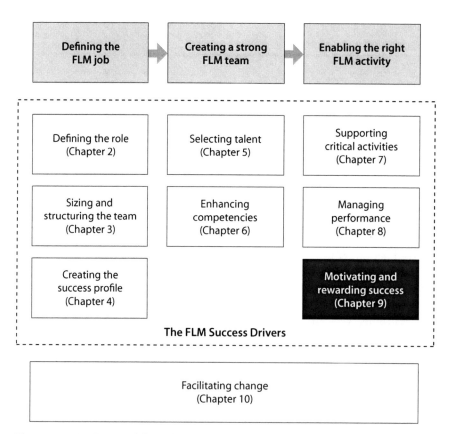

Figure 9-2 An Approach for Building a Winning Sales Management Team

Enhancing Motivation Through the FLM Success Drivers

Every FLM success driver impacts FLM motivation to some degree, either directly or indirectly. Building and sustaining a highly motivated FLM team (and therefore a highly motivated sales force) requires sales leaders to manage the success drivers to create a motivating sales culture. This includes the following:

- Defining a motivating FLM job by defining the role, sizing and structuring the team, and creating the FLM success profile
- Creating a strong team of motivated FLMs by selecting the right talent for the job and developing the competencies that allow the new FLMs to succeed
- Enabling FLMs to carry out the activities required to drive results by supporting critical needs and managing performance

Figure 9-3 suggests how the FLM success drivers combine to motivate FLMs who seek power, achievement, and social affiliation.

Enhancing FLM Motivation Through the Job Definition

Don, who has 20 years' experience in the FLM role, told us: "I can honestly say I love my job. I get satisfaction from leading my team and helping salespeople

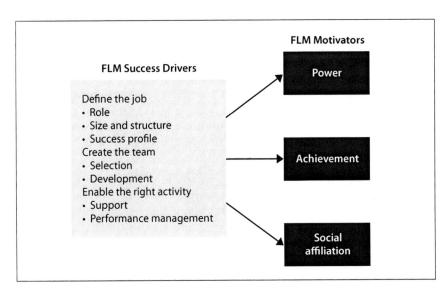

Figure 9-3   How Key FLM Success Drivers Impact Three FLM Motivators

grow. I get to learn about my customers' businesses and help them solve interesting problems. Running a district is like running your own business—there's a new and exciting challenge practically every day. It's been a great year. I hired a new salesperson and helped him get off to a fast start. I spent time coaching one of my lagging performers, and now she is on track to make quota for the first time. I helped my team land a major new account. I developed a sound business plan, and we are well on our way to implementing that plan with great success. I look forward to the challenges that lie ahead."

Don is motivated by achievement, social affiliation, and power. But Don is also intrinsically motivated by the work itself—a very powerful motivator that doesn't require extrinsic financial rewards or recognition. Psychology professor Mihaly Csikszentmihalyi describes this ultimate level of motivation as *flow*: "an optimal state of *intrinsic motivation*, where the person is fully immersed in what he or she is doing . . . characterized by a feeling of great absorption, engagement, fulfillment, and skill."[2]

In a winning sales management team, the *job itself* is a powerful motivator of FLM behavior, as it appeals to the three motivators in various ways:

- **Achievement.** Ultimately, the FLM job is about achievement, making district sales and profit goals. As people managers, FLMs achieve by helping members of their team succeed. As customer managers, they achieve by helping their customers accomplish business goals. As business managers, they achieve by contributing to company goals. By creating an FLM success profile that lets FLMs know what it takes to succeed, and by using it to guide FLM selection and development, sales leaders appeal to the achievement motivator.

- **Social affiliation.** As people managers, FLMs lead a team of salespeople. As customer managers, they interact frequently with customers. And as business managers, they engage with people in other company functions in meetings and other contexts. By defining an FLM role that emphasizes opportunities for interaction with customers, salespeople, and others at the company, while minimizing administrative demands, sales leaders appeal to the social affiliation motivator.

- **Power.** As people managers, FLMs are empowered to manage their team of people. As customer managers, they have some control over the company's relationships with customers. As business managers, they have power to make decisions about district strategies and resources and to share insights that shape company strategies. By clarifying role expectations and defining the right FLM span of control and structure, sales leaders let FLMs know

[2]Mihaly Csikszentmihalyi, *Flow: The Psychology of Optimal Experience* (New York: Harper and Row, 1990).

what is required of them. The FLMs know what business and activity they "own" and how much control they have over their people, thus appealing to the power motivator.

The FLM job can also include challenges that detract from the motivators. Here are some examples:

- **Achievement.** FLMs may see others achieving while they are not. They may feel that their district goals are too high, making it impossible for them to succeed.
- **Social affiliation.** Problematic salespeople can create stresses, unfriendly customers can exert their power, and working remotely in the field can be lonely.
- **Power.** FLMs may feel their people aren't listening to them, that customer buying decisions are determined largely by factors they cannot control, or that the company is not providing adequate support and resources.

Sales leaders must use the FLM success drivers to minimize the impact of motivation detractors that are inherent to the FLM job. "Despite having the perfect job description, reward and recognition systems, and a wonderful supportive boss, if it is too difficult or cumbersome to fulfill expectations, the FLM will not be motivated," says Liza Clechenko, former Vice President of Sales, East/Gulf Coast at BP. "One way to minimize the impact of detractors is to ensure that FLMs have efficient processes, systems, and tools to get the job done effectively."

Enhancing FLM Motivation Through Selection and Development

The FLM success drivers that create the team — selecting talent and developing competencies — contribute to FLM team motivation.

FLM Selection

The easiest way to ensure that an FLM team is highly motivated is to include the right characteristics in the FLM hiring profile (characteristics such as "ambitious," "self-motivated," or a "leader") and to screen effectively for those characteristics. A strong selection process (see Chapter 5) ensures that only intrinsically motivated people who desire a healthy balance of power, social affiliation, and achievement get selected for the FLM role.

FLM Development

Training and development programs (see Chapter 6) can be effective motivators for FLMs for several reasons. Development opportunities can

- Enlarge the comfort zone for FLMs, helping them overcome performance deficiencies, feel empowered to confidently lead their teams, and achieve higher performance levels
- Be an ego booster for achievement-oriented FLMs who are chosen for high-visibility, selective training programs — for example, programs that train the company's future elite leaders
- Create opportunity for social interaction (when training is done as a group), helping create a more cohesive bond among FLM team members

Enhancing FLM Motivation Through Support and Performance Management

Two FLM success drivers that enable FLM activity — supporting critical activities and managing performance — contribute to FLM team motivation.

FLM Support

An ideal environment for a motivated sales force includes excellent support for enabling FLMs to do their jobs well (see Chapter 7). By providing the right information and tools and access to support personnel and resources, sales leaders empower FLMs (appealing to the power motivator) and enable strong achievement. In addition to enhancing FLM motivation, supportive environments increase FLM efficiency and effectiveness.

FLM Performance Management

A good performance management process is crucial for FLM motivation (see Chapter 8), as it can appeal to all three of the FLM motivators. It provides social affiliation by providing FLMs with attention and feedback from their managers. It enhances achievement by reinforcing positive FLM behaviors and providing coaching and guidance on how an FLM can improve. And it appeals to the power motivator when FLMs are empowered to lead their teams in pursuit of agreed-on goals.

Creating a Motivating Sales Force Culture

All of the FLM success drivers contribute to the sales force culture. Culture is defined by shared beliefs, values, and attitudes in a sales force. It affects the way FLMs and others in the sales organization interact with one another and with customers. Culture creates an unwritten set of rules that guides the behavior of all sales force members.

A motivating work culture embodies the positive aspects of the motivators. Consider how two dissimilar sales cultures appeal to different motivators:

- Insurance company AFLAC has a sales culture that builds on the competitive nature and entrepreneurial spirit of sales force employees and the tens of thousands of independent sales agents who sell life insurance and supplemental policies. The culture is reinforced through programs aimed at making the sales force successful at growing business. There are literally hundreds of sales contests and awards for agents and sales managers, including an annual convention trip for top performers, awards for the best sales managers, and membership in the prestigious President's Club, for which less than 1 percent of agents and managers qualify. Winners of all awards get recognized in the quarterly sales agent magazine and on a company web site. AFLAC's competitive and entrepreneurial culture appeals especially to the achievement motivation of sales force members.

- Leaders at package-delivery company UPS describe their sales culture as "customer-service focused" and "team-oriented." "We don't see ourselves as having a lot of superstars, but rather as being a lot of good people *working together* to accomplish the right objectives," says former CEO Jim Kelly. This message is communicated through the sales force from the vice president of sales to the regional managers to the district managers (FLMs) and ultimately to the UPS people on the street who interact with customers. UPS's team-oriented and service-focused culture encourages achievement while also appealing to the social affiliation motivation of sales force members.

FLMs play a key role in propagating the sales force culture throughout the sales ranks. In their role as a link between the company and the field, FLMs share company cultural values with the salespeople they manage, acting as role models in carrying out culture-appropriate behaviors. FLMs are also key implementers of decisions, programs, processes, and systems that reinforce cultural values. For example, "FLMs play a critical role in recognizing the salespeople they manage," says John Barb, a former Vice President of Sales for the xpedx distribution division of International Paper. This helps to reinforce a motivating culture.

A positive sales culture is enabled by excellence in the FLM success drivers. Thoughtful execution of all the drivers appeals to a diverse group of FLM team members motivated by each of the three key motivators: achievement, social affiliation, and power.

FLM Motivation Programs

With the right FLM success drivers in place to create a motivating culture, sales leaders can further enhance FLM engagement through an array of recognition

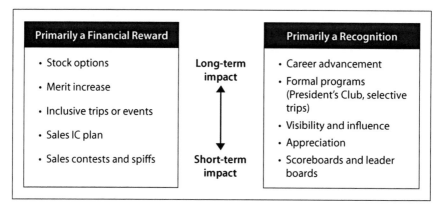

Figure 9-4 Some Common FLM Motivation Programs and the Timing of Their Impact

and financial reward programs that serve as motivators. Figure 9-4 shows some common FLM motivation programs and the timing of their impact.

The various recognition and financial reward programs combine to motivate FLMs who seek power, achievement, and social affiliation (see Figure 9-5).

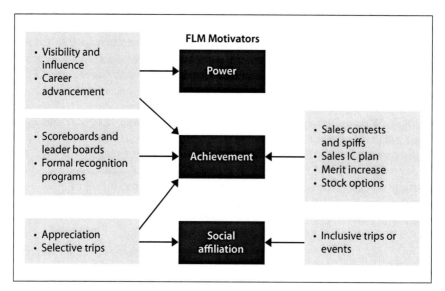

Figure 9-5 How Recognition and Financial Reward Programs Impact the Three FLM Motivators

Motivating FLMs with Recognition: An Often-Overlooked Motivation Tool

"Recognizing the exceptional performance of an FLM broadly within the organization can be a powerful motivator," says Jay Sampson, Executive Vice President, Global Sales, Marketing and Advertising at Machinima Inc. and former General Manager of U.S. Emerging Media Sales at Microsoft.

Conrad Zils, Global Director of the Commercial Center of Excellence for GE Healthcare, agrees. "Most sales organizations can do a lot more with recognition," he says. "Many of our managers work remotely or in smaller offices so they're closer to customers. We don't want them feeling like they're on an island. They react positively to recognition."

Recognition provides a significant opportunity to impact FLM job satisfaction and motivation, yet many companies underutilize the power of this often easy-to-implement tool. Recognition comes in many forms, ranging from formal recognition programs for top sales management contributors to opportunities for visibility and influence within the company to a thank-you for a job well done. Here we discuss how various types of recognition affect FLM motivation.

Formal Recognition Programs

Most sales forces have some type of formal recognition program, such as the President's Club, the Inner Circle, or the Million Dollar Roundtable. Salespeople and managers earn this formal recognition by exhibiting effective behaviors and competencies and strong results over a period of time—usually one year. These salespeople and managers may receive cash, merchandise, or travel awards, but the most important part of the recognition is the highlighting of their achievements before peers, management, or customers. Recognition programs not only reward top performers; they are also a way for management to signal to the rest of the sales force what it takes to be successful; it's a way of saying, "These are our winners, our role models, and our culture builders."

In most sales forces, FLMs are eligible to participate in the same recognition programs that salespeople participate in. The level of selectivity is similar for salespeople and managers (top 5 to 10 percent is typical), although it is not uncommon for a slightly higher percentage of managers than salespeople to be recognized. Sometimes, to ensure a balanced representation of FLMs, companies will use guidelines such as "at least one FLM from each sales region gets to go on the award trip" or "only the top FLM from each sales region gets into the President's Club."

Formal recognition programs have the highest motivational impact when selection is based on clearly articulated objective criteria and metrics that are accurate and fair to all FLMs. Usually, selection is based on a combination of factors, including results metrics (for example, sales, sales growth, gross margin, quota attainment) and other criteria that are considered important for FLMs to be good role models (such as teamwork, leadership, citizenship, excellence in coaching). Using the right combination of selection factors is critical to ensure that the selection reflects true performance differences. With more subjective factors, it is important to gather input using a structured process that minimizes management bias and favoritism.

Scoreboards and Leader Boards

Some sales organizations recognize FLM achievement by force-ranking FLMs on metrics such as sales, sales growth, or quota attainment and then publishing the ranked list. As one sales leader says, "Our managers are competitive. Just like in sports, they want to know where their team stands. They will work harder to move up in the rankings."

Although published forced ranking has motivational power, it also has downsides. By definition, there will be visible winners and losers. This can create internally focused rivalry, as FLMs soon forget that the competition is out in the marketplace, not within the company among peers. An "every man for himself" attitude can develop, hindering the teamwork needed to serve customers effectively and beat competitors. In addition, most FLMs feel unsuccessful unless they are ranked at or near the top. Published rankings can be demotivating to some FLMs—particularly the "middle" performers (75th to 25th percentile), a large group important to company success.

Whether to use forced ranking as a motivational tool for your FLMs depends largely on your sales culture. Ranking can work well in competitive, entrepreneurial cultures, but it can destroy team-oriented cultures. For more information about how to make forced ranking work in your sales organization, see Chapter 8.

Visibility and Influence

"It's easy to overlook the importance of recognizing FLMs for their successes in front of their peers," says John Barb, formerly of xpedx. "Seek out opportunities to recognize excellence in leadership within the FLM team."

The best sales leaders give successful FLMs visibility both among their peers and with company leadership. "Microsoft rewards managers not just for what results they achieved but also for how they got those results. We will put strong FLMs on panels as speakers to share best practices," says Jay Sampson. Similarly, at Boston Scientific, "We conduct 'meet the experts' events where FLMs who have excelled in certain areas present and share their expertise with the rest of the team," says Chris Hartman, Vice President, Central Zone, Cardiology, Rhythm and Vascular Group. "We also select high-performing FLMs to participate on an advisory board that meets twice a year with senior sales and functional leaders to provide input on strategic issues that the sales organization faces. FLMs on the board have input into the agenda for these meetings, lead many of the presentations, and 'own' many of the action items that are identified throughout the course of the meeting. Over time, we have evolved the Advisory Board into a truly action-oriented group that engages FLMs in discovering opportunities and delivering solutions."

The benefits of programs like these go beyond recognition. Through the sharing of best practices, learning gets propagated among all FLMs (see Chapter 6), and through participation on advisory boards, FLMs bring field perspective to the decision-making process and can act as ambassadors for change among their peers (see Chapter 10).

Many sales forces use sales meetings and newsletters to enhance the visibility of FLMs and other sales force members who are successful. The use of these media is an integral part of recognition programs and also fosters connection to the company and to others in the sales force. When recognition programs are used frivolously or too frequently, though, they can serve as shallow, "rah-rah" motivators rather than appealing to deep motivations. A serious, professional look and feel for these types of communications programs, and an optimal frequency, provide the best motivation.

Appreciation: Saying "Thank You"

Words of appreciation are an easy and important way to give FLMs an immediate motivational boost that often has a lasting impact on FLM engagement as well. "Just a simple 'thank you' when an FLM has to go through something tough can go a long way," says Chris Hartman. "Just pick up the phone and say 'I appreciate what you did.' A five-minute phone call of appreciation — especially from leadership beyond the sales organization (for example, from the president or CEO) — can be highly motivational for an FLM and has no impact on the budget."

For recognition in the form of praise and appreciation to have impact, it has to be genuine. People will see through insincere or forced praise. Words of appreciation are most effective when they are an ongoing part of the sales force culture.

Career Advancement

Well-defined career tracks that provide a clear vision of future opportunities are an important long-term motivational tool for FLMs. A promotion to FLM is a visible sign of career progression and is often the first promotion in a salesperson's career. The new job brings greater power and recognition of achievement. "Some FLMs will be 'pillars' who stay in the job until they retire; others will be 'movers' for whom the job is a stepping-stone on a career path to a higher level job," says Fred Wagner, a former Vice President of Sales for Johnson & Johnson's Ethicon

Endo-Surgery division. Both "pillars" and "movers" add value to the FLM team, and sales leaders should be prepared to manage to the different motivations of those in each group.

Motivating FLMs with Financial Rewards

Many types of programs use cash, trips, merchandise, or other tangible rewards to motivate FLM performance over varied time horizons (see Figure 9-4). The programs are listed roughly in order of timing of impact, from the most immediate to the longest-term impact.

Sales Contests and Spiffs

Most sales contests and spiffs are designed primarily for salespeople, not managers. Often, however, companies will make FLMs eligible to participate in the same contests and spiffs that salespeople are eligible for; this ensures that FLMs get excited about the programs and encourage their salespeople to participate.

Sales contests and spiffs are useful for motivating the sales force around specific near-term tactical events that might otherwise get insufficient attention — for example, launching a new product, combating a competitive entry, or providing a midyear boost to lagging sales. Most contests and spiffs last not more than a few months, and prizes can include cash, merchandise, and travel awards. The programs can be effective at relatively low cost. It's important to strategically align contests and spiffs with overall company objectives to ensure they don't redirect sales force effort away from core products, customers, and activities and dilute the impact of the main incentive compensation plan.

Sales Incentive Compensation Programs

The vast majority of U.S. sales forces use some form of variable incentive compensation tied to the achievement of performance outcomes. Incentive programs pay out over varied time periods, but most are designed to impact sales force motivation over a short- to medium-term time horizon (3 to 12 months). Almost all FLMs participate in their company's sales force incentive compensation (IC) plan. Typically, the IC plan for FLMs reflects, in large part, the design of the IC plan for the salespeople they manage. The company "pays for performance" by paying salespeople commissions or bonuses for bringing in sales and profits; FLMs, in turn, are rewarded for leading a team that contributes to company financial goals.

There is unanimous agreement that IC impacts sales force motivation, for better or for worse. FLMs may be motivated by the money itself, but IC plans have other indirect effects on motivation as well. Many FLMs are motivated by a large incentive component of pay because money serves as a measure of success and achievement. The perceived fairness of pay also impacts motivation; for example, FLMs who feel underpaid may slack off to make their compensation seem "fair."

The right IC plan can be a powerful tool for driving sales force motivation and therefore results. "But IC plan design is extremely complex, as the dynamics—economic, administrative, behavioral, and technical—that underlie sales compensation decisions are universally multifaceted and opaque," says Chad Albrecht, a Principal in the Sales Compensation Practice at ZS Associates. The wrong design can easily lead to undesired consequences, especially if it encourages sales force members to engage in activities that maximize their short-term incentive pay while compromising long-term customer and company interests.

The best sales organizations design FLM IC plans that encourage the right FLM behaviors while at the same time anticipating any undesired consequences of the plan and managing to avoid those risks. Although a detailed discussion of sales force incentive compensation is outside the scope of this book, an appendix to this chapter highlights some key design decisions for FLM IC plans.

Inclusive Trips or Events

When designed right, trips or events that include all FLMs are a powerful way to impact motivation and engagement across the entire FLM team. Appealing especially to the social affiliation motivator, such events have the most impact when they have clearly defined objectives and a focused agenda that encourages all FLMs to engage and participate (rather than simply listening to others talk). In addition to motivating, inclusive trips and events are useful for informing FLMs about and gaining their commitment to sales force changes and for educating and training FLMs on new skills and knowledge. (The inset box on page 208 describes an inclusive enhancement workshop for FLMs at Boston Scientific.) Inclusive events can provide an opportunity to showcase or recognize the best FLMs by having them lead best-practice sharing sessions for their peers. Inclusive events can also provide a setting for soliciting feedback from the FLM team about customers and other field issues.

Inclusive trips and events can require a significant investment of time and money, but with careful planning, they can be memorable events that impact FLM motivation for many months or even years after the event is over.

Merit Increases

Merit-based salary increases are linked to the FLM performance management process. The amount of an FLM's raise should align with feedback that the FLM receives during performance evaluations with a supervisor. Top performers who

An Enhancement Workshop for FLMs at Boston Scientific

This multiday development workshop for all FLMs focuses on skill improvement and reinforces best practices in critical sales effectiveness areas.

Purpose
This forum to develop FLMs takes them out of the field, elevates their knowledge, and educates them in approaches to issues that frequently are left on the back burner as they deal with the day-to-day challenges of running their regions and hitting their revenue goals.

Topics
Groups choose the most critical issues to focus on, selecting from a list of topics that includes hiring, coaching, targeting, sizing and structuring the sales force, aligning territories, helping salespeople prioritize their time, increasing manager effectiveness (time and effort allocation), implementing incentive compensation programs, and setting goals.

Methodology
Workshops include groups of 8 to 30 managers. Topics are addressed by

- Sharing best practices among participants, accomplished in subgroups of four to six people who later share with the larger group
- Conducting moderator-led lecture/discussion of best practices
- Discussing among participants — either in a single large group or in subgroups that later share with the large group — how to adapt and apply best practices in their regions

At the end of the workshop, participants write down one, two, or three ideas they will implement as a result of the workshop. As a group, participants identify support the company must provide to help them, such as information, tools, or processes that are outside an individual manager's control.

Feedback
From course sponsor Chris Hartman: "The program was designed by regional managers for regional managers. They took ownership and developed action items that were successfully implemented. Sales manager and salesperson selection, recruiting, and talent management improved significantly as a result of the workshop."

From course designer Marshall Solem, Principal, ZS Associates: "Lots of ground was covered in three days, and the exposure provided good development for people. Everyone took at least one idea (and often a few ideas) away from the workshop. Managers appreciated the chance to share best practices among themselves as much as they valued learning from the moderators. And they appreciated the time out of the field to focus on bigger issues and personal development."

consistently exceeded performance standards get larger raises, while poor performers get smaller or no raises.

Merit increases should reward FLMs for focusing on district success over a time horizon of a year or more, rather than for simply driving current period results. A best practice is to tie merit increases to metrics that reflect longer-term, sustained performance (MBO achievement, for example) while using incentive compensation to reward for short-term financial contributions, such as quarterly quota achievement. As one company's compensation policy states: "The *incentive plan* rewards FLMs for helping the company achieve sales objectives. *Salary* compensates FLMs for job activities such as growing the franchise, strengthening customer relationships, recruiting, training and developing talented salespeople, conducting marketing programs, handling administrative duties, maintaining product expertise, working with others to present a unified corporation to customers, controlling district spending, and managing salesperson turnover."

Merit increases are motivational when implemented effectively. FLMs desiring achievement and success will work harder for a larger raise. At the same time, a poor-performing FLM who receives no merit increase gets the message that performance improvement is imperative to survival in the job.

Merit increases are most motivational when FLMs perceive a strong link between their performance and the amount of their raise. If salary increases are allocated largely based on seniority, length of service, performance metrics such as district sales volume that don't account for differences in market opportunity, or the degree to which FLMs influence their boss, the motivational power is diminished.

Too often, sales leaders lack the managerial courage to give poor performers no merit increase, instead electing to spread rewards around to all FLMs to avoid conflict. Yet a discriminating approach to merit pay has clear advantages for FLM motivation. It optimizes the impact of salary-budget dollars, it sends the right message to the FLM team, and it avoids funding poor-performing FLMs at the expense of high performers.

Stock Options

Some companies will provide FLMs with stock or stock options, giving them an opportunity to "own a piece of the business," to encourage loyalty and long-term focus. This practice is especially popular in growing industries and economies and in tight labor markets, as it can be used to prevent good people (FLMs and sometimes salespeople as well) from leaving their jobs to join growing competitors. Stock options are generally used as a retention strategy for top performers. The number of stock options an FLM receives is usually based on a combination of the person's performance and tenure.

Conclusion

The right combination of motivation programs appeals to a diverse group of FLM team members. "Sales leaders must know their people and what works effectively for each type," says John Barb. "Some programs reach across the entire team. For example, almost all FLMs respond to recognition in front of their peer set. But in the end, a multitiered recognition and reward program works best."

Figure 9-6 summarizes the programs that will likely be most effective for FLMs who are motivated by each of the three motivators.

Motivation programs that provide recognition and financial rewards focus primarily on the achievement motivator. Consequently, sales leaders must look beyond these types of programs when motivating FLMs who seek social affiliation and power in addition to achievement. This requires using the FLM success drivers to motivate.

	Social Affiliation	Achievement	Power
Recognition programs			
Scoreboards and leader boards		★★	
Appreciation	★	★★	
Visibility and influence		★	★★
Formal recognition programs		★★	
Selective trips	★	★★	
Career advancement		★★	★
Financial reward programs			
Sales contests and spiffs		★★	
Sales IC plan		★★	
Inclusive trips or events	★★		
Merit increase		★★	
Stock options		★★	

Program impact: ★ = motivating; ★★ = highly motivating

Figure 9-6 Programs That Appeal to the Three FLM Motivators

It is important to align motivation programs with other FLM success drivers. "Aligning reward and recognition systems sends a strong cultural message to the sales force," says Liza Clechenko of BP. "For example, if you evaluate on results and behaviors but promote only on results, people get the message pretty quickly that behaviors don't really matter."

By using the FLM success drivers to create a motivating sales culture, and by reinforcing the culture with effective motivation programs, sales leaders appeal to three fundamental FLM motivators — achievement, social affiliation, and power — and thus encourage the right sales management activity to ultimately drive company results.

Appendix: Incentive Compensation Programs That Motivate and Direct FLM Activity

Almost all first-line sales managers (FLMs) participate in their company's sales force incentive compensation (IC) plan. Usually, the IC plan for FLMs is similar to the IC plan for salespeople but has been adapted to align with the FLM role. Companies pay salespeople incentives to motivate them to produce territory sales and profits. They pay FLMs incentives to lead a team of salespeople who contribute to sales and profits at the district or regional level.

The right IC plan can be a powerful tool for driving FLM motivation and therefore results. But a plan that is designed to drive sales and profits can also lead to undesired consequences, especially if it encourages FLMs to engage in activities that maximize their short-term incentive pay while compromising long-term

FLM IC Plan Design Feature	Rationale	Potential Undesired Consequence
FLMs get incentives tied to quarterly district profit	"Our FLMs are business managers who have price control. The company achieves its financial goals when FLMs lead teams of salespeople that produce sufficient short-term profit."	Some FLMs make short-term decisions that compromise long-term success. For example, they wait until next quarter to fill a territory vacancy in order to cut this quarter's district expenses and maximize their short-term earnings.
FLM IC pay is a multiple of the average IC pay for the FLM's direct reports	"The approach is easy to administer, aligns the motivations of FLMs and salespeople, and encourages FLMs to deliver results while also focusing on developing their people."	Some FLMs focus on helping only those performers who are most likely to reach performance hurdles for accelerated commission rates. These FLMs neglect below-average performers —especially those for whom goal hurdles are out of reach—even though those salespeople can benefit from FLM coaching.

Figure 9-7 Typical Design Features for Two FLM IC Plans and the Undesired Consequences That Can Result

customer and company interests. Figure 9-7 provides two examples of typical design features for FLM IC plans, their rationale, and the undesired consequences that could result and therefore need to be managed.

The best sales organizations design IC plans that encourage the right FLM behaviors while at the same time anticipating and managing to avoid any undesired consequences of the plan.

This appendix discusses the following topics:

- The characteristics of a good FLM incentive plan
- Some key incentive plan design decisions
- The importance of good sales force goal setting

The FLM incentive compensation plan is one among several important components of your approach to driving FLM performance.

Characteristics of a Good FLM Incentive Plan

Good FLM incentive compensation plans share several characteristics.

Alignment with the FLM Role

Alignment with the role encourages FLMs to engage in activities that are consistent with what sales leaders expect them to do to support the execution of the company's sales strategy. Consider how the IC plan aligns with the FLM role at three companies:

- **Company 1:** FLMs are primarily people managers. They get a moderate-size quarterly incentive tied to the results their sales team produces. They have MBOs for salesperson retention and key management activities, such as coaching and filling territory vacancies. MBO achievement influences annual FLM salary review and promotion decisions but does not impact incentive pay.

- **Company 2:** FLMs have a large customer management role. They earn most of their pay through incentives tied to sales performance — with both the customers that they have primary responsibility for and the customers assigned to the salespeople they manage.

- **Company 3:** FLMs have pricing authority in a business management role. They get a moderate-size incentive tied to district profitability, with a sizable salary component so that they don't overemphasize short-term results at the expense of price maintenance.

Alignment with the IC Plan for Salespeople

Alignment with the IC plan for salespeople encourages consistency in the motivations of FLMs and the people they manage. That is not to say that the salesperson and FLM plans must be identical; rather, the plans should be aligned with one another, with the respective roles of salespeople and FLMs, and with the sales strategy. For example, some companies pay salespeople on territory sales and managers on district gross margin, creating a healthy tension that encourages salespeople to drive sales and managers to encourage profitable sales that maintain price. Too much disparity between the salesperson and FLM plans, however, creates conflict if it encourages managers to engage in one kind of behavior and salespeople to engage in a different and incompatible behavior.

Motivational Power and Fairness

By meaningfully differentiating IC payouts between top-performing and poor-performing FLMs, those who go the extra mile to reach high performance thresholds are rewarded for their efforts. And to be motivating, an IC plan needs to be fair. It should reward results that come from each FLM's hard work and abilities, not from factors that are beyond the FLM's control (for example, above-average regional market growth or district size and market potential).

Simplicity

If understanding the plan requires too much energy, FLMs either will pay no attention to the plan or will misinterpret its intent. As a result, the plan will not motivate FLM behavior as desired. And worse, if FLMs don't understand the plan for their salespeople, they will not be able to implement the plan effectively.

Key Incentive Plan Design Decisions

Designing an FLM incentive compensation plan requires several decisions (see Figure 9-8).

Figure 9-9 compares two examples of FLM incentive compensation plans from different companies, characterized according to these key decisions.

FLM Pay Level

Total pay—including salary plus incentives—is largely determined by the market. You'll want to pay enough to attract and keep strong talent in the job. "At GE, we benchmark pay for all sales positions (including the FLM position) against competitors. We have a defined strategy for where we want to be in the market, and we set target pay levels accordingly. We track where good people go when

Decision		Sample Choices	
FLM pay level		• Above, below, or comparable to benchmarks • High, low, or moderate variation across FLMs	
FLM pay mix		• High or low leverage (% incentive vs. % salary) • More, less, or similar leverage to benchmarks	
FLM plan design	*Metrics*	• Revenue • Margin	• Market share • MBOs
	Plan type	• Commission	• Quota bonus
	Payout curve	• Thresholds • Accelerators	• Decelerators and caps
FLM plan timing		• Monthly • Quarterly	• Annual

Figure 9-8 Designing a Sales IC Plan for FLMs

they leave GE and where we hire our experienced talent from. This helps us determine where we need to be more competitive," says Conrad Zils, Global Director of the Commercial Center of Excellence for GE Healthcare.

You'll also want to compare the target pay level for FLMs to the target level for salespeople. FLMs typically have a higher target pay level than the salespeople they manage, with the full pay increase getting implemented over time, not when an FLM first gets promoted. In some sales environments, the best salespeople outearn their managers. Companies in this situation often seek to identify salespeople with management potential early in their careers—before they are making so much money that they would have to take a pay cut if they accept a management position. This strategy helps these companies attract the best management talent.

In addition to setting an average target level for total FLM pay, you'll need to determine an appropriate variation in pay across the FLM team. In other words, how much should you pay your best-performing FLMs relative to average and low performers? Because an FLM's results depend on the performance of many salespeople—typically some high, some average, and some lower performers—the law of averages compresses the range of performance at the FLM level. For example, if quota attainment for salespeople ranges between 70 and 130 percent, quota attainment for managers may vary between 90 and 110 percent. Sales leaders should account for the compression when designing IC plans for FLMs; payout

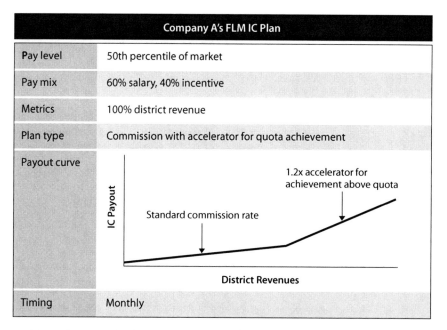

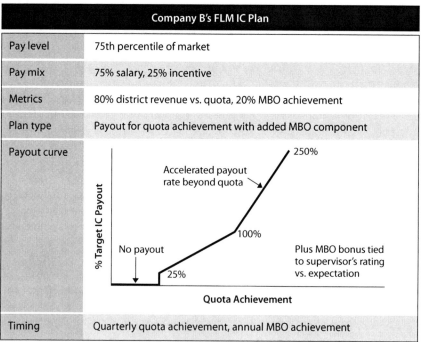

Figure 9-9   Two FLM IC Plans

curves should generally be steeper for FLMs than they are for salespeople to create enough variation in FLM pay.

Some argue that the best FLMs deserve the same multiple of target pay as the best salespeople. Others argue that because FLMs have passed a performance hurdle to get into their jobs, it is appropriate to have a tighter pay range for FLMs than for salespeople. The appropriate approach depends on the situation; the goal is to create an FLM pay spread that reflects an accurate variation in performance across the FLM team.

FLM Pay Mix

Pay mix reflects the proportion of FLM pay that is salary versus the proportion made up of incentives. Sales force pay mix varies substantially across industries and companies, depending on the sales process and the role of the sales force, the measurability of results, industry practice, and company history, culture, and management philosophy. The average for salespeople in the United States is about 40 percent of total pay coming from incentives. Generally, within a sales force, FLM pay mix is similar to salesperson pay mix or perhaps somewhat less leveraged (a slightly larger salary portion and smaller incentive portion for FLMs versus salespeople).

Pay mix should align with the FLM role. Many companies link the salary portion of FLM pay to aspects of the role that drive longer-term, sustained performance (such as recruiting and developing salespeople, sharing market insights with the company, and nurturing long-term relationships with customers) while linking the incentive portion of pay to aspects of the role that drive short-term financial contributions, such as the achievement of quarterly quotas.

FLM Plan Metrics

The metrics in your FLM incentive compensation plan should reinforce the characteristics of a good IC plan described earlier in the chapter. This includes the following:

- **Alignment with the FLM role.** Choose metrics and weights for the metrics that reflect the desired focus of FLM responsibility.
- **Alignment with the IC plan for salespeople.** Although the metrics in the salesperson and FLM plans do not need to be identical, they do need to align to encourage consistency in the motivations of FLMs and salespeople.
- **Motivational power and fairness.** Use metrics that account for differences across districts. For example, set district quotas that acknowledge district differences, then pay incentives on district quota attainment. In addition, metrics are motivating and fair only when FLMs can control them. For example, pay on gross margin (rather than on sales) if FLMs have control

over pricing decisions. And if FLMs have the authority to cut price by 10 percent, for example, but salespeople only have the authority to cut it by 5 percent, consider giving gross margin more weight in the FLM plan than it gets in the salesperson plan.

- **Simplicity.** Select metrics that FLMs understand, and include just a few. FLMs will either ignore or misinterpret the intent of metrics that are overly complex. And a single metric that has less than 15 percent weight in the IC plan will likely be ignored.

Incentives are especially effective at keeping a sales force focused on accomplishing short-term financial objectives. In many sales environments, results metrics such as district sales revenue or gross margin are objectively measurable and can be impacted by the sales force in a short time frame (within a month or a quarter, for example). In such environments, it is best to tie all or almost all short-term FLM incentives to financial performance metrics.

Some sales forces will tie a portion of FLM incentive pay to MBO achievement. MBOs usually focus on FLM responsibilities with longer-term impact, such as driving salesperson satisfaction or retaining major accounts. If financial results are measurable at the district level, it is usually best to keep the incentive portion that is tied to MBO achievement small (not more than 20 percent). Recognize MBO achievement during annual performance reviews through career progression and salary increases. Keep the FLM incentive compensation plan focused on short-term financial achievement only (for example, Company A in Figure 9-9) or tie only a small portion of IC pay to MBO achievement (for example, Company B in Figure 9-9).

FLM Plan Type and Payout Curve

Incentive compensation plans can include commissions, bonuses tied to quota achievement, or various combinations of these elements. The payout curve used in most FLM plans is similar to the payout curve used for the salespeople whom the FLM manages. Figure 9-10 highlights some of the most common differences between payout curves for salespeople and their managers.

FLM Plan Timing

Most companies have an annual planning period for their FLM incentive compensation plans, but shorter planning periods are appropriate in volatile markets where sales are difficult to forecast. Frequency of payout is typically tied to the pay mix. Sales forces with a small incentive component (10 percent or less) usually receive payouts annually. Those with a large incentive component (50 percent or more) usually receive payouts monthly. Payout frequency for FLMs

Plan Element	Definition	Typical Practice in a Salesperson IC Plan	Typical Practice in an FLM IC Plan
Threshold	Minimum performance level before receiving any incentives	Set at "carryover" sales level to reflect sales attributable to prior years' sales effort and non–sales force factors.	Set higher than the salesperson threshold because of the law of averages. Rule of thumb: two-thirds of the way between salesperson threshold and 100% (for example, if sales-person pay starts at 70% achievement, FLM pay starts at 90%).
Goal	Objective or quota for expected performance	Tie IC pay to goal achievement *usually*.	Tie IC pay to goal achievement *almost always*.
Accelerator	Higher commission rate for reaching a goal or performance hurdle	Reward top 10% for exceptional effort by accelerating their pay (usually at least 2x target opportunity) to reflect their contribution.	Reward top 10% for exceptional effort by accelerating their pay to reflect their contribution. Because of the law of averages, the performance hurdle for top managers should be set lower than the hurdle for top salespeople.
Decelerator	Lower commission rate beyond a performance hurdle	Usually no decelerator unless windfalls can be very large.	
Cap	Maximum payout for excellent performance	Usually no cap unless windfalls can be very large.	

Figure 9-10 Common Differences in Payout Curves for Salespeople and FLMs

generally mirrors that for salespeople, but in some cases FLMs receive payouts less frequently, particularly if FLMs have a larger salary component than salespeople do or if FLM performance measures vary significantly from those used for salespeople.

The Importance of Good Goal Setting

Over 90 percent of U.S. sales forces set sales goals for their people, and most link incentive pay for FLMs and salespeople to goal achievement. FLM motivation is directly impacted by the quality of district sales goals. Sales leaders enhance FLM motivation by setting district goals that are challenging, fair, and attainable. At the same time, FLMs impact the motivation of the salespeople they manage by allocating their district sales goals appropriately among their people. Several goal-setting best practices can help sales leaders set the right goal levels for FLMs; they can also help FLMs allocate their district goals appropriately to salespeople.

- **Start with a reasonable national goal.** Good goal setting for FLMs and salespeople is impossible if the national sales goal is not right. If the national goal is too aggressive, goals for FLMs and salespeople will be consistently too high. The sales force is likely to perceive goals as unachievable, and FLMs and salespeople may disengage, leading to sales levels that are even lower than they would have been had the goals been reasonable. If the national goal is too low, FLM and salesperson goals will be too easily achieved. The sales force will earn high incentive pay without having to work hard, and again, sales levels will be lower than what they could have been had goals been set correctly. Investments to create challenging yet realistic national forecasts based on data analysis and input from Marketing and Sales are an essential element of an effective sales force goal-setting process.

- **Use data-based formulas that incorporate measures of potential, as well as sales force input, to allocate the national goal out to FLMs and salespeople.** When allocating a national goal among sales force members, create a reasonable starting point using a formula-based approach that divides up goals based on territory- and district-level data. There are many formula-based goal-setting methods. The best approaches incorporate measures of future district and territory potential, as well as historical sales performance. Although using data is important for achieving fair and objective goals, the company shouldn't rely entirely on formula-based goals. Goals are more motivating when there is transparency in the goal-setting process and when the goals incorporate field input about local issues and conditions.

- **Don't overtax your stars.** Sales leaders sometimes allocate a disproportionately large share of the national goal to the strongest FLMs. Similarly, FLMs give their best-performing salespeople a larger share of their district goal. The reasoning is simple: "If I want to make my goal, it's best to challenge the ones I can rely on to deliver." Yet too often, this approach sets star FLMs and salespeople up for failure. Weak sales force members get easier goals, and the best are not rewarded enough for their hard work and superior results. Strong performers observe poor performers making more money for less work, and the impact on morale can be devastating. Always give your star performers challenging, yet reasonable, goals. Use accelerators in the IC plan to motivate peak performance.

- **Avoid systematic padding.** To ensure a safe cushion for goal achievement, many companies will sequentially pad sales goals from the top down. "Unfortunately, the practice of padding sales goals often backfires," says Chad Albrecht of ZS Associates. Suppose a vice president of sales adds 5 percent onto a reasonable company goal before passing it down to the regional level, and then regional directors tack on another 5 percent before allocating goals to their FLMs. FLMs now have goals that are 10 percent more than the original company goal; it is quite likely that FLMs will perceive these goals to be unrealistic. And if FLMs add another 5 percent safety net before allocating goals to their salespeople, territory goals will be 15 percent more than the original company goal, and salespeople will certainly perceive the goals to be unrealistic. With out-of-reach goals, salespeople may hold over sales until future incentive periods, leading to sales levels that are even lower than they would have been had goals been reasonable. In addition, out-of-reach goals can negatively impact sales force morale and retention.

- **Educate FLMs.** FLMs play a big role in sales force goal setting, so it's important to educate them on the goal-setting process. "There is often a knowledge gap about goal setting at the regional and district manager level regarding how goals are set and how they are tied to financial plans. FLMs really need to understand the process and inputs so they can set appropriate goals and communicate with and gain buy-in from their salespeople," says Sandy Cantwell, Vice President of Sales Operations at Cardinal Health.

Conclusion

Sales IC is a complex topic, yet numerous frameworks and analytic approaches exist to help sales leaders get the most from this important sales effectiveness driver. A useful reference for anyone contemplating IC plan assessment and change is *The Complete Guide to Sales Force Incentive Compensation: How to Design and Implement Plans That Work* (Zoltners, Sinha, and Lorimer, 2006).

Although IC can be a powerful driver of sales results, sales leaders should see it as just one component of an effective system for building a winning sales management team. Many sales effectiveness issues are commonly misdiagnosed by sales leaders as IC plan problems, when in fact additional, and sometimes better, remedies exist within other sales force decision areas. Be cautious when trying to solve sales management problems by changing the IC plan; more than likely, the primary source of the problem is something other than IC. Look to other types of motivation programs described in Chapter 9, as well as to other FLM success drivers described in the other chapters, and consider broader solutions in addition to incentives.

CHAPTER 10

The Sales Manager: An Essential Facilitator of Change

Three Stories About Sales Force Change

Three global companies — BP, GE, and Novartis — have implemented recent sales force changes. Their stories highlight the pivotal role that FLMs play in facilitating successful sales force change.

Implementing a New Sales Approach at BP

Customer demographics were changing in the branded fuels business, as many smaller, independent accounts consolidated and as family businesses moved on to the next generation. The resulting customer base had fewer, more sophisticated customers. To align with the evolving needs of these customers, BP sales leaders replaced a traditional relationship-based sales approach with a new value-based model in which salespeople focused on the business value that BP created for customers.

BP sales leaders made many sales force changes to successfully implement the new sales model. They redefined the competencies required for sales success. They rated current sales force members on the competencies, identified competency gaps, and created new training programs to fill the gaps. They built new tools to enable salespeople to conduct structured business conversations with customers. They revamped reward structures to tie sales force incentives and other rewards to bottom-line performance instead of just revenues.

"Our first-line sales managers were very engaged in the change process," says Liza Clechenko, a former Vice President of Sales, East/Gulf Coast at BP. "We asked managers for their input on what their customers needed and how we could get the sales force to become more value-focused. We gave them tools for tracking P&L for the first time. It was important to get the managers on board early and encourage them to become champions of the effort and own the solutions. We engaged them in workshops throughout the process. It took a year to complete the transition, but with the support of the first-line management team, we built acceptance of the new approach within the first six months."

Restructuring the Sales Force at GE Healthcare

As hospitals consolidated and centralized their buying processes, GE Healthcare transformed its sales force structure to align with the new and evolving needs of customers. Prior to 2009, the GE Healthcare sales organization was comprised almost entirely of product sales specialists, each of whom sold a particular product or service offering from GE's broad and diverse portfolio. In some cases, as many as 10 or more different GE product sales specialists called on the same hospital. Customers wanted better coordination of this sales effort across all GE Healthcare offerings.

The restructured sales organization now includes fewer product sales specialists, who continue to work with departmental decision makers, and more account managers, who work directly with the CXO of the largest customer organizations. Account managers are charged with understanding each hospital's overall needs and presenting "one face to the customer" to coordinate activity across all GE product sales specialists. The account manager's job requires a much higher degree of business acumen but less in-depth product knowledge than what is required of product sales specialists.

Account managers and product sales specialists report into their own first-line management team (region managers). To facilitate a team selling approach, GE leaders created a structure with 5 zones and 18 regions, deploying account managers and product sales specialists within common regional boundaries. They also introduced a team component to the sales compensation plan and aligned the compensation structure with each sales role. Within 12 months, a majority of the sales force was trained on the new sales approach.

"A key success factor was getting our first-line managers involved in the implementation and rollout of the new sales force structure," says Conrad Zils, Global Director of the Commercial Center of Excellence for GE Healthcare. "We redefined roles and responsibilities for product sales specialists and account managers within the context of the new selling model. We revised our competency, hiring, training, and coaching models accordingly. We even went as far as to prescribe the sales team's operating rhythm—a series of meetings and discussions through which managers should communicate information about the changes to their salespeople—in order to jump-start the implementation of the new model. Managers knew in advance what topics to cover, what questions to answer, who should participate, and how to communicate the benefits of the change. This ensured consistency of the message delivered across the sales force."

Improving Global Sales Force Effectiveness at Novartis

Sales leaders at Novartis seek to constantly improve global sales force performance through an annual sales force effectiveness review process. One initiative that came out of this process, described in Chapter 4, involved identifying seven first-line sales manager (FLM) success principles that sales leaders propagated among FLM team members to improve the effectiveness of the entire team. The FLM success principle initiative grew out of an earlier study at Novartis that focused on discovering the success principles that drove "effective selling behavior" among Novartis salespeople in the United States. Although the goal of this earlier study was to improve salespeople (not FLMs), Novartis FLMs played a key role in implementing the prescribed selling behaviors across the global sales force.

In the effective selling behavior study, an analysis team identified a group of top-performing Novartis salespeople (called *performance frontier salespeople*), then selected a group of average-performing salespeople for comparison purposes. Analysis team members observed salespeople from both groups on the job in order to understand the behaviors that salespeople used when interacting with customers. The team identified a set of success principles: specific behaviors that top-performing salespeople used to build value for customers that were different from the behaviors of average-performing salespeople. (See Chapter 4 for a description of this type of "performance frontier" analysis and how Novartis used it as part of the later FLM success principle initiative.) Novartis built a selling skills training program around the success principles, ran a successful pilot with 300 salespeople, and then trained the entire U.S. sales force on the principles. The training resulted in a more favorable perception of Novartis salespeople among physicians and also to better sales results.

With the success of the program in the United States, Novartis sales leaders set out to adapt the success principles for effective selling behavior and the training approach for global markets. They set an ambitious goal of implementing the program in the 10 largest global markets in just one year.

"There were approximately 1,100 first-line managers in our top 10 global markets, and each of these individuals was a key part of the initiative," says Quinton Oswald, a former Vice President and business unit leader for Tissue Growth and Repair at Novartis. "We created enrollment among managers by keeping them informed about what we were doing and why we were doing it through six monthly 'Top Ten Head of Sales' meetings. We hired an adult education expert from P&G, Larry Green, to oversee the program development and roll-out. We purposely stayed away from the cadre of usual suspects in pharmaceutical training circles who might have been daunted by the ambitious roll-out schedule. We developed a training program in each native language, and the trainer conducted 'train the trainer' sessions to prepare all managers to train their people on the success principles. We didn't want to delegate the training to the corporate training department; it was important that the local field managers be the advocates of the program. Successful change management is all about alignment and agreement, so sales manager engagement in the program was critical to its success."

The Focus of This Chapter

The stories about BP, GE, and Novartis illustrate how FLMs play an important role in helping a company design sales force changes that affect customers and then implementing those changes within the sales force. This chapter focuses on the FLM's responsibility as a facilitator of sales force change. In the chapter we will

- Outline some of the major forces of change that challenge sales organizations today

- Discuss two types of sales force change: (1) sales force transformations that involve major redesign in most strategic and operational sales force decision areas and (2) evolutionary sales force improvements that seek to proactively and continually increase sales effectiveness

- Discuss why FLM engagement is so critical for successful sales force change and describe the role of the FLM in designing and implementing sales force transformations and improvements

- Share practical advice from sales leaders on strategies for enabling FLMs as change facilitators

Sales leaders encourage successful sales force change when they align the FLM success drivers with the FLM's role as a facilitator of change (see Figure 10-1).

The Forces of Change

Sales leaders share their insights about the changing sales environment and its impact on sales management:

- "Change is everywhere today, and first-line sales managers need help with prioritizing, filtering, and navigating the ever-changing waters," says Chris Hartman, Vice President, Central Zone, Cardiology, Rhythm and Vascular Group at Boston Scientific.

- "In today's complex world, change is the norm. It's no longer an event—it's a daily occurrence," says Sandy Cantwell, Vice President of Sales Operations at Cardinal Health. "Managers need to embrace this and become comfortable with leading their teams in a continuously changing environment. This asks a lot of FLMs."

- "The next decade promises to be a period of more intense competition than current managements have yet experienced. The signals are now clearly discernible: a rising flood of new products and imports, a growing saturation of markets for older products, an increasing invasion of markets by firms

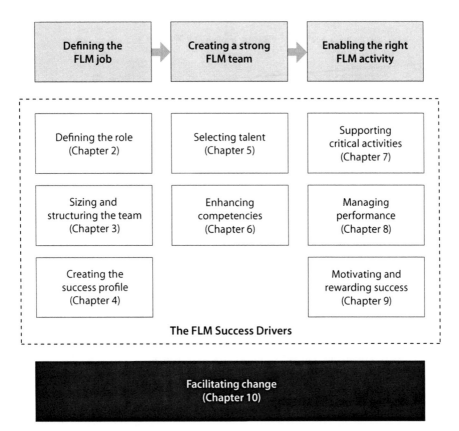

Figure 10-1 An Approach for Building a Winning Sales Management Team

formerly regarded as non-competitive, and the spread of automation with its enormous output potential. . . . Management must be ready."[1]

The first two statements were made by sales leaders in 2011. The last one comes from a 1961 *Harvard Business Review* article. Throughout history, technological and economic change has always challenged the capacity of businesses to be flexible and adaptive. Unless companies constantly innovate, they cannot remain competitive and successful for long.

The changing sales environment affects customers, salespeople, and the company. It affects what FLMs must do to manage their people, and how sales leaders manage the FLM team. Figure 10-2 shows examples of the many forces of change that impact sales forces today.

[1]George N. Kahn and Abraham Shuchman, "Specialize Your Salesmen," *Harvard Business Review* 39, no. 1 (1961): 90–98.

Figure 10-2 Forces of Change That Impact the Sales Force

A Changing World Economy

The changing world economy creates both opportunities and challenges for sales forces. Global markets are opening up to provide new sources of revenue growth. At the same time, more companies are leveraging the power of outsourcing and offshoring to build expertise and capacity while reducing long-term costs.

The evolving global economy creates new challenges as well, as more and smarter global competitors come on the scene. As economic growth in the United States slows, global forces create a redistribution of work and wealth across industries, countries, and continents. These economic forces impact customers, salespeople, and the company.

Advancing Technology

"With technology, the speed and magnitude of change has increased," says Sandy Cantwell of Cardinal Health. Technology creates opportunities for companies to improve sales productivity and effectiveness. More and more companies are harnessing the power of social media and online communities to connect and strengthen relationships with customers and prospects around the globe. The explosion of new customer and market data, made possible through technology, has enabled many sales forces to capture the power of analytics and information for driving sales force performance and building competitive advantage.

But technology creates new challenges for sales forces and for FLMs as well. "Technology has huge impact on transparency," says Chris Hartman of Boston Scientific. "Through the power of the Internet, anyone—including a customer, a competitor, and even a member of the media—can gain access to information that in the past may have been considered private or confidential. And they can do so at a rapid rate. Salespeople in our industry must be aware of the transparent environment that exists today and ensure that their communications do not expose the company to risk. That necessitates a new level of awareness for FLMs, who must know how to manage in a new, highly connected environment."

More Knowledgeable Customers Who Buy Based on Business Value

In today's technology-enabled, connected world, customers are better informed than before. Through the power of the World Wide Web and social networks, they can access a wealth of information about a company's offerings and even get independent reviews and assessments. Some customers, armed with this information, want to make purchase decisions without the help of a salesperson, as they seek to buy as cheaply and as conveniently as possible. Other customers want help with sifting through the flood of information and misinformation available; they look to salespeople for advice and guidance in making purchase decisions. These customers expect salespeople to add value beyond the mere sharing of information; they want salespeople who are partners and consultants, who understand their business, and who can help them solve complex challenges and find solutions that create business value.

Sales leaders comment on how these more sophisticated needs and expectations place new demands on FLMs in leading their sales teams:

- "It's no longer enough for an FLM to be a good people manager," says Chris Ahearn, currently a Senior Advisor at TPG Capital, and formerly the Senior Vice President of Corporate Sales and Marketing for Oakwood Worldwide. "Customers today are more sophisticated, better informed, and have more complex buying processes that often include gatekeepers and multiple influencers of the buying decision. Changes in the buying process require changes to the sales process and the supporting internal systems; this impacts the FLM role. The best sales managers need to be general managers with a broader skill set and strong business acumen—people who can coach salespeople on how to understand customer needs and demonstrate business value."

- "The healthcare industry has become increasingly more regulated, so the days of securing time with your customers by buying a ticket to a ballgame or paying for a round of golf are gone," says Conrad Zils of GE Healthcare. "It's becoming harder and harder to sell based on relationships. Relationships are obviously still important, but salespeople need to quickly understand the customer's business and be able to architect a more complete solution with economic value to the customer. The new sales environment requires more account planning, precall planning, and solution development; it's no longer just about maximizing time in front of customers. All this impacts the FLM role. FLMs must facilitate bringing more resources to bear in front of customers to support a value-based sales process."

- "Changes in the U.S. healthcare environment have led to increased variation in customer needs across the country," says Quinton Oswald, who has held leadership positions at Novartis, Genentech, and SARcode BioScience. "Sales managers today need to be more than good executors of national strategy. A talented first-line sales manager is a powerful tactical weapon for a company—someone who can adapt sales strategies and resource allocation decisions to match the needs of the local market."

A New Generation of Tech-Savvy Salespeople with Different Work Priorities and Communication Styles

Managers have always faced the challenge of managing workers of different generations who have diverse priorities and work styles. Due largely to the accelerating pace of technological innovation, differences among workers in the workforce today are more dramatic than ever before. Sales leaders share their observations about the changing workforce:

- "Sales force composition includes more varied experiences and cross-generational influences, particularly in the last five years," says Sandy Cantwell. "FLMs have to successfully manage people with dissimilar attitudes about issues such as work and life balance and different preferred communication methods and styles. More than ever, FLMs today have to embrace diversity."

- "Many of our junior managers have different goals and priorities than those of previous generations," says Chris Hartman. "They seek work-life balance and prioritize quality of life and family time over 'doing what it takes' to advance in their careers. More often, salespeople are reluctant to move to take a promotion to manager; rather, they are willing to wait until a local position opens up."

- "Many of our younger managers are very technologically savvy," says Chris Ahearn of TPG Capital. "They are 'digital natives' who grew up with the Internet and seem wired to adopt new technologies quickly. Those of older generations are 'digital immigrants' who have to learn how to live in a technology-enabled world."

- "Managers need to be very cognizant of the importance of embracing technology advances and effectively balancing different communication styles and preferences within their diverse teams," says Sandy Cantwell. "During conference calls, for example, some of our salespeople and managers will multitask, actively engaging in side conversations through instant messaging. Some are email-centric, others not. During live meetings, some managers leverage technology and use fully animated slide presentations, video streaming, polling questions, and other web- and software-enabled features to communicate. Others prefer to use a flip chart and markers. Sales managers must develop skills that enable them to effectively leverage varied techniques to deliver their message. They need strategies for structuring both live and virtual meetings to get effective feedback and encourage idea sharing with a diverse audience."

Focus on Profitability and Effectiveness

Slowing economic growth impacts the sales force and how FLMs manage their teams. Many companies have responded to economic pressures with initiatives to cut costs and improve productivity. Here are a few examples:

- "At Boston Scientific, five years ago our focus was squarely on revenue growth. Today, we take a more balanced approach, where sales leaders are also expected to deliver P&L results. To underscore that shift, we have modified our compensation model to reward revenue growth *and* profitability," says Chris Hartman.

- "Pressure to cut costs results in reductions of headquarters staff who support the field, and this impacts FLM workload," says Fred Wagner, former Vice President of Sales for Johnson & Johnson's Ethicon Endo-Surgery division. "User-led HR systems have become the norm for many companies. As an example, when a sales job opens up, the FLM has to post the job and do the supporting tasks that HR used to do. This is an administrative burden for FLMs who already have too much on their plates. Managers today have a lot more administrative work, and this changes the success profile for FLMs."

- "There is new emphasis on improving sales effectiveness," says Denise O'Brien, Vice President of Business Development, Global Sales and Client Development at ARAMARK. "Our goal is to define a common language around effectiveness for our function and to execute the one best way in a consistent and scalable way across all of our businesses."

Two Types of Change

Fueled by an evolving world economy and rapid technological innovation, the pace of change in the business environment is perhaps greater today than at any point in history. The best sales forces are dynamic. They respond to forces of change in the environment that impact customers, salespeople, and the company. At the same time, they proactively adapt their strategies to continually improve effectiveness and exploit new opportunities.

Sales force change initiatives can be transformational or evolutionary (see Figure 10-3). A sales force transformation involves major and (usually) event-driven change. It generally starts with a new sales strategy, which leads to substantial modifications in all or almost all strategic and operational sales force decision areas. Evolutionary sales force improvement, on the other hand, is less disruptive. It involves the ongoing fine-tuning of strategic sales force decisions along with constant improvement of the operational sales force processes, systems, and programs that enable execution of sales strategy. By encouraging ongoing

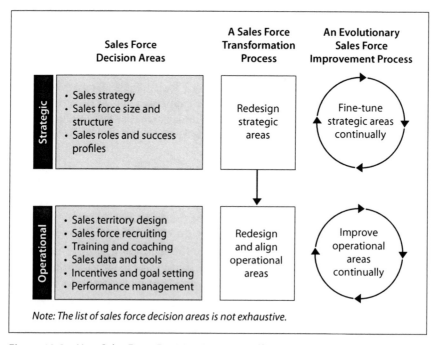

Figure 10-3 How Sales Force Decision Areas Are Affected by Sales Force Transformation and Evolutionary Sales Force Improvement

evolutionary improvement, sales forces stay aligned with evolving customer and company needs and can reduce the necessity for and frequency of sales force transformations.

Sales Force Transformation

The BP and GE Healthcare stories in the introduction to this chapter are examples of sales force transformations. Both involved substantial change in strategic sales force decision areas. At BP, sales leaders transformed the selling process and the competencies required for sales success in order to align sales force effort with new customer buying processes. At GE Healthcare, sales leaders restructured the roles and responsibilities of salespeople to meet evolving customer needs. At both BP and GE, most operational sales force processes, programs, and systems were redesigned to support the new sales strategy and organization. BP sales leaders implemented changes in operational areas such as competency models, training programs, tools, and reward structures. The GE transformation led to a realignment of sales territories and regions, as well as to revisions to many sales force development and support programs, including the competency, hiring, coaching, training, and compensation models.

Sales force transformations often create a need to change out a sizable number of salespeople and sales managers to fit with new sales roles and success profiles. Recall from Chapter 4 that when United Airlines implemented a sales force transformation that involved moving from a relationship-based sales approach to a value-based approach, every sales force member had to reinterview for the job. Approximately 30 percent of the managers and salespeople did not have the capability or motivation to adapt to the new sales model and were replaced.

A sales force transformation is usually triggered by an external event, such as a merger or an acquisition, a new company strategy, a major new product launch, missed financial goals, or a change in company leadership. Such events often come about in response to a market shift that acts as a catalyst for change.

Evolutionary Sales Force Improvement

Change does not have to be transformational to have a significant impact on the sales organization. Many sales force productivity-enhancement initiatives are evolutionary. They come about as sales leaders continually seek to fine-tune strategic sales force decisions and improve operational sales force decisions, processes, programs, and systems. For example, the Novartis sales force training initiative described in the introduction to this chapter brought about evolutionary improvement by propagating success principles for effective selling behavior among Novartis salespeople across the globe. The initiative was part of a deliberate effort to enhance the effectiveness of the global sales organization.

Several evolutionary improvements came out of this effort at Novartis, including a project to help salespeople in the United States increase productivity through smarter customer targeting and a project that identified and propagated seven FLM success principles that enhanced the effectiveness of the global FLM team (see Chapter 4).

Evolutionary improvement is often implemented without major change to the selling process or to the sales force success profile; consequently, it can usually be implemented without changing the people on the sales and sales management teams. Most companies make some evolutionary sales force improvements at least every year. The best companies are committed to making regular evolutionary improvements to increase sales force effectiveness and productivity.

The Role of the FLM in Facilitating Change

FLMs have a dual responsibility as facilitators of both transformational and evolutionary change. First, they are active participants in *designing* change. They can provide input about specific customer and sales force needs and can help the company ensure that changes will work locally. Second, FLMs have a key role in *implementing* change with their salespeople and customers. Figure 10-4 provides several examples of ways that FLMs can contribute as designers and implementers of change across a range of strategic and operational sales force decision areas.

The FLM Role in Designing Sales Force Change

When a company is designing any sales force change, its FLMs are uniquely positioned to provide input that can help the company make decisions that align with customer needs. "Often, there is a disconnect between the perspective of those at headquarters and the field's understanding of what the customers' issues truly are," says Quinton Oswald of SARcode BioScience. "FLMs are in the best position to convey the message to the company that customers want to buy in a different way. By framing their communication within the context of problems that customers face in the buying process, FLM feedback becomes concrete. This creates shared understanding so that headquarters and field personnel can work together to align strategy and tactics around a common goal of customer success."

In addition to providing input about customer needs that helps to shape the overall design of a sales force change, FLM input is useful for testing a design at the local level. For example, FLMs can tell you what a proposed change in sales force size and structure means for sales headcount and customer coverage in their districts and can describe how the change will impact specific salespeople and customers. They can tell you which salespeople have competency gaps and how a new sales force training program can benefit those people and their customers.

Sales Force Decision Area	FLM's Activities When Designing the Change	FLM's Activities When Implementing the Change
All decision areas	• Share insight on field impact of change	• Share rationale for change with salespeople and customers • Encourage and model sales force commitment
Sales strategy	• Provide field input	• Adapt strategy to local needs • Coach and manage salespeople to execute strategy effectively • Execute sales process in key accounts
Sales force size and structure	• Provide field input on best size and structure • Recommend local headcount changes	• Hire, let go, and reassign people locally as needed
Sales territory design	• Recommend territory design changes to optimize local coverage	• Identify account assignment changes • Help transition customer relationships between salespeople
Sales force recruiting	• Provide field input on the salesperson hiring profile	• Assess competencies of current salespeople and replace those who no longer fit the profile • Build applicant pool and select and attract salespeople who fit the profile
Sales training and coaching	• Identify salesperson competency gaps	• Coach and train salespeople • Reinforce classroom training through field coaching
Sales data and tools	• Provide field input on data and tools to help the sales force	• Learn new data and tools and help salespeople use them to drive sales • Use data and tools for coaching and managing performance
Incentives and goal setting	• Provide field input on incentive plan changes and goal setting	• Understand incentive plan changes and train salespeople • Suggest territory sales goal adjustments to reflect local conditions • Share new goals with salespeople
Performance management	• Provide field input on metrics and performance management processes	• Educate and manage salespeople on new metrics and processes

Figure 10-4 FLM Activities When Designing and Implementing Sales Force Change

FLM input helps you take a design that looks good on paper and make it more tangible by evaluating it from a practical sales force and customer perspective.

Finally, asking FLMs for input helps mobilize the FLM team around a transformational change or improvement initiative. FLM commitment is critical for gaining broader sales force acceptance. "By involving FLMs, you increase their buy-in, which in turn increases the likelihood of buy-in across the sales force," says Lauren Lamm, Manager at ZS Associates. "This decreases the time to implementation and lessens the time of uncertainty and lower productivity during the transition."

Designing a Sales Force Transformation

A sales force transformation that involves a rethinking of sales strategies, organization structure, and sales roles is more likely to succeed when the design incorporates input from many sources. Input from customers, consultants, and market or competitive research is important for shaping the design of a sales force transformation. Company leaders from many areas — including sales, marketing, customer service and support, human resources, and finance — can also provide input for sales force transformation design.

It's often not possible or practical to involve FLMs in designing a sales force transformation, especially when the proposed changes are likely to affect the FLM role and success profile. However, if it's possible to get input from some select FLMs — especially those who have the characteristics likely for success in the transformed sales organization — that input can be quite valuable. FLM input helps ensure that proposed changes to sales strategies, structures, and roles align with customer buying needs and can work effectively in local markets.

Designing Evolutionary or Operational Improvements

FLMs are in a good position to help you design evolutionary sales force improvements — for example, a new coaching process for developing sales competencies, a new incentive plan for driving profitability, or a new tool for improving territory planning. In many cases, FLMs can also help in the latter stages of a sales force transformation design by providing input about operational processes required to support a new sales strategy or structure.

Boston Scientific has an FLM advisory board that regularly provides input for designing sales force changes. "We get FLMs involved in the execution plan and give them ownership of changes by asking them to participate," says Chris Hartman. "We share with FLMs the reason for the change, the challenges we are facing, and ask for their help in figuring out how to do it. By creating an environment where FLMs influence and own the plan, the sales force is less likely to view it as something that's simply passed through from headquarters."

"There are certain FLMs who are the go-to people — the ones whom others look up to and who have the most influence on the rest of the sales team," says

Chris Hartman. "We make sure we involve them. This group of 'go-to' people includes 18 members of an FLM advisory board who get together once a quarter to share field insights and collaborate with headquarters on field action items. We use the advisory group as a sounding board *and* as a problem-solving board. We share what headquarters is thinking with board members and get their reactions. Additionally, if there are projects or programs that we need to create to improve our success in the marketplace, we engage members of the FLM advisory board on task force teams to develop those solutions. Without question, it is an action-oriented, 'roll up your sleeves' group that has a tremendous amount of influence on the Boston Scientific sales organization. FLMs on the advisory board go back to their regions and let others know that we are listening to field input and engaging their peers to develop sales action plans. The tone of the advisory board represents a dramatic shift from the more passive, 'for your information' advisory boards of the past. It has definitely strengthened the relationship and alignment between headquarters and the field sales team."

Regardless of whether FLMs help with designing new sales force operational programs, systems, and processes, it is critical that FLMs are involved in designing how to *implement* the changes. "We recently changed our sales culture to emphasize forecast attainment rather than past revenue growth as a driver of company success," says Fred Wagner of Ethicon Endo-Surgery. "We changed the performance metrics tied to sales force rewards and recognition. FLMs were a key part of the advisory group that created the rollout plan."

The FLM Role in Implementing Change

Because of their role linking salespeople, customers, and the company, FLMs are ideally positioned as the key implementers of sales force change. Sales force transformations and evolutionary sales force improvements can impact the people, customer, and business manager roles and all the connections that were introduced in Chapter 2, as shown in Figure 10-5. Any change that affects the interaction between salespeople and customers is likely to affect all three FLM roles.

Implementing Change as a People Manager

For an FLM in a people manager role, implementing change can mean informing salespeople about new assignments. In the case of transformational change, it can mean changing out some team members who do not fit with a new sales force success profile. This can require some difficult decisions that take time and managerial courage to implement. Implementing change as a people manager usually requires coaching and training salespeople on new skills and knowledge. It can mean adapting to and educating salespeople on revised metrics, redesigned incentive compensation plans, and new approaches for managing and motivating team performance. To implement change, FLMs must walk salespeople through the

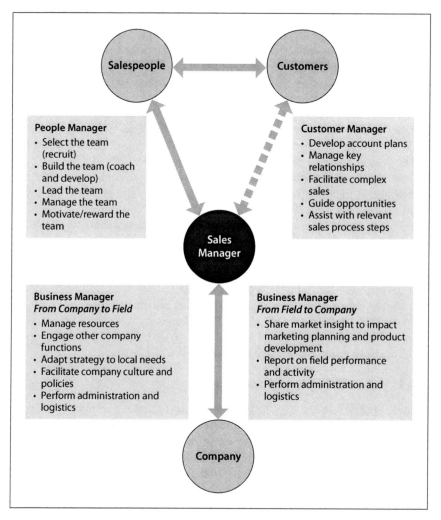

Figure 10-5   Three Main Roles of Sales Managers

details of how change affects day-to-day sales force activity—how change affects the sales process and key operational processes (for example, contract management and marketing communications), and how it affects salespeople's relationships with headquarters departments (for example, Marketing, Supply Chain, and Customer Support). As people managers, FLMs must lead their teams by sharing the rationale for changes, gaining the commitment of their people, and keeping their people energized by celebrating early successes as changes are implemented.

Implementing Change as a Customer Manager

For an FLM in a customer manager role, implementing change can mean learning a new selling process and a new FLM role in that process. Implementing change can require FLMs to help customers adapt and understand the benefits of change. FLMs may need to facilitate a smooth transition of customer–sales force relationships after a sales force restructuring or realignment that affects which salesperson or sales team each customer works with. FLMs may have to reassure customers that their needs will continue to be met during a transition period. Especially when transformational change takes place, FLMs may need to increase the amount of time they spend in a customer management role.

Implementing Change as a Business Manager

For an FLM in a business manager role, implementing change can mean adapting a new sales strategy for the local market, realigning sales territories, or setting revised territory sales goals. The responsibility of FLMs as a communication link between headquarters and the field is crucial in the business management role. FLMs are the primary communicators of revised company goals, strategies, and tactics to salespeople and customers. "Many of our salespeople work remotely or in smaller offices so they're closer to customers. We don't want them feeling like they're on an island when it comes to change. They go to their managers for answers, and it's critical that managers have those answers. Salespeople need to feel even more engaged during times of change, which is why employee engagement is something we survey on an ongoing basis," says Conrad Zils. And after a change is implemented, FLMs can provide feedback to let headquarters know if new strategies are working in the field. They can share feedback on how customers react to the change and can suggest modifications or adjustments that align business strategies with customer and field needs.

The Power of the FLM as a Change Implementer

Competency at managing during times of change usually varies across FLM team members. But it is important to engage all FLMs effectively in the sales force change process—including those who are not as well suited to the change facilitator role. A comparison of conversations that took place in two sales districts after a company implemented a sales incentive plan change illustrates this point. The new plan had more challenging goal hurdles that salespeople and managers had to reach before commissions kicked in. Salespeople were unhappy about the change. To earn the same amount of incentive money, they would have to work harder and reach beyond their comfort zone of selling to the longtime customers who provided a continuous and stable source of revenue and income.

A Conversation in District 1

SALESPERSON 1:   The new plan is unfair. How can the company do this to me?

FLM 1:   The world is changing, and our markets aren't growing anymore. We are facing new competition, and unless we can drive new account growth, we will not survive long term. The people at headquarters listened to my input when they created this plan. I believe that this change will help us stay competitive. It will mean some changes in the way we work, but I am committed to helping you. I know you can continue to be successful in this new world.

A Conversation in District 2

SALESPERSON 2:   The new plan is unfair. How can the company do this to me?

FLM 2:   I agree with you—the plan is unfair to me, too. Once again, headquarters doesn't understand the challenges we face in the field.

Don't underestimate the power of an FLM team that is committed (or not committed) to a sales force change initiative.

Engaging FLMs in Change

The best sales leaders enable FLMs in their role as both designers and implementers of sales force change. Here sales leaders share some ideas on ways to engage FLMs in successful sales force change.

When Change Is Transformational, Get the Right FLMs on the Team

Changes in sales strategy, structure, and roles often affect the FLM role and success profile. Before you can mobilize an FLM team around a transformational change, you will need to define the FLM role that can enable execution of a new sales strategy and then take steps to ensure that you have people on the FLM team who have the characteristics it takes to succeed in the new environment.

At temporary housing provider Oakwood Worldwide, the FLM role and success profile changed considerably when the company transformed its sales process from a relationship-based approach to a consultative approach. "FLMs needed a broader skill set so they could coach and teach salespeople how to execute the new consultative sales process," says Chris Ahearn, former Senior Vice President of Corporate Sales and Marketing. "We created training programs to help existing FLMs gain the necessary business skills, but not all FLMs had the abilities and personal characteristics needed for success in the new environment. In the end, we changed out a large percentage of our FLMs, keeping those who matched well with the new success profile."

When change in the FLM role and success profile is significant, it can make sense to require current FLMs to go through a selection process (see Chapter 5) to determine which ones have the characteristics required for success in the new job and which are better suited to a different role either inside or outside the company.

Help Your FLMs Put a Change Management Process into Action

"There is a real fear of disrupting customer relationships in sales forces, and this inhibits companies from implementing many positive sales force changes," says Chris Ahearn. "Usually, the fear is irrational. With a strong FLM team that is skilled at change management, successful change is possible."

Chris Ahearn used several change management best practices to help the Oakwood sales force adopt a multichannel model that included a new telesales team. Even though almost half of the sales force turned over within one year, customer feedback about the change was very positive. "We started the process by listening to customers to ensure we addressed their needs," says Chris Ahearn. "The new sales model helped to drive double-digit growth at the company." According to Chris, keys to a successful implementation with the sales force included the following:

- Emphasizing a window of opportunity that necessitated action
- Using a one-page road map that showed everyone where the company was and where it was going in the implementation process
- Getting FLMs involved up front and seeking their input throughout

"We gave FLMs guidance on how to put the corporate change model into action and how to use it to do something purposeful to drive sales force change," says Chris.

BP sales leaders also used a corporate change model to provide structure for the company's sales force transformation. "Often the corporate change model focuses only on internal change, and yet the change may have an impact on customers and suppliers external to the organization," says Liza Clechenko. "For the sales force, we adapted the model to be relevant externally as well, so that sales force members could help their customers deal with change."

Communicate, Communicate, Communicate

Communication between sales leadership and the FLM team is vital for engaging FLMs in successful change implementation. Sales leaders share insights on the importance of good communication:

- "We start with transparency at the top, which builds trust throughout the organization," says Jay Sampson, Executive Vice President, Global Sales, Marketing and Advertising for Machinima, Inc. "By repeating the message of our goals over and over, we make sure the sales force can explain our strategy or the changes to our strategy to customers in the right way."

- "You cannot overcommunicate when there is change," says John Barb, former Vice President of Sales for the xpedx division of International Paper. "It is important for everyone to know exactly what is changing, how it fits the strategy, and what they need to do to win. This ensures alignment across the organization."

- "But it's important to avoid overloading FLMs with too much information," says Quinton Oswald. "We tell them what they need to know but try to keep it fairly simple."

Sales leaders can support FLMs in communicating change to their salespeople. By helping FLMs with the message, sales leaders encourage communication that is effective and consistent across the sales organization.

- "We always help FLMs with talking points they should use to explain change to salespeople," says John Barb.

- "Headquarters can provide a good broad-brush starting point for FLMs to use in communicating to their teams, but the best FLMs will tailor the corporate message to their specific situation," says Chris Ahearn. "Those who make the communication personal and relevant for their team are most successful in implementing change."

Liza Clechenko says that leaders at BP followed some best practices for communicating change when they rolled out their new selling process to the sales force, including the following:

- Provide context for the communication.
- Make the message meaningful to the team.
- Show how the change fits into the bigger picture.
- Facilitate two-way communication and dialogue with team members.
- Find some champions who can help you communicate the change to create acceptance.

The best champions are also key influencers—sales force members to whom others are most likely to look for guidance. Key influencers can help communicate positive aspects of change either virally or during "water cooler conversations" and other informal networks.

Web-enabled technologies can enhance sales force communication during change implementation. "When the medical business segment at Cardinal Health implemented a sales technology and process change initiative, the FLMs became key in communicating the changes to the sales force," says Sandy Cantwell. "We began the effort in a pilot region, and the FLMs and other sales force members from this region became champions of the project. We created 30-minute 'ask the expert' webcasts to use as a resource for the entire sales force."

Online communities or discussion boards are an effective tool for communicating during times of change, as long as the content is managed to avoid the spread of misinformation and to keep the site productively focused.

Help FLMs Develop Change Management Competency

Sales leaders can help FLMs by giving them the tools they need to deal with managing change. "A critical characteristic to screen for in FLMs is willingness to embrace change and open-mindedness," says Liza Clechenko. "You hire for the right mind-set. Then you can train FLMs for steps in the change management process."

Many companies provide FLMs with training on change management skills, enabling them to better engage their salespeople in the change process. "Recognizing that we are going to be facing continuous change, it's important for FLMs to improve their change management skills," says John Barb. "Training helps FLMs understand how others react to change and what they need to do to become more effective change leaders."

"Cardinal Health provides FLMs with training that helps managers understand how to manage inclusion and diversity," says Sandy Cantwell. "We do role-playing exercises to build sensitivity to the perspectives of different cultures, generations, and communication styles. This helps FLMs see that how they are perceived is sometimes different from what they intended."

Give FLMs the Support They Need to Enable Change

Sales leaders can provide support resources to give FLMs the help, information, and confidence they need to implement changes successfully with their people and customers.

As an example, sales force change frequently involves realignment of sales territories. Major territory alignment changes occur when a sales force transformation involves a change in sales force size or structure. Evolutionary territory alignment changes will also occur regularly, in response to specific personnel or market factors. In Chapter 7, we described some support processes, people, and tools that companies can provide to help sales managers implement territory realignments effectively and efficiently. These resources can enable FLMs in their role as change facilitators.

"The commitment of FLMs is critical for ensuring that the sales organization captures the effectiveness gains expected from territory realignment and that the impact of disruption to customers and salespeople is minimized," says Tony Yeung of ZS Associates. "An effective implementation process heavily involves the FLM team in making critical alignment decisions that affect their sales districts."

In the case of minor territory alignment adjustments, mapping tools, coupled with structured processes, help FLMs evaluate different alignment scenarios and recommend salesperson-account assignment changes to sales leaders who can approve changes based on company guidelines. Occasionally, FLMs are the users of these tools; in most cases, however, the user is an analyst at headquarters who is an expert in using the tools to support the FLM team.

"In a major realignment, it is most effective to bring the FLM team together for work sessions on territories and personnel," says Tony. "This provides an opportunity to clearly explain the specifics and the case for change. Through a structured process, FLMs can make refinements to the planned territory structure and help make personnel decisions. This ensures the right decisions get made and also encourages FLMs to become owners and advocates for the change within their sales districts. Within a single day, ownership for the change is transferred from headquarters to the field."

By providing the right support resources, sales leaders enable FLMs to be implementers of sales force change with their people and customers.

Conclusion

The world of sales is ever changing. The recipe for sales success is complex, and every sales force must respond to forces of change that impact customer needs, the sales talent pool, and company priorities.

At every company contemplating sales force change, the input and commitment of the first-line sales management team is critical for implementing change successfully. In their roles as people, customer, and business managers, sales managers are essential facilitators of sales force change. Without the feedback and support of the sales management team, any sales force improvement or change initiative is destined to fail.

Sales leaders must prepare the sales management team—the force behind the sales force—to face change in the business environment. By embracing the role of essential facilitator of change, an FLM team becomes a key success factor for enabling both transformational and evolutionary change in the sales force, thereby helping you gain competitive advantage in a changing environment.

The Path Forward: An Assessment Tool for Creating an Action Plan

Boosting the Effectiveness of Your FLM Team Through Evolutionary Improvement

Throughout this book, we have shared stories and insights from sales leaders that demonstrate the critical role that first-line sales managers (FLMs) play in driving sales force performance. We've shared dozens of practical approaches and concrete ideas that you can employ immediately to begin enhancing the FLM success drivers—the decisions, programs, processes, systems, and tools you use to define, create, and enable your FLM team. Many of these ideas are listed in "A Summary of Best Practices for Managing FLM Success Drivers" at the end of this section. Only by creating excellence in the success drivers can you build and sustain a winning sales management team—a force behind your sales force that can enable you to succeed in the marketplace.

But where do you start? In the case of transformational change, the sequential approach outlined in this book makes sense; begin with Chapter 2 ("Defining the Role"), and work through the chapters in order until all eight FLM success drivers have been addressed. But what if you want to bring about evolutionary sales force improvement? A sequential and comprehensive line of attack may not be the best approach. To continually improve your FLM team, you're likely to get the best results if you prioritize the FLM success drivers and focus your improvement efforts on the most important ones first. Then, you can regularly assess and enhance every success driver to constantly improve your FLM team and to ensure continued excellence as your business environment and company strategies change.

An FLM Performance Assessment

An FLM Performance Assessment can help you prioritize the eight FLM success drivers so you can focus your improvement efforts first on the success drivers likely to have the highest impact on your sales organization. The assessment profiles each FLM success driver in terms of two measures:

- **Competency.** How competent or capable is your organization currently at managing each FLM success driver?

- **Impact.** How important is each FLM success driver for your sales force's ability to succeed?

First, we describe the FLM Performance Assessment that one company developed and used to prioritize evolutionary improvements in the FLM success drivers. Then, we show you how to create your own FLM Performance Assessment for setting your priorities for building excellence in the FLM success drivers for your sales organization.

An Example of an FLM Performance Assessment

Figure A shows an FLM Performance Assessment that one company developed to create a snapshot of the sales organization's competency and the impact of the FLM success drivers at a particular point in time.

Sales leaders at this company developed a ranking of the eight FLM success drivers on two dimensions: competency and impact. They felt the organization did the best job of managing "size and structure," so that driver received a "1" competency ranking; they felt it did the poorest job of managing "selection," so that driver received an "8" competency ranking. Similarly, sales leaders felt that "selection" was most important for sales force success, so that driver received a "1" impact ranking; they felt that "support" was least important for success, so they gave that driver an "8" impact ranking. Sales leaders plotted the rankings on the assessment grid. Each FLM success driver's position on the grid suggests an action.

- **Low impact and high competency** (such as "size and structure"). Maintain at current levels for the time being.
- **High impact and high competency** (such as "role definition"). Monitor to ensure that competency stays high.
- **Low impact and low competency** (such as "support"). Monitor to see if impact increases as needs change.
- **High impact and low competency** (such as "selection" and "success profile"). Make improving these FLM success drivers a top priority, as they provide the greatest opportunity for improving the FLM team to drive performance.

The FLM Performance Assessment was specific to this company and its condition at the time of the assessment. FLM success driver competency ranks can change as performance improves in some areas and slips in others. Competency ranks can also change as the environment changes and impacts the effectiveness of current practices. Impact ranks can change, too, as the sales environment and company strategies evolve. The sales leaders at this company gained particular insight by conducting assessments like this on a regular basis and by tracking changes over time. The assessment became the cornerstone of an evolutionary

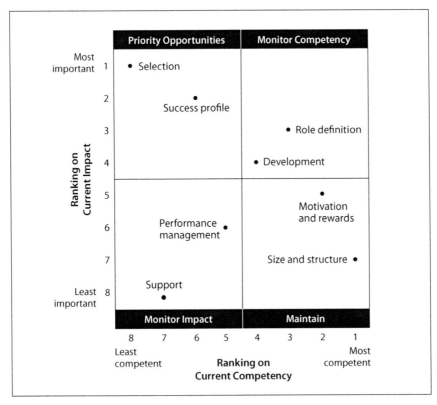

Figure A   An FLM Performance Assessment Developed and Used by One Company

sales force improvement effort that enabled the sales organization to constantly improve the effectiveness of its FLM team.

Creating Your Own FLM Performance Assessment

Use the worksheet in Figure B to create an FLM Performance Assessment for your sales organization. Conducting the assessment requires three steps.

Step 1: Rank the FLM Success Drivers from 1 Through 8 on Competency

For example, give the driver that you feel your organization does the best job of managing a "1" competency ranking; give the driver that you feel your organization does the poorest job of managing an "8" competency ranking.

To develop your competency rankings, do the following:

- Read Chapters 2 through 9 of this book to help you understand and assess how competent your company is at each FLM success driver.

- Consult the summary of FLM success driver best practices provided at the end of this section. Base your rankings on an assessment of the extent to which your organization follows the best practices for each driver.
- Gather input from your leadership team and others in your company. For example, have members of the leadership team rank the FLM success drivers independently and then meet as a group to discuss and arrive at a consensus opinion.

Step 2: Rank the FLM Success Drivers from 1 Through 8 on Impact

For example, give the driver that you feel is most important for your sales force's success a "1" impact ranking; give the driver that you feel is least important for your sales force's success an "8" impact ranking.

To develop your impact rankings, gather input from your leadership team or consult outside experts. Also collect input from sales force members. For example, ask FLMs how much more efficiently they could operate with better support mechanisms, or ask salespeople how much more they could sell with better coaching from their sales managers.

Developing impact rankings usually requires a good deal of management judgment, as rankings are conditional on the situation. Consider these examples:

- Some FLM success drivers are likely to have high impact in all conditions because they are essential for sustaining ongoing sales force operations. These include selecting talent, supporting critical activities, managing performance, and motivating and rewarding success.
- Some drivers are likely to become more salient when the sales environment is changing. For example, changing conditions can make it necessary to redefine the FLM role and success profile, to reevaluate FLM team size and structure, and to enhance competencies in light of the changing conditions.
- Some drivers become more important when the sales process is complex or when there are multiple types of sales specialists. In complex conditions, drivers such as defining the role, sizing and structuring the team, enhancing competencies, and supporting critical activities can have higher impact.

Consider the situation you face when developing your impact rankings, and reassess impact rankings whenever conditions change.

Step 3: Plot Your Rankings on the Grid

You can use the suggested abbreviations in the ranking table to label each FLM success driver.

Abbr.	FLM Success Driver	Competency Ranking (How good are we at managing this FLM success driver?) 1 = most competent 8 = least competent	Impact Ranking (What is the impact of this FLM success driver on sales force success?) 1 = highest impact 8 = lowest impact
ROL	Defining the role		
SS	Sizing and structuring the team		
PRO	Creating the success profile		
SEL	Selecting talent		
DEV	Enhancing competencies		
SUP	Supporting critical activities		
PM	Managing performance		
MOT	Motivating and rewarding success		

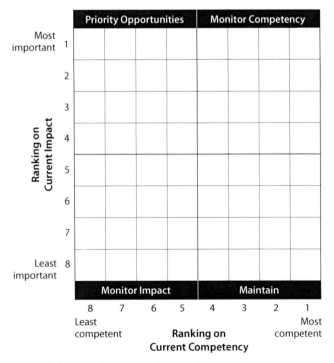

Figure B   A Worksheet for Creating an FLM Performance Assessment

An Alternative Assessment Approach Using a Rating System

The example in Figure A and the worksheet in Figure B use a ranking approach for assessing competency and the impact of the FLM success drivers. The approach asks sales leaders to differentiate among the drivers by force-ranking them to develop competency and impact scores.

Some sales organizations prefer to use a rating approach for assessing competency and impact. For example, one organization used a five-point scale where 1 equals low impact or competency and 5 equals high impact or competency. Then sales leaders rated each FLM success driver on the 1 to 5 scale, without forcing the ordered differentiation that ranking requires.

A rating approach is usually harder to implement than a ranking approach. To work well, a rating approach requires leaders to be specific about what competency and impact look like at each level in the rating scale. For example, what best practices must the organization follow to earn a "5" competency rating for a certain driver, such as "selecting talent"? (You can use the list of best practices at the end of this section as a starting point for answering this question.) And what does a "2" impact rating mean in terms of how a driver affects sales, profits, or other measures of sales force success? Sales leaders need a common language and understanding of what the ratings mean.

In addition, good results with a rating approach require sales leaders to discriminate among success drivers through their ratings. An assessment has limited value if it indicates that the organization is "highly competent" on every success driver or that every driver is "very important."

We have observed both rating and ranking approaches working well.

A Summary of Best Practices for Managing FLM Success Drivers

In Chapters 2 through 9, we suggested many best practices for managing the FLM success drivers. Here we summarize the key ideas from each chapter. Use the following lists to help you assess your sales organization's competency on each driver. Give a high ranking to FLM success drivers for which you follow all or almost all of the best practices. Give a low ranking to FLM success drivers for which you follow few best practices.

Best Practices for Defining the Role (Chapter 2)

1. Have an FLM role description that keeps FLMs focused on the activities that enable effective execution of the sales strategy. Include an appropriate mix of people, customer, and business management responsibilities.

2. Periodically assess how sales managers spend their time, and look for opportunities to increase their focus on high-impact tasks and reduce the time spent on low-value activities.

3. Identify your best-performing managers, and use their behaviors as a model for defining the FLM role.

4. Revisit the FLM role description periodically, and make adjustments as the environment and company strategies change.

Best Practices for Sizing and Structuring the Team (Chapter 3)

1. Use analytic approaches, such as workload buildup to link span of control to the time it takes FLMs to complete tasks required for their roles as people, customer, and business managers.

2. Use feedback from customers and salespeople, industry benchmarks, financial guidelines, and the experience of successful FLMs as guidelines for determining span of control and reporting structure.

3. When multiple types of sales specialists share customer responsibility, create a sales force reporting structure that aligns with customers' need for a coordinated sales effort and specialized sales expertise.

4. Provide sales force support mechanisms (for example, information support, incentives, or development programs) that reduce any stresses that the sales-reporting structure creates for customers or salespeople.

5. Adapt span of control and sales-reporting structures as the environment and company strategies change.

Best Practices for Creating the Success Profile (Chapter 4)

1. Create a sales manager success profile or competency model that aligns with the FLM role.

2. Distinguish between characteristics (inherent traits) and competencies (learned skills and knowledge) in the profile.

3. Include a manageable number of characteristics and competencies in the profile.

4. Study the characteristics and competencies of your current FLMs, and identify those that distinguish the best performers. Include these in your profile.

5. Revisit the FLM success profile periodically, and make adjustments as the environment and company strategies change.

Best Practices for Selecting Talent (Chapter 5)

1. Use the success profile to guide FLM selection. Screen for characteristics (inherent traits); if candidates have the right characteristics, you can develop their competencies.

2. Create a strong applicant pool. Identify internal candidates early in their careers, and provide them with opportunities to demonstrate managerial characteristics and competencies (look beyond sales results). Identify external candidates through referrals from trusted sources, such as employees or customers.

3. Use multiple techniques to evaluate candidates, including observation of the candidate's work (can use case studies) and structured interviews.

Best Practices for Enhancing Competencies (Chapter 6)

1. Design the content of new FLM development programs around competency gaps. Those new to management need to develop management skills; those new to the company need to develop company product, sales process, and culture knowledge.

2. Periodically assess FLM team performance, and direct development resources to the most important competencies on which performance needs to improve.

3. Provide ongoing development content for experienced managers to continually improve competencies and to fill competency gaps that emerge as business needs change.

4. Use a blended learning approach that combines classroom, on-the-job, and self-taught learning methods to provide continual reinforcement of learning and to balance effectiveness and efficiency.

5. Provide opportunities for best-practice sharing among FLMs, especially in smaller sales forces that don't have sufficient scale to run more formal programs.

6. Revisit FLM development content and methods regularly, and make adjustments as business needs change.

Best Practices for Supporting Critical Activities (Chapter 7)

1. Match support processes and systems, people, and data and tools to the three FLM roles to help FLMs succeed and be efficient as people managers, customer managers, and business managers.

2. Create new support mechanisms to address emerging needs and challenges.

3. Periodically test existing support mechanisms for FLM usage, impact on sales force and FLM activity, and customer impact. Regularly eliminate support mechanisms that no longer add enough value.

4. Create sales force dashboards that integrate data measuring customer potential, sales effort, and sales results. Avoid overload by limiting the number of dashboards and tools and keeping them focused on strategic and meaningful metrics. Provide resources to support ad hoc sales force analytic needs.

5. Help FLMs prioritize their time by limiting the amount of "non-sales stuff" (customer service requests, headquarters requests, nonessential email, and so on) that goes to FLMs.

Best Practices for Managing Performance (Chapter 8)

1. Focus on both inputs (FLM capabilities and activities) and outputs (sales force satisfaction and activity, customer satisfaction, and contribution to company results) when evaluating FLM performance.

2. Create and track performance metrics that align with the FLM role, are measurable, and are impacted by FLMs (not by factors that are beyond FLM control).

3. Provide frameworks (such as competency models, MBO frameworks, and balanced scorecards) that encourage consistency of metrics and evaluation across FLMs and over time.

4. Recognize the power of culture in managing FLM performance. Build a positive sales culture that encourages FLMs to "do the right thing" at all times.

Best Practices for Motivating and Rewarding Success (Chapter 9)

1. Provide a mix of motivation programs that appeal to FLMs who are motivated to varying degrees by achievement, social affiliation, and power.

2. Manage the FLM success drivers to create a motivating sales culture that appeals to FLMs' desire for achievement, social affiliation, and power, while minimizing the impact of motivation detractors that are inherent to the FLM job.

3. Provide a mix of recognition programs and financial rewards that motivate FLM success in both the short term and the long term.

4. Recognize FLMs for their successes regularly within the organization and in front of their peers.

5. Align the FLM sales incentive plan with the FLM role and the desired sales culture. Tie FLM incentive pay to results metrics; tie FLM salary increases and career progression to capability and activity metrics and assessments.

6. Use analytics to support the process of setting results goals for FLMs. Avoid goals that are not challenging enough or that are perceived as unattainable or unfair.

Index

CPSIA information can be obtained at www.ICGtesting.com
Printed in the USA
BVOW02*1357190715

408901BV00007B/245/P